CHOSEN But Free

A Selection of Books by Norman L. Geisler

Legislating Morality (Bethany House, 1998)

Creating God in the Image of Man? (Bethany House, 1997)

When Cultists Ask (Victor, 1997)

Love Is Always Right (Thomas Nelson, 1996)

An Encyclopedia of Christian Evidences (Victor, 1996)

Roman Catholics and Evangelicals (Baker, 1995)

In Defense of the Resurrection (rev. by Witness Inc., 1993)

Answering Islam (Baker, 1993)

When Critics Ask (Victor, 1992)

Miracles and the Modern Mind (Baker, 1992)

Matters of Life and Death (Baker, 1991)

Thomas Aquinas: An Evangelical Appraisal (1991)

In Defense of the Resurrection (Quest, 1991)

The Life and Death Debate (Greenwood, 1990)

When Skeptics Ask (Victor, 1990)

Gambling: A Bad Bet (Fleming H. Revell, 1990)

Come Let Us Reason (Baker, 1990)

Apologetics in the New Age (Baker, 1990)

The Battle for the Resurrection (Thomas Nelson, 1989)

Christian Ethics (Baker, 1989)

The Infiltration of the New Age (Tyndale, 1989)

Knowing the Truth About Creation (Servant, 1989)

World's Apart (Baker, 1989)

Christian Apologetics (Baker, 1988)

Signs and Wonders (Tyndale, 1988)

Philosophy of Religion (revised, 1988)

Introduction to Philosphy (Baker, 1987)

Origin Science (Baker, 1987)

The Reincarnation Sensation (Tyndale, 1986)

A General Introduction to the Bible (revised, Moody Press, 1986)

False Gods of Our Time (Harvest House, 1985)

To Drink or Not to Drink (Quest, 1984)

Explaining Hermeneutics (ICBI, 1983)

Is Man the Measure? (Baker, 1983)

Miracles and Modern Thought (Zondervan, 1982)

What Augustine Says (Baker, 1982)

The Creator in the Courtroom—Scopes II (Baker, 1982)

Decide for Yourself (Zondervan, 1982)

Biblical Errancy (Zondervan, 1981)

Options in Contemporary Christian Ethics (Baker, 1981)

Inerrancy (Zondervan, 1980)

To Understand the Bible, Look for Jesus (Baker, 1979)

The Roots of Evil (Zondervan, 1978)

A Popular Survey of the Old Testament (Baker, 1977)

From God to Us (Moody Press, 1974)

DR. NORMAN GEISLER

CHOSEN
But Free

BETHANY HOUSE PUBLISHERS
MINNEAPOLIS, MINNESOTA 55438

Published by Bethany House Publishers
A Ministry of Bethany Fellowship International
11400 Hampshire Avenue South
Minneapolis, Minnesota 55438
www.bethanyhouse.com

Printed in the United States of America

Library of Congress Catalogin-in-Publication Data

Geisler, Norman L.
    Chosen but free / by Norman L. Geisler .
      p. cm.
    Includes bibliographical references.
    ISBN 0–7642–2198–1 (hardcover)
    1. Predestination. 2. Free will and determinism. 3. Providence and government of God. 4. God—Omniscience. 5. Calvinism. 6. Arminianism. I. Title.
BT810.2.G45   1999
233'.7—dc21
                                                            99–6420
                                                                            CIP

To all my students
who for the past thirty-five years
have asked more questions about this
than any other topic.

DR. NORMAN L. GEISLER is author or coauthor of some fifty books and hundreds of articles. He has taught at the university and graduate level for nearly forty years and has spoken, traveled, or debated in all fifty states and in twenty-five countries. He holds a Ph.D. in philosophy from Loyola University and now serves as Dean of Southern Evangelical Seminary in Charlotte, North Carolina.

ACKNOWLEDGMENTS

My appreciation to my wife, Barbara, for her patient proofing of the manuscript, and my secretary, Laurel, for her expert typing of the text.

This manuscript was improved considerably by the keen insights and many helpful suggestions of Professors Robert Culver, Fred Howe, and Thomas Howe, along with Bob and Gretchen Passantino.

CONTENTS

CHAPTER ONE

WHO IS
IN CHARGE?

In his widely acclaimed book *The Knowledge of the Holy*, A. W. Tozer writes: "What comes into our minds when we think about God is the most important thing about us."[1] And so before we examine God's sovereignty in coherence with human free will, we will in chapter 1 allow God's own Word to educate us as to His nature and attributes.

THE CHARACTERISTICS OF GOD

When anyone who is thoroughly acquainted with the Bible thinks about God, one of the first things that comes into the mind ought to be God's *sovereignty*. God's sovereignty is deeply rooted in His attributes. Several of them are crucial to His ability to reign over all things.

God is before all things

God is *"before all things"* (Col. 1:17).[2] Or, as the first verse of the Bible puts it, "In the beginning God...." Before there was any-

---

[1] A. W. Tozer, *The Knowledge of the Holy* (New York: Harper & Row, 1978), 9.
[2] Unless otherwise noted, Bible quotations are from the New International Version of the Bible. Also, unless otherwise noted, all italics within Scripture reference are the author's.

thing else, there was God, the Uncreated One. The psalmist said, "From everlasting to everlasting, thou art God" (Ps. 90:2 KJV). There never was a time when God was not. In fact, He existed forever before all things. He is called "the First," "the Beginning," and "the Alpha" (Rev. 1:8; 1:17; 21:6). Often the Bible speaks of God as being there "before the world began" (John 17:5; cf. Matt. 13:35; 25:34; John 17:24; Rev. 13:8; 17:8).

God was not only before all things, but He was before all time. That is, He is eternal. For God was there *"before the beginning of time"* (2 Tim. 1:9). In fact, God brought time into existence when He "framed the worlds" (literally, "the ages," Heb. 1:2, *Rotherham* trans.). God "alone has immortality" (1 Tim. 6:16 NKJV). We get it only as a gift (Rom. 2:7; 1 Cor. 15:53; 2 Tim. 1:10). And our immortality has a beginning; God's does not.

God created all things

Not only is God before all things, but He created all things. "In the beginning God created the heaven and the earth" (Gen. 1:1 KJV). *"Through him [Christ] all things were made;* without him nothing was made that has been made" (John 1:3). "For by him all things were created: things in heaven and on earth, visible and invisible, whether thrones or powers or rulers or authorities; all things were created by him and for him" (Col. 1:16).

God upholds all things

God not only created all things, He also upholds all things. Hebrews declares that God is *"sustaining all things* by his powerful word" (Heb. 1:3). Paul adds, "He is before all things, *and in him all things hold together"* (Col. 1:17). John informs us that God not only brought all things into existence but He keeps them in existence. Both are true for "they *were created* and *have their being"* from God (Rev. 4:11). There is "one Lord, Jesus Christ, through whom all things came and *through whom we live"* (1 Cor. 8:6; cf. Rom. 11:36). Hebrews asserts "it was fitting that God, for whom and *through whom everything exists,* should make the author of their salvation perfect through suffering" (Heb. 2:10).

God is above all things

The God who is before all things that He created and who is upholding all things is also beyond them. He is transcendent. The apostle affirmed that there is "one God and Father of all, who is *over all* and through all and in all" (Eph. 4:6). The psalmist declared: "O

LORD, our Lord, how majestic is your name in all the earth! You have set your glory *above the heavens*" (Ps. 8:1). "Be exalted, O God, *above the heavens*; let your glory be over all the earth" (Ps. 57:5). "For you, O LORD, are the Most High *over all the earth*; you are *exalted far above all gods*" (Ps. 97:9; cf. 108:5).

God knows all things

What is more, the God of the Bible knows all things. He has omniscience (*omni*=all; *science*=knowledge). That God is all-knowing is clear from numerous passages of Scripture. The psalmist declared: "Great is our Lord, and mighty in power; *His understanding is infinite*" (Ps. 147:5 NKJV). God *knows "the end from the beginning"* (Isa. 46:10). He knows the very secrets of our heart. The psalmist confessed to God: "Before a word is on my tongue *you know it completely*, O LORD. . . . *Such knowledge is too wonderful for me*, too lofty for me to attain" (Ps. 139:4, 6). Indeed, "Nothing in all creation is hidden from God's sight. *Everything is uncovered and laid bare before the eyes of him* to whom we must give account" (Heb. 4:13). The apostle exclaimed: "Oh, the depth of the riches of the wisdom and knowledge of God! *How unsearchable his judgments*, and his paths beyond tracing out!" (Rom. 11:33). Even those who would eventually be saved were known by God (1 Peter 1:2) before the foundation of the world (Eph. 1:4). By His limitless knowledge God is able to predict the exact course of human history (Dan. 2, 7), including the names of persons generations before they were born (cf. Isa. 45:1). Nearly two hundred predictions were made by God about the Messiah, not one of which failed. God knows all things past, present, and future.

God can do all things

Furthermore, God is all-powerful. He not only knows all things eternally and unchangeably, but God is omnipotent (*omni*=all; *potent*=powerful). Before performing a great miracle, God promised Abraham, " '*Is anything too hard for the* LORD? I will return to you at the appointed time next year and Sarah will have a son' " (Gen. 18:14). In fact, "Nothing is impossible with God" (Luke 1:37).

He is not only infinite (not-limited) in His knowledge, He is also infinite in His power. God declares: " 'I am the LORD, the God of all mankind. *Is anything too hard for me?*' " (Jer. 32:27). God's power is supernatural as is evident by the miracles He performs that overpower the forces of nature. Jesus the Son of God walked on water (John 6), stilled the storm (John 6), and even raised the dead (John 11).

What is more, God's omnipotent power is manifested in the creation of the world from nothing. He simply spoke and things came into being (Gen. 1:3, 6, 9, 11). Paul describes Him as "God, who said, 'Let light shine out of darkness' " (2 Cor. 4:6). The writer of Hebrews declares that *God is "sustaining all things by his powerful word"* (Heb. 1:3).

Of course, God cannot do what is actually impossible to do. Since it is impossible for God to do things contrary to His unchanging nature, it is understandable that He cannot do any contradictory thing. The Bible says, "God cannot lie" (Titus 1:2 NASB), because "it is impossible for God to lie" (Heb. 6:18). For " 'He who is the Glory of Israel does not lie or change his mind; for he is not a man, that he should change his mind' " (1 Sam. 15:29).

For example, He cannot make a square circle. Nor can He make a triangle with only two sides. Likewise, God cannot create another God equal to Himself. It is literally impossible to *create* another being that is *not created*. There is only one Uncreated Creator (Deut. 6:4; Isa. 45:18). Everything else is a creature.

Nonetheless, God can do whatever is possible to do. He can do anything that does not involve a contradiction. There are no limits on His power. The Bible describes Him as "the Almighty" (almighty) in numerous places (e.g., Gen. 17:1; Ex. 6:3; Num. 24:4; Job 5:17).

God accomplishes all things

God's sovereignty over all things implies also that He accomplishes all things that He wills. Isaiah declares, "The LORD Almighty has sworn, 'Surely, as I have planned, so it will be, and *as I have purposed, so it will stand.* . . . For the LORD Almighty has purposed, and *who can thwart him?* His hand is stretched out, and who can turn it back?' " (Isa. 14:24, 27). Again, " 'I am God, and there is no other; I am God, and there is none like me. . . . *My purpose will stand, and I will do all that I please. . . . What I have said, that will I bring about; what I have planned, that will I do'* " (Isa. 46:9–11). Paul adds, "In him we were also chosen, having been predestined according to the plan of him *who works out everything in conformity with the purpose of his will*" (Eph. 1:11). Peter confirms this, saying of Christ's crucifiers that " *'they did what your power and will had decided beforehand should happen'* " (Acts 4:28; cf. 2:23).

THE SOVEREIGNTY OF GOD

A God who is before all things, beyond all things, creates all things, upholds all things, knows all things, and can do all things is also in control of all things. This complete control of all things is called the sovereignty of God. As the *Westminster Confession of Faith* puts it, "God, from all eternity, did, by the most wise and holy counsel of His own will, freely, and unchangeably ordain whatever comes to pass" (chapter 3). Nothing catches God by surprise. All things come to pass as He ordained them from all eternity.

God rules over all things

The Bible affirms God's sovereignty in many ways. Just as earthly sovereigns control their domain, even so the heavenly King is in charge of His creation. Isaiah's vision of God was of a heavenly king whose train filled the temple (Isa. 6). Yahweh is called *"the great King"* (Ps. 48:2). His reign is eternal for *"the LORD is enthroned as King for ever"* (Ps. 29:10). And He is King over all the earth, for *"The LORD is King for ever and ever;* the nations will perish from his land" (Ps. 10:16). He is also the almighty King: "Who is this King of glory? The LORD strong and mighty, *the LORD mighty in battle"* (Ps. 24:8). As such, God rules over all things: "Yours, O LORD, is the greatness and the power and the glory and the majesty and the splendor, for *everything in heaven and earth is yours.* Yours, O LORD, is the kingdom; *you are exalted as head over all.* Wealth and honor come from you; *you are the ruler of all things"* (1 Chron. 29:11–12).

God is in control of all things

Not only is God in charge of all things, He is also in control of them. Job confessed to God: *"I know that you can do all things; no plan of yours can be thwarted"* (Job 42:2). The psalmist added, "Our God is in heaven; *he does whatever pleases him"* (Ps. 115:3). Again, *"The LORD does whatever pleases him,* in the heavens and on the earth, in the seas and all their depths" (Ps. 135:6). As Daniel put it, *"He does as he pleases* with the powers of heaven and the peoples of the earth. No one can hold back his hand or say to him: 'What have you done?' "* (Dan. 4:35).

Earthly kings are under God's control

Solomon declared that *"The king's heart is in the hand of the* LORD; he directs it like a watercourse wherever he pleases" (Prov. 21:1). God is the Sovereign over all other sovereigns. He is *"King of kings and Lord of lords"* (Rev. 19:16). There is no human that is not under God's power.

Human events are under God's control

God not only controls the hearts of kings, He is in charge of all human events. He ordains the course of history before it occurs, as He predicted through Daniel the great world kingdoms of Babylon, Medo-Persia, Greece, and Rome (Dan. 2, 7). Indeed, the great King Nebuchadnezzar learned the hard way that " *'the Most High is sovereign over the kingdoms of men* and gives them to anyone he wishes and sets over them the lowliest of men' " (Dan. 4:17). The Lord says, " 'So is my word that goes out from my mouth: It will not return to me empty, but [it] *will accomplish what I desire and achieve the purpose for which I sent it'* " (Isa. 55:11).

The good angels are under God's control

God not only rules in the visible realm but also in the invisible domain. He is "over all creation" including "visible and invisible, whether thrones or dominions or principalities or powers" (Col. 1:15–16). The angels come before His throne to get their orders to obey (1 Kings 22; Job 1:6; 2:1). They constantly worship God (Neh. 9:6). Indeed, they are positioned before the throne of God, and "day and night they never stop saying: 'Holy, holy, holy is the Lord God Almighty, who was, and is, and is to come' " (Rev. 4:8).

The evil angels are under God's control

God's sovereign domain includes not only the good angels but also the evil ones (Eph. 1:21). They too will bow before God's throne one day in total subjection to Him, for *"at the name of Jesus every knee should bow,* in heaven and on earth and under the earth [evil spirits]" (Phil. 2:10; cf. Isa. 45:22–23). Indeed, the evil spirits who deceived King Ahab were dispatched from the very throne of God. The Scriptures inform us:

> I saw the LORD sitting on his throne with all the host of heaven standing round him on his right and on his left. And the LORD said, "Who will entice Ahab into attacking Ramoth Gilead and going to his death there?" One suggested this, and another that. Finally, a spirit came forward, stood before the LORD and said, "I will entice him." "By what means?" the LORD asked. "I will go out and be a lying spirit in the mouths of all his prophets," he said. "You will succeed in enticing him," said the LORD. "Go and do it" (1 Kings 22:19–22).

Even Satan is under God's control

Even Satan came along with the good angels before God's throne in the book of Job (Job 1:6; 2:1). And although he wished to destroy Job, God would not permit him. Satan complained, saying to God, " 'Have you not put a hedge around him and his household and everything he has? You have blessed the work of his hands, so that his flocks and herds are spread throughout the land' " (Job 1:10). God has power to bind Satan any time He desires, and He does it for a thousand years in the book of Revelation (20:2).

Also, the devil's demons who fell with him (Rev. 12:9; Jude 6) know they are eventually doomed. One cried out to Jesus, " 'What do you want with us, Son of God? . . . Have you come here to torture us before the appointed time?' " (Matt. 8:29). And eventually Satan and all his hosts will be destroyed. The devil himself "knows that his time is short" (Rev. 12:12). While he is presently roaming the earth (1 Peter 5:8), he does so only on a leash held firmly by God's sovereign hand.

Christ came to destroy the works of the devil (Heb. 2:14), which He did officially on the Cross (1 John 3:8). And Christ will return to defeat the devil actually. John foretells how "the devil, who deceived them, was thrown into the lake of burning sulfur, where the beast and the false prophet had been thrown. They will be tormented day and night for ever and ever" (Rev. 20:10).

Even human decisions are under God's control

Perhaps the most difficult thing to understand is that God is in sovereign control of everything we choose, even our salvation. For "in him we were also chosen, having been predestined according to the plan of *him who works out everything in conformity with the purpose of his will. . .*" (Eph. 1:11). "For those God foreknew he also predestined to be conformed to the likeness of his Son, that he might be the firstborn among many brothers. And those he predestined, he also called; those he called, he also justified; those he justified, he also glorified" (Rom. 8:29–30). According to Paul, "he chose us in him before the creation of the world" (Eph. 1:4). Peter said of Jesus to the Jews, " 'This man was handed over to you *by God's set purpose and foreknowledge;* and you, with the help of wicked men, put him to death by nailing him to the cross' " (Acts 2:23). Indeed, only those who are elect will believe, for Luke wrote that "all who were appointed for eternal life believed" (Acts 13:48).

Other verses affirm God's actions on the human will, even in matters of salvation. John declares that we are "children [of God] born not of natural descent, *nor of human decision* or a husband's will, but born of God" (John 1:13). Likewise, Paul affirms that *"it is not of him who wills,* nor of him who runs, but of God who shows mercy" (Rom. 9:16 NKJV). He adds even more difficult words: "God has mercy on whom he wants to have mercy, and he hardens whom he wants to harden" (Rom. 9:19; see appendix 1).

God's sovereignty over human decisions includes both those for Him and against Him. Peter, quoting from Isaiah (8:14), writes of Christ: He is " 'a stone that causes men to stumble and a rock that makes them fall.' They stumble because *they disobey* the message—which is also what *they were destined* for" (1 Peter 2:8). Likewise, God has destined the "vessels of wrath" who were "prepared for destruction" (Rom. 9:22 NASB) as well as the "vessels of mercy" (Rom. 9:23 NASB)—each according to His will.

Whatever else may be said, God's sovereignty over the human will includes His initiating, pursuing, persuading, and saving grace without which no one would ever will to be saved. For "there is no one who understands, *no one who seeks God*" (Rom. 3:11). "We love Him" only because *"He first loved us"* (1 John 4:19 NKJV). Indeed, no one comes to the Father unless he is drawn by God (John 6:44).

HOW THEN ARE WE FREE?

If God is sovereign, how then can we be free? Does not divine sovereignty make a sham of human responsibility? Is not a sovereign God a Giant Puppet Master, pulling the strings of human "puppets" at His will? If God is in complete control of everything, including human choice, then how can we be truly free? Are not sovereignty and significant free will mutually exclusive? These questions are the subject of the rest of this book. And we begin in the next chapter with what the Bible says about free choice.

CHAPTER TWO

WHY BLAME ME?

I have never forgotten a placard I saw in a Presbyterian church foyer over forty years ago: "We believe in predestination, but drive carefully because you may hit a Presbyterian!" On the other side of the coin from divine sovereignty (see chapter 1) is human responsibility.

WHO DONE IT?

If God is in control of everything, then why should we be blamed for anything? If an all-knowing God knows what we are going to do before we ever do it—and if He cannot be wrong—then is not this the way it's going to happen regardless of what we do?

Or to put the problem another way, if God is in control of all events, then how can I be responsible for anything that happens, even my evil actions? It would seem that His sovereignty eliminates my responsibility.

THE DEVIL MADE ME DO IT

Some believers have been known to excuse their sin, claiming: "The devil made me do it!" But the problem here is even greater, because logically one cannot stop at this point. For if God is in sovereign control of all things, then instead it would appear that, ultimately, *"God* made me do it."

Indeed, one response to the problem of divine sovereignty and human responsibility is that of extreme Calvinism.[1]

This response claims that free choice simply is doing what we desire, but that no one ever desires to do anything unless God gives him the desire to do so.[2] If all of this were so, then it would follow that God would be responsible for all human actions.

If it were true, then the Bible should say that God gave Judas the desire to betray Christ. But it does not. Rather, it says, "the devil had already prompted[3] Judas Iscariot, son of Simon, to betray Jesus" (John 13:2).

Nor does it help to claim that God gives only good desires but not evil ones and that all other choices result from our evil natures. For neither Lucifer nor Adam had an evil nature to begin with, and yet they sinned.

WHO MADE THE DEVIL DO IT?

For the strong (extreme) Calvinists the ultimate question is: Who made the devil do it? Or, more precisely, who caused Lucifer to sin? If free choice is doing what one desires, and if all desires

---

[1]We use the term "extreme" rather than "hyper" since hyper-Calvinism is used by some to designate a more radical view known as "superlapsarianism," which entails double-predestination (see appendix 7), denies human responsibility (see Edwin Palmer, *The Five Points of Calvinism* [Grand Rapids, Mich.: Baker Book House, 1972], 85), or nullifies concern for missions and evangelism (see Iain H. Murray, *Spurgeon v. Hyper-Calvinism: The Battle for Gospel Preaching* [Carlisle, Pa.: Banner of Truth Trust], 1995).

We should note that theologians we classify as extreme Calvinists consider themselves simply "Calvinists" and would probably object to our categorizing them in this manner. In their view, anyone who does not espouse all five points of Calvinism as they interpret them is not, strictly speaking, a true Calvinist. Nonetheless, we call them "extreme" Calvinists because they are more extreme than John Calvin himself (see appendix 2) and to distinguish them from moderate Calvinists (see chapter 7).

[2]Edwin Palmer, an extreme Calvinist, insists "that man is free—one hundred percent free—free to do exactly what he wants." But this is seriously misleading in view of what is said only a few lines later, namely, "Man is totally unable to choose equally as well between [the] good and the bad." He adds, "the non-Christian is free. He does precisely what he would like. He follows his heart's desires. Because his heart is rotten and inclined to all kinds of evil, he freely does what he wants to do, namely, sin." See Edwin H. Palmer, *The Five Points of Calvinism* (Grand Rapids, Mich.: Baker Book House, 1972), 35–36.

[3]Further, it is noteworthy that it says the devil "prompted," not forced, Judas to betray Christ. The act of Judas was free and uncoerced. This is evident from the use of the word "betray" (Matt. 26:16, 21, 23 NASB), for betrayal is a deliberate act (cf. Luke 6:16). And though the devil had put the idea into his heart (John 13:2), Judas performed the act freely, admitting later that he had "sinned" (Matt. 27:4). Jesus said to Judas, "What you are about to do, do quickly." Mark even says that what Judas did he did "conveniently" (Mark 14:10–11 KJV).

come from God, then it follows logically that God made Lucifer sin against God![4] But it is contradictory to say that God ever could be against God. God is essentially good. He cannot sin (Heb. 6:18). In fact, He cannot even look with approval on sin. Habakkuk said to God: "Your eyes are too pure to look on evil; you cannot tolerate wrong" (1:13). James reminds us that "When tempted, no one should say, 'God is tempting me.' For God cannot be tempted by evil, nor does he tempt anyone" (1:13).

So, if for no other reason, the strong Calvinist's position must be rejected because it is contradictory. And the Bible exhorts us to "avoid contradictions" (1 Tim. 6:20 NKJV). Opposites cannot both be true at the same time and in the same sense. God cannot be good and not good. He cannot be for His own essential good and be against it by giving Lucifer the desire to sin against Him. In short, God cannot be for Himself and against Himself at the same time and in the same sense.

Consequently, some less strong Calvinists claim that God does not give any evil desires but only good ones. However, this view has two problems. First, why would God give a desire to do good only to some and not to all? If He is all-loving, then surely He would love all, as the Bible says He does (John 3:16; 1 Tim. 2:4; 2 Peter 3:9). Second, this does not explain where Lucifer got the desire to sin. If it did not come from God, then it must have come from himself. But in that case, his original evil act was self-caused, that is, caused by himself—which is exactly the view of human free will the strong Calvinist rejects.[5]

WHO MADE THE DEVIL?

If God did not make the devil do it, then who did? More simply, who made the devil? The biblical answers to these questions are:

---

[4]Jonathan Edwards mistakenly believed that a man never, in any instance, wills anything contrary to his desire, or desires anything contrary to his will (Jonathan Edwards, "Freedom of the Will," in *Jonathan Edwards: Representative Selections*, eds. Clarence H. Faust and Thomas H. Johnson [New York: Hill and Wang, 1962], 267–68). But this is contrary to both Scripture (Rom. 7:15) and our conscious experience. John Locke was correct when he said, "the will is perfectly distinguished from desire" (John Locke, "An Essay Concerning Human Understanding," in *The Empiricists*, ed. Richard Taylor [Garden City, N.Y.: Doubleday & Company, Inc., 1961], 2.21.30).
[5]In spite of the fact that his mentor, Jonathan Edwards, rejects the view of human freedom called self-determination, R. C. Sproul speaks of free will as "self-determination" (R. C. Sproul, *Willing to Believe* [Grand Rapids, Mich.: Baker Book House, 1997], 158), but Sproul simply means it is not determined (caused) by anything external to itself. It is determined by things internal to itself, namely, by its nature. This is not what is meant in this discussion by a "self-determined action," which is one freely caused by the self (the I) without either external or internal constraint (see appendix 4).

God did not make the devil, and He did not make the devil do it. Rather, God made a good angel called Lucifer, and he sinned freely.

God made only good creatures

The Bible affirms that God made only good creatures. After almost every day of creation it says, "and it was good" (Gen. 1:4, 10, 12, 18, 21, 25). And after the last day, it declares, "It was very good" (1:31). Solomon added, "This only have I found: God made mankind upright . . ." (Eccl. 7:29). We are told explicitly that "every creature of God is good" (1 Tim. 4:4 KJV). And an absolutely good God cannot make an evil thing. Only a perfect creature can come from the hands of a perfect Creator.

God gave free choice to good creatures

One of the things God gave His good creatures was a good power called free will. Mankind intrinsically recognizes freedom as being good; only those who usurp and abuse power deny it, and yet even these value and seek it for themselves. And people never march against freedom. One never sees a crowd carrying placards: "Down with freedom!" or "Back to bondage!" And even if someone did speak against freedom, he would thereby be speaking for it, since he values his freedom to express that idea. In short, free choice is an undeniable good, since it affirms its own good even when attempting to deny it.

Free choice is the origin of evil

However, the power of moral free choice entails the ability either to choose the good God designed for us or to reject it. The latter is called evil. It is good to be free, but freedom makes evil possible. Free will is good in itself, but entailed in that good is the ability to choose the opposite of good, which then makes evil possible.

If God made free creatures, and if it is good to be free, then the origin of evil is in the misuse of freedom. This is not hard to understand. We all enjoy the freedom to drive, but many abuse this freedom and drive recklessly. Yet we should not blame the government that gives us the license to drive for all the evil we do with our cars. Those whose *irresponsible* driving kills others are *responsible* for what has happened. Remember: the government that gave us the permission to drive has also given us laws on how to drive safely.[6]

---

[6]Of course, both the government and God put limits on those who abuse their freedom. Human finitude, divine judgment, and eventual death place limits on all free choices.

Likewise, God is morally accountable for giving the good thing called free will, but He is not morally responsible for all the evil we do with our freedom. Solomon said it well: "This only have I found: God made mankind upright, *but men have gone in search of many schemes*" (Eccl. 7:29). In brief, God made the *fact* of freedom; we are responsible for the *acts* of freedom. The fact of freedom is good, even though some acts of freedom are evil. God is the cause of the former, and we are the cause of the latter.

DID GOD MAKE ME DO IT?

Staunch Calvinist[7] Jonathan Edwards "solved" the problem of predestination and free will by claiming that: (1) Free will is doing what we desire; (2) But God gives us the desire to do good. What about the desire to do evil? That comes from our fallen nature, which desires only evil. Apart from God giving us the desire to do good, we naturally desire to do evil.[8]

However, the faithful followers of Edwards admit this does not solve the issue of where Lucifer and Adam got the desire for their first sin. R. C. Sproul calls this an "excruciating problem," adding: "One thing is absolutely unthinkable, that God could be the author or doer of sin."[9] Yet this problem is "excruciating" only because Sproul believes in the law of noncontradiction,[10] and it appears to be a contradiction to hold, as he does, all of these premises:

(1) God cannot give anyone the desire to sin;

(2) Originally, neither Lucifer nor Adam had a sinful nature;

(3) The will does not move unless given a desire by God or by its own nature.

And here is the unmistakable conclusion: both Lucifer and Adam sinned. But Sproul is not willing to give up on premises 1 or 2 under any circumstances. Therefore, premise 3 must be false, since it is contradictory to the other premises he believes are absolutely true. For it is certain that Lucifer neither had an evil

---

[7]Some Calvinists, like W. G. T. Shedd, are more moderate at this point (see his *Dogmatic Theology*, 2nd ed., vol. 3 [Nashville: Thomas Nelson Publishers, 1980], 298f.

[8]See Jonathan Edwards, *Freedom of the Will*, eds. Arnold S. Kaufman and William K. Frankena, reprint ed. (New York: Irvington Press, 1982).

[9]R. C. Sproul, *Chosen by God* (Wheaton, Ill.: Tyndale House Publishers, 1986), 31.

[10]Sproul declared: "I don't like contradictions. I find little comfort in them. I never cease to be amazed at the ease with which Christians seem to be comfortable with them.... What I want to avoid is a God who is smaller than logic and a faith that is lower than reason" (ibid., 40–41).

nature, nor did God give him the desire to sin.

Conversely, if the followers of Jonathan Edwards insist on clinging to their flawed view of human freedom, then their God must take the rap for giving Lucifer and Adam the desire to sin. For if the original perfect creature's will is in neutral and is unmoved until God moves on it (having no sinful nature to move it toward sin), then there is only one person left in the universe to do it—God! And as "excruciating" as it is, they must either blame God for the origin of evil, or else they must give up their view of free will as doing what one desires according to one's nature or God's giving of those desires.

WHO MADE ME DO IT?

If neither the devil nor God made me do it, then who did? The biblical answer is that *I* did. That is, the "I" or "self" is the cause of evil. How? By means of the good power of free choice that God gave me.

Doesn't every event have a cause?

Strong Calvinists object to this reasoning, claiming that every event has a cause—even our actions. And to claim that God did not cause our actions would mean that there is an effect without a cause—which is absurd. In response to this reasoning, several things should be noted.

First, every *event* does have a cause. But not every *cause* has a cause, as even the strong Calvinists agree. Every painting has a painter, but every painter is not painted. Further, if every cause had a cause, then God could not be the first Uncaused Cause that He is. Hence, it is even more absurd to ask: "Who made God?" God is the *Unmade* Maker. And it is absurd to ask, "Who *made* the *Unmade?*" No one made the Unmade; He is simply *unmade*.

Pursuing the question any further is like insisting that there must be an answer to the question "Who is the bachelor's wife?" Bachelors do not have wives, and the Uncaused Being does not have a cause.[11] Likewise, if the creature, by means of the good power of

---

[11]It should not be hard for an atheist to believe that something can be uncaused, since many believe that the universe itself is uncaused. But if the universe can be uncaused because it was always there, then so can God because He was always there. Of course, the problem with the atheist's claim is that there is strong evidence that the universe had a beginning, since it is running down (see William Lane Craig, *The Kalam Cosmological Argument* [London: The Macmillan Press, Ltd., 1979]).

free choice, is the first cause of evil, then no cause of this evil action should be sought other than the person who caused it.

Second, the extreme Calvinist's objection wrongly assumes that either an evil action must be caused by some other person or thing or else it is not caused at all since, the thinking goes, every event is either caused or uncaused, and there allegedly are no other logical alternatives. Neither the extreme nor moderate Calvinist (or even Arminian) believes that evil actions have no cause for at least two basic reasons. For one, it is a violation of this fundamental rule of reason: Every effect has a cause. Even the renowned skeptic David Hume denied that he ever asserted such an "absurd" thing that things arise without a cause.[12]

What is more, if evil actions have no cause, then no one can be held responsible for them. But both good moral reason and Scripture inform us that free creatures are held morally responsible for their choices. Lucifer was condemned to eternal separation from God for his rebellion against God (Rev. 20:10; 1 Tim. 3:6), as were the angels who fell with him (Rev. 12:4, 12; Jude 6–7). Likewise, Adam and Eve were condemned for their actions (Gen. 3:1–19; Rom. 5:12).

However, if our actions are not uncaused, then is not the extreme Calvinist's view correct that they must be caused by another? Not at all. For this perspective overlooks one very important alternative, namely, that they were caused by ourselves. True, every action is either uncaused or caused. This exhausts the logical possibilities. But it does not follow that every action is either *uncaused by anyone* or *caused by someone else*. It may have been *caused by me*, i.e., by my Self. There are three possibilities: My actions are (1) uncaused; (2) caused by someone (or something) else; or (3) caused by my Self. And there are many reasons to support the last view.

WHO CAUSED ME TO DO IT?

Again, extreme Calvinists object that a self-caused action is a contradiction in terms. According to this line of thought, nothing can cause itself. We cannot, for example, lift ourselves by our own bootstraps. A cause is always prior to its effect (in being, if not in time). But we cannot be prior to ourselves. Thus, it would seem to

---

[12]Hume wrote to a friend: "But allow me to tell you that I never asserted so absurd a Proposition as that anything might arise without a cause" (*The Letters of David Hume*, ed. J. Y. T. Greig, 2 vols. [Oxford: Clarendon Press, 1932], I.187).

follow that a self-caused action is impossible, being rationally absurd.

Here again, extreme Calvinism exhibits a fundamental misunderstanding. A self-caused *being* is impossible for the reason they give, but this is not true of a self-caused *action*. It is true that we cannot exist before we exist or be before we have being. But we can and must *be* before we can *do*. That is, we must *exist* before we can *act*.

Therefore, self-caused actions are not impossible. If they were, then even God, who cannot do what is impossible (cf. Heb. 6:18), would not have been able to create the world. For there was no one or nothing else to cause the world to exist before it existed, except God. If the act of Creation was not self-caused by God, then it could not have been created, since He, the Uncaused Cause, is the only one who could have performed it.

Likewise, if self-caused actions are not possible, then there is no explanation for Lucifer's sin. For again, a sinless God could not have caused Lucifer to sin (James 1:13). And since Lucifer was the first one to sin, then his action must have been self-caused or else he would never have been able to sin. It follows that self-caused actions are possible. Even moderate Calvinists, like W. G. T. Shedd, admit this, saying, "A positive act of angelic self-determination is requisite.... Nothing but the spontaneity of will can produce the sin; and God does not work in the will to cause evil spontaneity" (*Dogmatic Theology*, 1.420).

Perhaps the reason it seems to some that self-caused actions are not possible is the term "self-caused" itself. It might be better understood were we to speak of our actions as "caused by myself" (as opposed to "caused by another"). Or, better yet, actions caused by my Self (that is, by *me, myself,* or *I*). Actions do not cause themselves, but a self can cause an action. Speaking this way would eliminate the ambiguity of language that gives rise to the false belief that a self-caused action is impossible.

WHY DID I DO IT?

But why do I do what I do? Don't my background, training, and environment *affect* what I do? Yes, they do, but they do not *force* me to do it. They *affect* my actions, but they do not *effect* (i.e., cause) them. They *influence* but do not *control* my actions. That I still have the power to make free moral choices is true for several reasons.

First, there is a difference between *inherited physical characteris-*

tics (like brown eyes), over which I have no control, and *inherited spiritual tendencies* (like lust), over which I ought to have control. We cannot avoid the basic size, color, talents, or ethnic group from which we have come. But we do have a choice as to whether to follow spiritual impulses we may have inherited, like impatience, anger, pride, or sexual impurity. None of these tendencies excuses evil actions that may follow from them; for instance, physical abuse, murder, or sexual perversion.

We may feel the impulse to strike back at someone who has said something nasty about us, but we can choose not to act on this impulse. Morally speaking, "irresistible urges" are urges that have not been resisted. People have died for lack of water and food, but no one has ever been known to die for lack of sex, alcohol, or other drugs to fulfill his cravings! We have a free choice in all these areas.

Second, there is a difference between moral and nonmoral (amoral) choices. Our preferences for color are nonmoral and largely determined. But a choice to be racist based on the color of one's or another's skin is not nonmoral, nor is it an act we could not avoid performing.

Finally, those who point out that all actions have a reason and that reason determines what we do often fail to properly distinguish a purpose from a cause. The purpose is *why* I act. The cause is *what* produces the act. A purpose is a *final cause* (that *for which* we act), but a cause is an *efficient cause* (that *by which* we act). No end or goal of an act *produces* a human free act. It is simply the *purpose* for which we *choose* to act. If we *choose* to cheat or steal, we do so freely, even though greed may have been the *purpose* for doing so. Moral actions spring from our free choices, no matter what the purposes for them may have been.

HOW CAN AN EVIL NATURE CHOOSE GOOD?

Extreme Calvinists, following Jonathan Edwards, object that will necessarily follows nature.[13] This basic argument states that what is good by nature cannot will evil, and what is evil by nature cannot will good. Unless God gives evil men the desire to will good, they cannot will good any more than dead persons can raise themselves back to life. Following the "later" Augustine (see appendix 3), before the Fall, Adam was able to sin or not to sin; after the Fall, *he was able to sin but unable not to sin*; after regeneration

---

[13]See R. C. Sproul, *Chosen by God*, 60–61.

man is able to sin or not to sin (like Adam before the Fall); and in heaven man will be both able not to sin and not able to sin.

In response, it should be observed that this is contrary to Augustine's own earlier position (see appendix 3) that we are born with a *propensity* but not a *necessity* to sin.[14] It makes sin unavoidable, rather than inevitable. That is, it is inevitable that we *will* sin, but it is not inevitable that we *must* sin. Even though we are depraved and by nature bent toward sin, nonetheless, each sin is freely chosen. In addition, there are several serious problems with this position.

First of all, it is self-contradictory, for it holds two logically opposite premises: (1) What is good by nature cannot will evil (since will follows nature); (2) Yet Lucifer and Adam, who *were* good by nature, willed evil.

Second, it logically removes all responsibility for evil actions by evil (unregenerated) creatures, since they have no real choice in the evil they do. They can't help but do what comes naturally.

Third, it confuses *desire* and *decision.* That evil men naturally *desire* to sin does not mean they must *decide* to sin. Both Scripture and experience inform us that there is a difference. Paul writes, "I do not understand what I do. For *what I want to do I do not do,* but *what I hate I do"* (Rom. 7:15).[15] Personal experience reveals that we sometimes act contrary to our strongest desire, such as to retaliate or to shirk responsibility.[16]

Fourth, this view is a form of determinism. It believes that our moral actions are determined (caused) by another, rather than self-determined (caused) by ourselves.

Fifth, if what is evil can't will good, and if what is good can't

---

[14]Augustine said of Adam and Eve, "The sin which they committed was so great that it impaired all human nature—in this sense, that the nature has been transmitted to posterity with a propensity to sin and a necessity to die" (Augustine, "City of God," in *A Select Library of the Nicene and Post-Nicene Fathers of the Christian Church,* ed. Philip Schaff, vol. 2 [Grand Rapids, Mich.: Wm. B. Eerdmans Publishing Co., 1956], 14.1).

[15]Sproul suggests that this passage is simply speaking of "conflicting desires" (*Chosen by God,* 59). But this is not consistent with the text, which says that what "I do" (i.e., *choose* to do) is often contrary to what I "want" (i.e., desire). Elsewhere, Sproul offers the implausible suggestion that Paul is simply experiencing the "all things being equal dimension" (*Willing to Believe,* 156). That is, we choose what we do not want to choose when all things are equal—but they are not always so! Hence, we always choose what we desire. It is painful to watch extreme Calvinists go through these exegetical contortions in order to make a text say what their preconceived theology mandates that it must say.

[16]Many extreme Calvinists claim (see Sproul, *Chosen by God,* 58–59) that whatever we ultimately decide to do is really our strongest desire, even when we decide to go against what we experience as our strongest desire. But this is really victory by stipulated definition and not a real argument. It is both a denial of our experience and is unfalsifiable.

will evil, then why do Christians who have been given good natures still choose to sin?

Many extreme Calvinists attempt to avoid this charge by redefining determinism. Sproul does so by suggesting, "Determinism means that we are forced or coerced to do things by external force."[17] This is the fallacy of special pleading. This particular reasoning admits that there is an *internal* determination but denies that it should be called "determinism" because there was no *external* determination. Yet a rose by any other name is still a rose. The bottom line is, they believe that irresistible forces were exerted upon free creatures in order to get them to do what God wanted them to do. With the exception of the later Augustine (see appendix 3) there was no major church father up to the Reformation who held this view (see appendix 1).

FOR HEAVEN'S SAKE, WHOSE FAULT IS IT?

The unpleasant truth is that even though I have an inherited sin nature (Eph. 2:3), I have no one to blame but myself (i.e., my *Self*) for my personal moral actions. This is clear for many reasons.[18]

Responsibility and the ability to respond

Both extreme and moderate Calvinists (*and* Arminians) agree that God holds free creatures morally responsible for their free choices. Indeed, the Bible is filled with references supporting this conclusion. This is true of Lucifer (1 Tim. 3:6), other angels who fell (Jude 6–7), Adam and Eve (1 Tim. 2:14), and of all human beings since the Fall (Rom. 3:19).

However, sound reason demands that there is no responsibility where there is no ability to respond. It is not rational to hold someone responsible when they could not have responded. And God is not irrational. His omniscience means God is the most rational Being in the universe. Therefore, reason also demands that all moral creatures are morally free; that is, they have the ability to respond one way or another.[19] Whatever evil we do and are respon-

---

[17]Sproul, *Chosen by God*, 59.

[18]This is not to say that Adam's sin has no effect on us; it does (Rom. 5:12). We are born in sin (Ps. 51:5) and are sinners by nature (Rom. 7:18). We are born with a bent to sinning. Nevertheless, in spite of this natural inclination, we are personally responsible for sins we commit. Again, this is the difference between desire and decision.

[19]Minimally, free will is the ability to do otherwise. The degree to which a person is free is debated among Christians who reject the extreme Calvinist's view (see appendices 1 and 4). What they agree on is that one cannot be both forced and free (see chapter 4).

sible for, we could have responded otherwise. When we did evil we could have *not* done it. This is what is meant by a "self-caused" action. It is an action that was not caused by another but by one's Self. It is an action that one could have avoided (see also appendix 4).

— *Ought implies can*

Not only are evil moral actions ones that *could* have been otherwise, but they *should* have been otherwise. There is agreement by both the extreme Calvinists and their opponents that a moral duty is something we *ought* to do. Moral laws are prescriptive, not merely descriptive. They prescribe actions that we *should* (or *should not*) do.

But here, too, logic seems to insist that such moral obligations imply that we have self-determining moral free choice. For *ought* implies *can*. That is, what we ought to do implies that we can do it. Otherwise, we have to assume that the Moral Lawgiver is prescribing the irrational, commanding that we do what is literally impossible for us to do. Good reason appears to insist that if God demands it, then we can do it. Moral obligation implies moral freedom.

The objection brought against this conclusion by the strong Calvinist calls for comment. For he insists that God often commands us to do the impossible and yet still holds us responsible for not doing it.[20] For example, God commanded: "Be perfect, therefore, as your heavenly Father is perfect" (Matt. 5:48). Yet we all are painfully aware that in our fallen state this is impossible. In fact, we are commanded never to sin, and yet as depraved beings we cannot avoid sinning. For we are sinners "by nature" (Eph. 2:3).

Two comments should be made, then, in response to this objection. First of all, when we say "*ought* implies *can*" we do not mean that whatever we ought to do we can do by our own strength.[21] This would be contrary to the clear teaching of Christ that "without me you can do nothing" (John 15:5). We can't do anything but, as Paul said, "[We] can do all things through Christ who strengthens [us]" (Phil. 4:13 NKJV). Sure, we are told to "work out [our] own salvation with fear and trembling" (Phil. 2:12), but only because "it is God who works in [us] to will and to act according to

---

[20]See R. C. Sproul, *Willing to Believe*, 99.

[21]This error is called Pelagianism, named after the early church teacher called Pelagius, against whose supposed views (really, his followers' views) Augustine wrote many works (see appendix 3).

his good purpose" (Phil. 2:13). Hence, *"ought* implies *can"* only in the sense that we can *by the grace of God.* Without His grace we cannot overcome sin.

Second, further evidence that we can do what we ought to do by God's grace is found in a familiar passage: "No temptation has seized you except what is common to man. And God is faithful; *he will not let you be tempted beyond what you can bear.* But when you are tempted, he will also provide a way out so that you can stand up under it" (1 Cor. 10:13). It couldn't be clearer: God never prescribes anything without providing the way to accomplish it. If we are morally bound, then we must be morally free.

Reward and punishment

Another evidence that we have morally self-determining free choice is that Scripture and common moral wisdom both inform us that praise and blame make no real sense unless those praised or blamed were free to do otherwise. Why eulogize Mother Teresa and vilify Hitler, if they could not help doing what they did? Why blame Adolf Eichmann and praise Martin Luther King, if they had no free choice in the matter? Yet they did, and we do. The Bible says plainly that God " 'will give to each person according to what he has done' " (Rom. 2:6).

An undeniable fact

Fatalists and determinists[22] have attempted in vain to deny human freedom—and this they have done without anyone forcing them to do so! The fact is that freedom is undeniable. For if everything were determined, then so would the determinists be determined to believe that we are not free. But determinists believe that determinism is true and non-determinism is false. Further, they believe that all non-determinists ought to change their view and become determinists. Yet this implies that non-determinists are free to change their view—which is contrary to determinism. Thus, it only follows that determinism is false, since it is contradictory to its own claim. (Of course, this is not to deny that all free acts are determined by God in the sense that He foreknew—for sure—that we would freely perform them [see chapter 3].)

---

[22]By "determinists" here we mean those who deny that in moral decisions we are free to do other than we do. A determinist, as opposed to a self-determinist, believes that all moral acts are not caused by ourselves but are caused by someone (or something) else.

WHAT SAITH THE SCRIPTURES?

From beginning to end the Bible affirms, both implicitly and explicitly, that human beings have free choice. This is true both prior to and after the Fall of Adam, although free will is definitely affected by sin and severely limited in what it can do.

Free will before the Fall

The power of free choice is part of mankind being created in the image of God (Gen. 1:27). Adam and Eve were commanded: (1) to multiply their kind (1:28) and (2) to refrain from eating the forbidden fruit (2:16–17). Both of these responsibilities imply the ability to respond. As noted above, the fact that they *ought* to obey these commands implied that they *could* obey them.

The text narrates their choice in the latter, saying, *"she* took some and *ate it.* She also gave some to her husband, who was with her, and *he ate it"* (Gen. 3:6). God's condemnation of them makes it evident that they were free. He asked, " 'Have *you eaten* from the tree that I commanded you not to eat from?' " (Gen. 3:11). "God said to the woman, 'What is this *you have done?'* The woman said, 'The serpent deceived me, and *I ate'* " (3:13).

The New Testament references to Adam's act make it plain that he made a free choice for which he was responsible. Romans 5 calls it "sin" (v. 16), an "offense" (v. 15 NKJV), and "disobedience" (v. 19). 1 Timothy 2 refers to Adam's act as a "transgression" (v. 14 NKJV). All these descriptions imply that it was a morally free and culpable act.

Free will after the Fall

Even after Adam sinned and became spiritually "dead"[23] (Gen. 2:17; cf. Eph. 2:1) and a sinner "by nature" (Eph. 2:3), he was not so completely depraved that he could neither hear the voice of God nor make a free response (see chapter 4). For "the LORD God called to the man, 'Where are you?' He answered, *'I heard you in the garden, and I was afraid because I was naked; so I hid'* " (Gen. 3:9–10). God's image in Adam was *effaced* by the Fall but not *erased.* It was marred but not destroyed. Indeed, the image of God (which includes free will) is still in human beings after the Fall. This is why murder (Gen. 9:6) and even cursing (James 3:9) of other people are sins, "for in the image of God has God made man" (Gen. 9:6).

---

[23]"Spiritual death" in the Bible does not mean annihilation, but separation. Isaiah said, "But your iniquities have separated you from your God" (Isa. 59:2). Likewise, the "second death" is not annihilation but conscious separation from God (Rev. 20:14; cf. 19:20; 20:10).

Fallen descendants of Adam have free will

Both Scripture and good reason inform us that depraved human beings have the power of free choice.[24] The Bible says fallen man is ignorant, depraved, and a slave of sin. But all these conditions involve a choice. Peter speaks of depraved ignorance as being ignorant "willingly" (2 Peter 3:5 KJV). Paul declared that unsaved people have "clearly seen" and "understood" the truth but they deliberately "suppress" it (or "hold it down" [Rom. 1:18–19]). As a result, they are "without excuse." Even our enslavement to sin is a result of a free choice. He adds, "Don't you know that when you offer yourselves to someone to obey him as slaves, you are slaves to the one whom *you obey*..." (Rom. 6:16). Even spiritual blindness is a result of the choice not to believe. For "The god of this age has blinded the minds of *unbelievers*, so that they cannot see the light of the gospel..." (2 Cor. 4:4).

With respect to *initiating* or *attaining* their own salvation, both Luther and Calvin were right in asserting that fallen humans are not free with regard to "things above," that is, achieving their own salvation.[25] However, contrary to strong Calvinism, in regard to the freedom of *accepting* God's gift of salvation the Bible is clear: Fallen beings are free. Thus, the free choice of fallen human beings is both "horizontal" (social) with respect to things in this world and "vertical" (spiritual). The former is evident in the choice of a mate: "But if her husband dies, she is *free* to marry anyone *she wishes*, but he must belong to the Lord" (1 Cor. 7:39). This is a freedom described as having *"no constraint,"* and where one has *"authority over his own will,"* and where one *"has decided this in his own heart"* (1 Cor. 7:37 NASB). This same horizontal freedom is described in an act of giving "entirely *on their own*" (2 Cor. 8:3) as well as *"spontaneous and not forced"* (Philem. 14). And the vertical ability to believe is everywhere implied in the Gospel call (cf. Acts 16:31; 17:30). Freedom for God's creatures, as it is for the God in whose image they are made, is described in James 1:18: *"Of his own will begat he us with the word of truth..."* (KJV).

Peter describes what is meant by free choice when he says it is *"not under compulsion"* but *"voluntary"* (1 Peter 5:2 NASB). Paul depicts the nature of freedom as an act where one *"purposed in his heart"* and *did not act under* "compulsion" (2 Cor. 9:7 NASB). In Phi-

---

[24]Even depravity involved a choice by Adam and by all his spiritual descendants (Rom. 5:12).

[25]See Martin Luther, *The Bondage of the Will*, trans. Henry Cole (Grand Rapids, Mich.: Baker Book House, 1976), 79; and John Calvin, *The Institutes of the Christian Religion*, trans. Henry Beveridge (Grand Rapids, Mich.: Wm. B. Eerdmans Publishing Co., 1957), vol. 2, 79.

lemon, he says it is an act of *"consent"* and *"should not be . . . by compulsion"* but *"of your own free will"* (NASB).

W. G. T. Shedd summed it up directly when he wrote:

> Though actuated by the Holy Spirit, the holy will is nevertheless a self-moving and uncompelled faculty. Holy inclination is the will's right self-motion because of the Divine actuation, or "God's working in the will to will." Sinful inclination is the will's wrong self-motion without Divine actuation. But the motion in both instances is that of mind, not of matter; spiritual, not mechanical; free, not forced motion (*Dogmatic Theology*, 3.300).

Even unsaved people have a free choice as to either receiving or rejecting God's gift of salvation (Rom. 6:23). Jesus spoke of those who rejected Him, saying, " 'O Jerusalem, Jerusalem . . . how often I have longed to gather your children together, as a hen gathers her chicks under her wings, but *you were not willing*' " (Matt. 23:37). And John affirmed that *"all who received him* [Christ], to those who believed in his name, he gave the right to become children of God" (John 1:12). Indeed, He desires that all unsaved people will change their minds (repent). For "He [God] is patient with you, not wanting anyone to perish, but everyone to come to *repentance*" (2 Peter 3:9). That is, to a change of mind.

Like the alternatives of life and death Moses gave to Israel, God says, *"Choose* life" (Deut. 30:19). Or, as Joshua said to his people, " '*Choose* you this day whom ye will serve' " (Josh. 24:15 KJV). Or, as God said to David, "This is what the LORD says: 'I am giving you three options. *Choose* one of them for me to carry out against you' " (2 Sam. 24:12). Morally and spiritually responsible alternatives are set before human beings by God, leaving the *choice* and *responsibility* to them. Jesus said to the unbelievers of His day, "If *you do not believe* that I am, you will indeed die in your sins" (John 8:24). Over and over He declared belief to be something they were to *do*: " '*We believe* and know that you are the Holy One of God' " (John 6:69); " 'Who is he, sir? . . . Tell me so that *I may believe* in him' " (John 9:36); "Then the man said, 'Lord, *I believe*,' and he worshiped him" (John 9:38); "Jesus answered, 'I did tell you, but *you do not believe*' " (John 10:25). This is why Jesus said, " '*Whoever believes* in him is not condemned, but whoever does not believe stands condemned already *because he has not believed* in the name of God's one and only Son' " (John 3:18). Plainly, then, belief is our responsibility and is rooted in our ability to respond. This view has overwhelming support by virtually all the great church fathers up to the sixteenth century (see appendix 1).

Can everyone believe?

Contrary to the extreme Calvinist's view, faith is not a gift that God offers only to some (see appendix 5). All are responsible to believe and "whoever" decides to believe can believe (cf. John 3:16).[26] Jesus says, " *'Whosoever believeth* in him shall have everlasting life' " (John 3:16 KJV). He adds, " *'Whoever believes* in him is not condemned' " (v. 18). And, " *'Whoever comes* to me I will never drive away' " (John 6:37). Revelation 22:17 also states: " *'Whoever* is thirsty, *let him come;* and whoever wishes, *let him take* the free gift of the water of life."

If everyone can believe, why then did Jesus assert of some " 'For this reason they could not believe, because, as Isaiah says elsewhere: "He has blinded their eyes and deadened their hearts, so they can neither see with their eyes, nor understand with their hearts, nor turn—and I would heal them" ' " (John 12:39–40)?

The answer is found in the context: (1) Belief was obviously their responsibility, since God held them responsible for not believing. Only two verses earlier we read, "Even after Jesus had done all these miraculous signs in their presence, *they still would not believe in him*" (John 12:37); (2) Jesus was speaking to hardhearted Jews who had seen many indisputable miracles (including the resurrection of Lazarus [John 11]) and who had been called upon many times to believe before this point (cf. John 8:26), which reveals that they were able to do so; and (3) It was their own stubborn unbelief that brought on their blindness. Jesus had said to them, " 'I told you that you would die in your sins; *if you do not believe* that I am, you will indeed die in your sins' " (John 8:24). Thus, it was chosen and avoidable blindness.

Can anyone believe unaided by God's grace?

While all truly free acts are self-determined and could have been otherwise, nonetheless, it is also true that no free human act can move toward God or do any spiritual good without the aid of His grace. This is evident from the following Scriptures:

---

[26]It is an intramural debate among those opposed to extreme Calvinism whether faith is a gift or not. The Bible is seriously lacking in any verses demonstrating that faith is a gift (see appendix 5). But if it is a gift, then it is one offered to all and can be freely accepted or rejected. Arminius spoke of "the gift of faith," but added that it must be "received" by free will (James Arminius, "Works," in *The Writings of James Arminius*, trans. James Nichols, vol. 1 [Grand Rapids, Mich.: Baker Book House, 1956], 2.52 [article 27]).

But who am I, and who are my people, that we should be able to give as generously as this? Everything comes from you, and we have given you only what comes from your hand (1 Chron. 29:14).

"No one can come to me unless the Father who sent me draws him, and I will raise him up at the last day" (John 6:44).

"I am the vine; you are the branches. If a man remains in me and I in him, he will bear much fruit; apart from me you can do nothing" (John 15:5).

[Jesus prayed:] "Holy Father, protect them by the power of your name—the name you gave me—so that they may be one as we are one" (John 17:11).

"While I was with them, I protected them and kept them safe by that name you gave me. None has been lost except the one doomed to destruction so that Scripture would be fulfilled" (John 17:12).

But by the grace of God I am what I am, and his grace to me was not without effect. No, I worked harder than all of them—yet not I, but the grace of God that was with me (1 Cor. 15:10).

Not that we are competent in ourselves to claim anything for ourselves, but our competence comes from God (2 Cor. 3:5).

But he said to me, "My grace is sufficient for you, for my power is made perfect in weakness." Therefore I will boast all the more gladly about my weaknesses, so that Christ's power may rest on me (2 Cor. 12:9).

Continue to work out your salvation with fear and trembling, for it is God who works in you to will and to act according to his good purpose (Phil. 2:12–13).

I can do everything through him who gives me strength (Phil. 4:13).

W. G. T. Shedd, who as stated previously is a moderate Calvinist, wraps it up this way:

If the sinner voluntarily rejects the offered mercy of God, he is culpable for so doing, and is therefore amenable to the charge of culpability and responsible before the divine tribunal because of it.... Man is responsible for sin because he is both the author and the actor of it; but he is not responsible for holiness, because he is only the actor and not the author.... "The sinner is free in accepting or rejecting the invitations of the gospel." If he accepts them, he does so freely under the actuation of the Holy Spirit. If he rejects them, he does so freely without this actuation and solely by his own self-determination (*Dogmatic Theology*, 3.298–299).

EITHER/OR OR BOTH/AND?

Sovereignty and free will. Is it one *or* the other, or is it both one *and* the other? The Bible says both. In the first chapter we saw that God is sovereign over all things, including human events and free choices. Nothing catches God by surprise, and nothing is outside His control (see chapter 1). On the other hand, in this chapter we have seen that human beings, even in their fallen state, have the God-given power of free choice. This applies to many earthly things here "below" as it does to heavenly things from "above," namely, with regard to *receiving* God's gift of salvation.

The mystery of the relationship between divine sovereignty and human free will has challenged the greatest Christian thinkers down through the centuries. Unfortunately, the extreme Calvinists have sacrificed human responsibility in order to preserve divine sovereignty (see chapter 4). Likewise, as we shall see later, extreme Arminians have sacrificed God's sovereignty in order to hold on to man's free will (see chapter 5). We believe that both of these alternatives are wrong and lead to inordinately extreme actions (see chapter 6).

CHAPTER THREE

VIEWING THE ALTERNATIVES

THE TWIN TRUTHS OF SOVEREIGNTY AND RESPONSIBILITY

The Bible emphatically declares that God has absolute sovereignty over all that happens, including the salvation of saints and the condemnation of unrepentant sinners (see chapter 1). Nevertheless, the same Scripture stresses that the moral responsibility for moral actions rests squarely with free moral agents and not with God (see chapter 2). It has been said that on the outside of the door of heaven it reads, "Whosoever will may enter," while on the inside is written, "I have chosen you." According to Scripture, both are true. This is one of the great mysteries of the Christian faith, along with the Trinity and the Incarnation (see 1 Tim. 3:16).

The Cross: both predetermined and freely chosen

One of the most powerful indications that the Bible sees no contradiction between God's predetermination and human free choice is found in Acts 2:23. On the one hand, it declares that Jesus' death was determined "by *God's set purpose* and foreknowledge." (This can also be rendered "determinate counsel" KJV or "God's definite plan"

TCNT.) Yet even though it was set and determined from all eternity that Jesus would die, nonetheless, Jesus says He did it freely: " 'I lay down my life—only to take it up again. *No one takes it from me,* but *I lay it down of my own accord' "* (John 10:17–18).

Nothing could be clearer. God determined it from all eternity, and yet Jesus did it freely. And if it can be true of Jesus' free choices, then there is no contradiction in asserting that our free actions are both determined and free. As far as the Bible is concerned, *there is no contradiction between divine predestination and human free choice!*

The crucifiers: both predetermined and free

Sometimes the twin truths of divine sovereignty and human responsibility are expressed in the same passage. In one of the texts just mentioned, both God's predetermination and man's wicked free choice are present: " 'This man [Jesus] was handed over to you by *God's set purpose and foreknowledge;* and *you . . . put him to death* by nailing him to the cross' " (Acts 2:23). As before, while God determined their actions from all eternity, nevertheless, those who carried out the crucifying of Jesus were free to perform these actions—and were morally responsible for them. Here again, it is not either sovereignty or free choice; it is both sovereignty and free choice.

In Acts 3, verses 12, 15, and 18 contain the same two truths. On the one hand, the *"Men of Israel"* had *"killed the Prince of life"* (NKJV). Yet on the other hand, "this is *how* God fulfilled *what he [God] had foretold* through all the prophets, saying that his Christ would suffer." So it had to happen because He foretold that it would, yet "this is how God fulfilled" it, by the Jews freely killing the Christ.

Jesus' betrayal: both necessary and freely chosen

Jesus proclaimed: " 'And truly the Son of man goeth, *as it was determined:* but *woe unto that man by whom he is betrayed!' "* (Luke 22:22 KJV). God determined that the betrayal must happen, but when it occurred it did so as a result of a free and responsible act of Judas. There is no contradiction between these two truths.

Stumbling over Christ: both disobedience and destiny

In his first letter, Peter cites Isaiah: He [Christ] is " 'A stone that causes men to stumble and a rock that makes them fall.' They stumble because *they disobey* the message—which is also what *they were destined* for" (1 Peter 2:8; cf. Isa. 8:14). With no sense of difficulty or disjunction, Peter records in the same verse that men reject Christ, the Stone, both because of their own disobedience and because God had destined them to it. There is no contradiction, since God knew exactly what they would freely do.[1]

Conspiracy against Jesus: both predetermined and pernicious

Peter also pairs divine sovereignty and human responsibility in Acts: " 'Indeed Herod and Pontius Pilate met together with the Gentiles and the people of Israel in this city to *conspire against* your holy servant Jesus, whom you anointed. *They did* what your *[God's] power and will had decided beforehand* should happen' " (Acts 4:27–28). Notice that Herod, Pilate, the Gentiles, and the Jewish leaders conspired and *"did"* it, but God's "power and will had decided beforehand" what would happen. Both are true.

Joseph's enslavement: intended both by his brothers and by God

Looking briefly at one example from the Old Testament, Genesis informs us that Joseph's brothers sold him into Egypt as a slave. But eventually Joseph said, "So then, *it was not you who sent me here, but God"* (Gen. 45:8). And later he added, " '*You intended to harm me,* but *God intended it for good* to accomplish what is now being done, the saving of many lives' " (Gen. 50:20). Again, both are true. One and the same event is the result of both God's plan and human free choice, even though God intended only good through it.

Salvation: both chosen by God and chosen by us

Another example of both God's sovereignty and our responsibility being found in the same scriptural text is found in Jesus' statement from John 6:37: " '*All that the Father gives me will come to me,* and *whoever comes to me* I will never drive away.' " On the one hand, only those the Father preordains to do so will come to Christ (John 6:44). On the other hand, it is also true that "whoever" chooses to come will be saved (Rom. 10:13).

Salvation: both ordained to it and persuaded into it

There is an interesting passage in Acts which states that "*all who were appointed [by God] for eternal life* believed" (13:48). Yet within a few verses of this text Luke says, "*they [Paul and Barnabas]*

---

[1]"The idea behind the words 'a stone of stumbling' . . . is that of a stone or rock which lies in the road so that travelers knock against it or get tripped up by it. It is thus that Christ, once He is revealed, inescapably stands in the way of those who refuse to respond to the testimony about Him. *The Word,* both spoken and living, becomes a stumbling-block to those who are *disobedient,* i.e., those who actively revolt against the gospel (see iv. 17)" (Alan M. Stibbs, *The Older Tyndale New Testament Commentary on First Peter* [Grand Rapids, Mich.: Wm. B. Eerdmans Publishing Co., 1959]).

spoke so effectively that a great number of Jews and Gentiles believed" (14:1). According to this rendering, in the first text only those who were preordained to be saved would come to faith. But it is also true that persuasive preaching is a means by which people come to faith in Christ. So the Bible teaches *both* divine sovereignty *and* human responsibility in the same overall passage. The same act can be determined by God as well as chosen by man. There is no contradiction between these as far as Scripture is concerned.

Some moderate Calvinists, like J. O. Buswell, deny this is a reference to predestination. He wrote, "Actually the words of Acts 13:48–49 do not necessarily have any reference whatever to the doctrine of God's eternal decree of election. The passive participle *tetagmenoi* may simply mean 'ready,' and we might well read, 'as many as were prepared for eternal life, believed.' " He adds, "Commenting on this word, Alford says, 'The meaning of this word must be determined by the context. The Jews had *judged themselves unworthy of eternal life* (v. 46); the Gentiles, "as many as were disposed to eternal life," believed. . . . To find in this text preordination to life asserted, is to force both the word and the context to a meaning which they do not contain.' "[2] Be this as it may, even if this text is taken as such, in the strong sense there is no contradiction between preordination and persuasion, since God preordained the means (persuasion) with the end (eternal life).

Rejection of Christ: both by God's destiny and by our disobedience

As mentioned before, the harmony between predetermination and free choice is clear in Peter's words: "They stumble because *they disobey* the message—which is also what *they were destined* for" (1 Peter 2:8). There is no inconsistency here: they were destined to disobey, and God knew for sure they would choose to reject Christ. Buswell comments that "Acts 13:46 notes that the Jews by their own choice rejected the message. Then, Paul turns to the Gentiles. Individual choice determined the rejection of the message, thus by inference it appears that when this rejection occurred, then the Gentiles moved into the sphere, so to speak, of God's appointed grace to them, and thus they also believed. Notice verse 48 states that the Gentiles *heard* the good news. *They were glad, they glorified the word of the Lord,* and *their belief thus moved them into the sphere of God's grace,* the appoint-

---

[2]James Oliver Buswell, Jr., *A Systematic Theology of the Christian Religion, vol. II* (Grand Rapids, Mich.: Zondervan, 1962–63), 152–53.

ment, so to speak, of eternal life. Even as *the Jews chose to reject,* so *the Gentiles chose, within God's grace, to believe."*[3]

A beautiful illustration

One final illustration of the congruency between predetermination and free choice is found in the shipwreck recorded by Luke in Acts 27. Paul assured his fellow travelers in advance that " 'not one of you will be lost; only the ship will be destroyed' " (v. 22). Yet a few verses later he warned them, " '*Unless these men stay with the ship, you cannot be saved*' " (v. 31). Both are true. God knew in advance and had revealed to Paul that none would drown (cf. v. 23). But He also knew it would be through their free choice to stay on the ship that this would be accomplished.

SOVEREIGNTY AND RESPONSIBILITY

No one has ever demonstrated a contradiction between predestination and free choice. There is no irresolvable conflict between an event being predetermined by an all-knowing God and it also being freely chosen by us. Even the famous Calvinistic *Westminster Confession of Faith* (1646) makes this point when it says, "Although in relation to the foreknowledge and decree of God, the first cause, all things come to pass immutably and infallibly, yet by the same providence he ordereth them to fall out, according to the nature of *second causes,* either necessarily, *freely,* or contingently" (emphasis mine).

The noted Puritan Calvinist Stephen Charnock held this same position, declaring:

> That is, he [God] did not only know that we would do such actions, but that we would do them freely; he foresaw that the will would freely determine itself to this or that ... and though God knows contingent things, yet they remain in the nature of contingencies; and though God knows free agents, yet they remain in the nature of liberty....
>
> God did not foreknow the actions of man, as necessary, but as free; so that liberty is rather established by this foreknowledge, than removed. God did not foreknow that Adam had not a power to stand, or that any man hath not a power to omit such a sinful action, but that he would not omit it.
>
> Thus, man hath a power to do otherwise than that which

---

[3]Ibid., emphasis mine.

God foreknows he will do. Adam was not determined by any inward necessity to fall, nor any man by any inward necessity to commit this or that particular sin; but God foresaw that he would fall, and fall freely.[4]

Consider the logic of this view:

God knows—for sure—precisely how we will use our freedom. It goes like this:

(1) God knows all things, including the future (Isa. 46:10; Ps. 147:5).

(2) God knew from eternity that Jesus would die on the Cross (Acts 2:23; cf. Rev. 13:8).

(3) Thus, Jesus *must* die on the Cross. (If he had not died on the Cross, then God would have been wrong in what He foreknew. But an all-knowing [omniscient] God cannot be wrong in what He knows.)

(4) But Jesus freely chose to die on the Cross (John 10:17–18).

(5) Therefore, one and the same event is both predetermined and freely chosen at the same time.

The same logic applies to predetermination and free choice in either salvation or condemnation. Consider the following:

(1) God knows all things.

(2) Whatever God foreknows must come to pass (i.e., is determined). If it did not come to pass, then God would have been wrong in what He foreknew. But an all-knowing Being cannot be wrong in what He foreknows.

(3) God knew Judas would betray Christ.

(4) Therefore, it *had to come to pass* (i.e., was determined) that Judas would betray Christ.

The logic is flawless. If God has an infallible knowledge of future free acts, then the future is completely determined. But what *does not* follow from this is that

(5a) Judas was not free to betray (or not to betray) Christ.

This is because there is no contradiction in claiming that God *knew for sure* (i.e., predetermined) that Judas would *freely* (i.e., with free choice) betray Christ.

What *is contradictory* to affirm—and the Bible never affirms it— is the following statement:

(5b) Judas was *coerced* to betray Christ *freely*.

One and the same act cannot be both forced and free at the same

---

[4]Stephen Charnock, *Discourses upon the Existence and Attributes of God* (Grand Rapids, Mich.: Baker Book House, 1979), 450.

time and in the same sense. For coerced acts are not free acts, as is clear from both the Bible and good reason. The Bible (see chapter 2) uses terms like *"no constraint"* and *"authority over [one's] own will"* (1 Cor. 7:37 NASB) or *"not under compulsion"* but *"voluntarily"* (1 Peter 5:2; 1 Cor 9:17). Free acts are acts of *"consent"* and *"should not be . . . by compulsion"* but *"of [one's] own free will"* (Philem. 14). At a minimum, freedom means the power of contrary choice; that is, an agent is free only if he could have done otherwise.

Further, good reason informs us that if someone is forced against his will to commit a crime, then he is not responsible for it. For example, if some three-hundred-pound muscleman forced your hand on a loaded gun and pointed it at someone else and squeezed your finger on the trigger, you are not responsible for the shot that killed him/her.

The same reasoning (showing there is no contradiction in affirming both that God determined Judas would betray Christ and yet that Judas did it freely) applies to those who accept Christ as well as to those who reject Him. An example can be briefly stated as follows:

(1) God knows all things.

(2) Whatever God foreknows must come to pass (i.e., is predetermined).[5]

(3) God foreknew the apostle John would accept Christ.

(4) Therefore, it had to come to pass (as predetermined) that John would accept Christ.

But here again John's acceptance is free. It is simply that God knowingly predetermined from all eternity that John would freely accept Christ.[6]

Mystery or contradiction?

Does not the law of noncontradiction demand that two opposite statements cannot both be true at the same time and in the same sense? Yes, of course it does.[7] But these two statements are not logically opposite.

---

[5]By "determined" here we do not mean that the act is directly caused by God. It was caused by human free choice (which is a self-determined act). By "determined" it is meant that the inevitability of the event was fixed in advance since God knew infallibly that it would come to pass. Of course, God predetermined that it would be a self-determined action. God was only the remote and primary remote cause. Human freedom was the immediate and secondary cause.

[6]This is not to say that John would *initiate* the move to Christ or that it could be done without the movement of the Holy Spirit on his heart and will. This is the subject of chapter 4.

[7]The Bible uses the term "mystery" of things that go beyond reason but not against reason. However, it never uses the words "paradox" or "antithesis" of things we are to believe. In fact, the only time the Greek word for antitheses (*antitheses*, i.e., contradictions) is used in the New Testament, we are told to "avoid" them (1 Tim. 6:20 NKJV). Since in the history of thought Zeno's "paradox" and Kant's "antinomies" or antitheses were logical contradictions, these terms should be avoided by Christians when speaking of the mysteries of the faith like the Trinity, the Incarnation, and the relation between sovereignty and free will.

Let's again illustrate the harmony of predetermination and free choice. Suppose you cannot watch your favorite sports event live on TV. So you videotape it. When you watch it later, the entire game and every play in it are absolutely determined and can never be changed. No matter how many times you rerun it, the final score, as well as every aspect of every play, will always be the same. Yet when the game happened, every event was freely chosen. No one was forced to play. Therefore, the same event was both determined and free at the same time.

Someone may object that this is so only because the event has already occurred, and that before the game occurred it was not predetermined. In response we need only point out that if God is all-knowing (omniscient), then from the standpoint of His foreknowledge the game *was* predetermined. For *He* knew eternally exactly how it was going to turn out, even though *we* did not. Therefore, if God has infallible foreknowledge of the future, including our free acts, then everything that will happen in the future is predetermined, even our free acts. This does not mean these actions are not free; it simply means that God knew how we were going to use our freedom—and that He knew it *for sure.*

However, this raises again the question of contradiction. How can one and the same event be both free and determined at the same time? The answer, as the early St. Augustine put it, is that our free actions are determined from the standpoint of God's foreknowledge, but they are free from the vantage point of our choice. He noted that "no one sins because God foreknew that he would sin." In fact, "when he sins, it is because He whose foreknowledge cannot be deceived foresaw. . . ." So, "No man sins unless it is his choice to sin; and his choice not to sin, that, too, God foresaw."[8] What St. Thomas Aquinas added—"Everything known by God must necessarily be"—is true if it refers to the statement of the truth of God's knowledge, but it is false if it refers to the necessity of the contingent events.[9] That is, our acts are free with respect to our choice, but they are determined with respect to God's foreknowledge of them.

To demonstrate the reasonableness of this conclusion, consider again the law of noncontradiction. The above affirmations (from Acts

[8]St. Augustine, "City of God," in *A Select Library of the Nicene and Post-Nicene Fathers of the Christian Church*, ed. Philip Schaff, vol. 2 (Grand Rapids, Mich.: Wm. B. Eerdmans Publishing Co., 1956), 5.10.

[9]Thomas Aquinas, "Summa Theologica," in *The Basic Writings of St. Thomas Aquinas*, ed. Anton C. Pegis, vol. 1 (New York: Random House, 1944), 1a. 14, 4.

2:23 and John 10:17)—(1) "Jesus' death on the Cross was determined by God" and (2) "Jesus' death on the Cross was freely chosen by Himself"—are not contradictory because they are said in a different relation (or "sense"). The law of noncontradiction is violated only if two logically opposite statements are said of the same thing at the same time and *in the same relationship*. But these two statements are said in a *different relationship*. In the one case, it is in relation to God's foreknowledge, but in the other it is in relation to Jesus' free choice.

Furthermore, in order to have a contradiction one statement must affirm what the other denies. They must be logically opposite, and this is not the case here. The two statements simply say: (1) God predetermined it; (2) Jesus freely chose it. These are not logically contradictory. What would be contradictory is this: (1) God predetermined it; (2) God did not predetermine it. Likewise, this would be contradictory: (1) Jesus did not freely choose it; (2) Jesus did freely choose it. But there is no contradiction in saying it was predetermined from God's standpoint and free from Jesus' perspective. It is determined in *the one sense* that God foresaw it. Yet it is also true in *another sense* that Jesus freely chose it. To be contradictory it must be both true and false at the same time and *in the same sense*. Therefore, no logical contradiction has been demonstrated between God's sovereignty and human free choice.

Now that we have seen that there is no contradiction between predetermination by God and free choice by man, it remains to explore the relationship between them. There are three basic views as to how divine sovereignty and human responsibility relate to God's foreknowledge of the events.

THREE VIEWS ON SOVEREIGNTY AND RESPONSIBILITY

The three basic views we will examine are represented respectively by extreme Calvinists, moderate Calvinists, and modern Arminians (Wesleyans).[10] First, a look at extreme Calvinism.

Extreme Calvinism: predetermination is in spite of foreknowledge

Statement of the extreme Calvinist view

According to this view, God's predetermination is done *in spite of* His foreknowledge of human free acts. God operates with such

---

[10]What is popularly known as "Arminianism" today is really Wesleyan (following John Wesley) and not what Jacobus Arminius and his immediate followers held (see chapter 6).

unapproachable sovereignty that His choices are made with total disregard for the choices of mortal men. Strong Puritan Calvinist William Ames asserts:

There is no foreknowledge which is prerequisite or presupposed for the decree of predestination besides that simple intelligence which relates to all things, since it depends upon no cause, reason, or outward condition, but proceeds purely from the will of him who predestines.

What is more, according to Ames, God determines to save whomever He wishes regardless of whether they choose to believe or not. In fact, God gives the faith to believe to whomever He wills. Without this God-given faith they could not and would not believe. In fact, fallen human beings are so dead in sin that God must first regenerate them before they can even believe. Dead men do not believe anything; they are dead![11]

There is an important corollary to this view. If free choices were not considered at all when God made the list of the elect, then irresistible grace on the unwilling follows. That is, man would have no say in his own salvation. Accordingly, the fact that all men do not choose to love, worship, and serve God will make no difference whatsoever to God. He will simply "doublewhammy" those He chooses with His irresistible power and force them into His kingdom against their will (see chapter 5).

The roots of this extreme Calvinistic view are found in the later Augustine. More recent versions have been expressed in the writings of John Gill, Jonathan Edwards, John Gerstner, and R. C. Sproul. Since Augustine came to believe that heretics could be coerced to believe *against* their free choice, he saw no problem in God doing the same for the elect (see appendix 3).

The problems with extreme Calvinism

There are, of course, serious problems with this position. First of all, it involves a denial of human free choice (that is, the power of contrary choice), which is supported by both Scripture and good reason (see chapter 2 and appendix 4). As even Augustine himself earlier stated, "He that is willing is free from compulsion. . . ."[12] In the final analysis, a person who is coerced, either externally or in-

---

[11]William Ames, *The Marrow of Theology*, trans. and ed. John D. Eusden (Durham, N.C.: The Labyrinth Press, 1983), 153.
[12]Augustine; see appendix 4.

ternally,[13] has no choice in his own salvation. Jonathan Edwards held that "free choice" is doing what we desire, and it is God who gives the desire. But since God only gives the desire to some (not all), this leads to another problem.

Second, "irresistible grace" on the unwilling is a violation of free choice. For God is love (1 John 4:16), and true love is persuasive but never coercive. There can be no shotgun weddings in heaven. God is not a cosmic B. F. Skinner who behaviorally modifies men against their will. C. S. Lewis has two of the finest passages in print against the idea of "irresistible force" used on unwilling unbelievers.[14] In *Screwtape Letters* Lewis concludes that "the Irresistible and the Indisputable are the two weapons which the very nature of His [God's] scheme forbids Him to use. Merely to override a human will ... would be for Him useless. He cannot ravish. He can only woo."[15] In *The Great Divorce* Lewis has another great passage showing how God will ultimately respect the free choice with which He has endowed His creatures. Said Lewis, "There are only two kinds of people in the end: those who say to God, 'Thy will be done,' and those to whom God says, in the end, 'Thy will be done.' All that are in Hell, choose it. Without that selfchoice there could be no Hell."[16]

In spite of some apparent inconsistency on this point (see his comments on Luke 14:23), John Calvin faced honestly the biblical teaching that the Holy Spirit can be resisted. He recognized that Stephen said of the Jews, " 'You stiff-necked people, with uncircumcised hearts and ears! You are just like your fathers: *You always resist the Holy Spirit!*' " (Acts 7:51).[17] Calvin remarked, "Finally, they are said to be *resisting the Spirit,* when they stubbornly reject what He says by the prophets." Calvin describes this resistance with phrases such as "stubbornly reject," "intentionally rebel," and "wage war on

---

[13]In a futile attempt to avoid being called determinists, R. C. Sproul (like other extreme Calvinists) defines free will as the ability to choose without *external* coercions. Then he proceeds to admit to believing that man is *internally* coerced by irresistible grace of regeneration on the unwilling. But coercion is coercion whether it is external or internal, and all coercion is contrary to free choice. This is the view of the New Testament (see chapter 2) and all major church fathers, including the early Augustine, Anselm, and Aquinas, up to the Reformation (see appendix 1).

[14]In another place Lewis used an unfortunate and misunderstood metaphor about his own conversion in which he claims to have been brought "kicking [and] struggling into the kingdom" (in C. S. Lewis, *Surprised by Joy,* [New York: Harcourt, Brace and Company, 1955], 229). But the aforementioned texts make it clear that he did not believe in irresistible grace on the unwilling.

[15]C. S. Lewis, *Screwtape Letters* (New York: The Macmillan Company, 1961).

[16]C. S. Lewis, *The Great Divorce* (New York: The Macmillan Company, 1946), 69.

[17]John Calvin, *Calvin's Commentaries: The Acts of the Apostles,* trans. John W. Fraser and W. J. G. McDonald, eds. David W. Torrance and Thomas F. Torrance (Grand Rapids, Mich.: Wm. B. Eerdmans Publishing Co., 1979), see on Acts 7:51.

God."[18] But if God's grace can be resisted, then it is not irresistible. Irresistible force used by God on His free creatures would be a violation of both the charity of God and the dignity of man. God is love. And true love never forces itself on anyone, either externally or internally. "Forced love" is a contradiction in terms.

Third, the extreme Calvinist's view leads logically to a denial of God's omnibenevolence (all-lovingness). For the Bible says, "God *is* love" (1 John 4:16) and that He "love[s] the world" (John 3:16). "For there is no respect of persons with God" (Rom. 2:11 KJV), not only in His justice but in all His attributes, including love (Matt. 5:45). In fact, if God is one indivisible being without any parts, as classical Calvinists believe,[19] then His love extends to *all* of His essence, not just part of it. Hence, God cannot be partly loving. But if God is all-loving, then how can He love only some so as to give them and only them the desire to be saved? If He really loves all men, then why does He not give to all men the desire to be saved? It only follows then that, in the final analysis, the reason why some go to hell is that God does not love them and give them the desire to be saved. But if the real reason they go to hell is that God does not love them, irresistibly regenerate them, and give them the faith to believe, then their failure to believe truly would result from God's lack of love for them (see chapter 2).

Suppose a farmer discovers three boys drowning in his pond where he had placed signs clearly forbidding swimming. Further, noting their blatant disobedience he says to himself, "They have violated the warning and have broken the law, and they have brought these deserved consequences on themselves." Thus far he is manifesting his sense of justice. But if the farmer proceeds to say, "I will make no attempt to rescue them," we would immediately perceive that something is lacking in his love. And suppose by some inexplicable whim he should declare: "Even though the boys are drowning as a consequence of their own disobedience, nonetheless, out of the goodness of my heart I will save one of them and let the other two drown."[20] In such a case we would surely consider his love to be partial and imperfect.

Certainly this is not the picture of the God of the Bible who "so loved the world" (John 3:16) and sent His Son to be a sacrifice not

---

[18]Ibid., emphasis mine.

[19]The simplicity (indivisibility) of God is embraced by traditional Calvinism, including John Calvin himself. See John Calvin, *Institutes of the Christian Religion*; Stephen Charnock, *Discourses Upon the Existence and Attributes of God*; and William Ames, *The Marrow of Theology*, 86–87.

[20]It makes no difference whether the boys are "drowning" or dead. The same logic applies if he has power to raise all but only raises one from the dead.

only for the sins of some "but also for the sins of the whole world" (1 John 2:2); whose Son "died for the ungodly" (Rom. 5:6) and not just for the elect. Indeed, the God of the Bible "wants all men to be saved and to come to a knowledge of the truth" (1 Tim. 2:4). Peter even speaks of those "denying the sovereign Lord who bought them" (2 Peter 2:1; see appendix 6).

Even John Calvin was not an extreme Calvinist on this point (see appendix 2), for he believed that by Christ's death "all the sins of the world have been expiated."[21] Commenting on the "many" for whom Christ died in Mark 14:24, Calvin said, "The word many does not mean a part of the world only, but the whole human race."[22] This means that people like Jonathan Edwards, John Gerstner, and R. C. Sproul, who believe in limited atonement, are more extreme than John Calvin! Hence, they have earned the title "extreme Calvinists."

Arminianism: God's predetermination is based on His foreknowledge

Statement of the Arminian view

While it is debatable whether Arminius meant this (see chapter 6), some of his Wesleyan followers are said to believe that God knows in advance (by His omniscience) just what choices everyone will make, whether to accept or to reject salvation. While Wesleyan "Arminians" believe that election is conditioned on foreseen faith, (see Richard Watson *Theological Institutes* [N.Y.: T. Mason and G. Lane, 1836], 2.350) some do not believe that God's act of election itself is conditional. Rather, they hold that God unconditionally willed that salvation would be received on the condition of faith. Consequently, on the basis of their foreknown free choice to accept Christ, God chooses (elects) to save them. Man is totally free to accept or reject God, being under no coercion from Him. On the other hand, since God is all-knowing He is in sovereign control of the whole universe. He knew exactly what everyone would choose to do, even before He created the world. In short, man is entirely free and yet God is in complete control of the universe. But the "control" is not based on coercion of the events but on the *knowledge* of what the free agents will do under whatever persuasive means He may use on them.

---

[21] John Calvin, *Calvin's Commentaries: The Epistles of Paul the Apostle to the Galatians, Ephesians, Philippians, and Colossians*, trans. T. H. L. Parker and eds. David W. Torrance and Thomas F. Torrance (Grand Rapids, Mich.: Wm. B. Eerdmans Publishing Co., 1979), 308.

[22] John Calvin, *Calvin's Commentaries: A Harmony of the Gospels Matthew, Mark, and Luke and the Epistles of James and Jude*, trans. A. W. Morrison and eds. David W. Torrance and Thomas F. Torrance (Grand Rapids, Mich.: Wm. B. Eerdmans Publishing Co., 1972), 138–39.

Problems with this Arminian view

The Arminian view faces several difficulties. First, the biblical data seem to say more than that God simply *knew* what was going to happen. It appears that God actually *determined* what would happen and that He even assures its accomplishment by effectively working to bring it about. As we saw earlier (in chapter 1), God's sovereignty means He is in control of all that happens, even the free acts of human beings. Paul was "confident of this, that he who began a good work . . . will carry it on to completion until the day of Christ Jesus" (Phil. 1:6). He added, "It is God who works in you to will and to act according to his good purpose" (Phil. 2:13).

Second, if God's choice to save was *based on* those who choose Him, then it would not be based on divine grace but would be based on human decisions. This flies in the face of the whole biblical teaching on grace (cf. Eph. 2:8–9; Titus 3:5–7; Rom. 11:6). It is contrary to the clear teaching of Scripture that salvation springs from the will of man. John said believers are "children born not of natural descent, *nor of human decision* or of a husband's will, but born of God" (John 1:13). Paul adds that salvation does not "depend on man's desire [will] or effort, but on God's mercy" (Rom. 9:16).

Third, in opposition to this Molinistic[23] view of middle knowledge,[24] which suggests that God's foreknowledge is dependent on our free choices, the classical view of God (held by both Calvinists and traditional Arminians) affirms that God is an eternal and entirely independent Being. He is not dependent on anything in the created universe for what He "is." And being a simple (indivisible) Being, whatever He "has" He is. That is, His attributes are identical to His essence or nature. So if God *has* knowledge, then He *is* knowledge. This means that while the objects of His knowledge are distinct from His nature, God's knowledge of them is identical to His eternal and independent nature. Thus, God's knowledge is independent of anything outside Himself. But if it is totally independent, then God's knowledge cannot be dependent on our free choices.[25]

Finally, the whole idea of there being a chronological or even logical sequence in God's thoughts is highly problematic for evan-

---

[23]Molinism is the view springing from the Spanish Jesuit theologian Miguel de Molinis (1640–97), who posited that God has "middle knowledge" of future free events. This knowledge is said to be dependent on the human free choices that would later be made.

[24]See William Lane Craig, *The Only Wise God* (Grand Rapids, Mich.: Baker Book House, 1987).

[25]Aquinas gives the reason that God's knowledge cannot be dependent on anything in the created world, including our free choices. His argument goes like this: Everything in creation is an effect that flows from the First Cause. What exists in the effect first preexisted in the First Cause. But in God, who is a totally independent Being, nothing is dependent. Therefore, God's knowledge of all free acts is totally independent knowledge (see *Summa Theologica*, 1a.14).

gelical theology. It runs contrary to the traditional doctrine of God's simplicity (absolute indivisibility) held by Augustine, Anselm, and Aquinas, and bequeathed to modern evangelicals through the Reformers. God's attention does not pass from thought to thought, for His knowledge embraces everything in a single spiritual co-intuition. For if God is simple, then His thoughts are not sequential but simultaneous. He does not know things inferentially but intuitively. On the contrary, if God is not simple, then He could think in temporal succession. And, as some have shown, if God is temporal, then He is also spatial. Indeed, such a God would even be material (which is contrary to Scripture, e.g., John 4:24). And if God is limited to the space/time world, then He could think no faster than the speed of light. Thus He would not even be able to know the whole universe at a given moment, to say nothing of having an infallible knowledge of the future. Furthermore, if God is limited, then He is subject to disorder and to entropy (that is, He is running out of usable energy). Thus, God will ultimately be exhausted.

Moderate Calvinism: God's predetermination is in accord with His foreknowledge

There is a third alternative. It postulates that God's election is neither *based on* His foreknowledge of man's free choices nor exercised *in spite of* it. As the Scriptures declare, we are "elect *according to* the foreknowledge of God" (1 Peter 1:2 NKJV). That is to say, there is no chronological or logical priority of election and foreknowledge. As John Walvoord insightfully commented on 1 Peter 1:2, it "teaches not the logical order of election in relation to foreknowledge but the fact that they are coextensive."[26] In other words, all aspects of the eternal purpose of God are equally timeless.

God is a simple Being, all of whose attributes are one with His indivisible essence. Hence, both foreknowledge and predetermination are one in God.[27] Whatever God knows, He determines. And whatever He determines, He knows.

More properly, we should speak of God as *knowingly determining* and *determinately knowing* from all eternity everything that happens, including all free acts. For if God is an eternal and simple Being, then His thoughts must be eternally coordinate and unified.

According to the moderate Calvinist's view, whatever God fore-

---

[26] In Lewis Sperry Chafer/John F. Walvoord, *Major Bible Themes*, rev. ed (Grand Rapids: Zondervan, 1974), 233.

[27] For further arguments for simplicity see Thomas Aquinas, *Summa Theologica*, 1.3.4.

chooses cannot be based on what He foreknows. Nor can what He foreknows be based on what He *forechose*. Both must be simultaneous, eternal, and coordinate acts of God. Thus, our actions are truly free, and God determined that they would be such. God is totally sovereign in the sense of actually determining what occurs, and yet man is completely free and responsible for what he chooses.

Evaluation of the moderate Calvinist's view

In spite of the fact that moderate Calvinists have repeatedly stated their view and distinguished it from the Arminian position, and in spite of the fact that extreme Calvinists have acknowledged this confessed difference, nonetheless, some choose to ignore it. Citing with approval his mentor, John Gerstner, Sproul affirms: "In Norman Geisler, the implicit Arminianism of Dispensationalism[28] has become explicit. Geisler writes, 'God would save all men if He could. . . .' God will save as many as God can 'without violating their free choice. . . .' No Arminian has ever been more specific in his denial of Calvinistic [read: "extreme Calvinistic"] doctrine than this self-designated dispensational Calvinist."[29] This statement concerning the ". . . implicit Arminianism of Dispensationalism" reveals an obvious lack of knowledge of dispensational thought. It ignores the primary source materials found in L. Sperry Chafer, John Walvoord, C. C. Ryrie, and other key dispensationalists. Their easily verifiable statements on the issue of God's sovereign grace and their cogent rejection of classical Arminian and Wesleyan thought are available for any researcher. A careful look at these sources would have avoided such an unwarranted proclamation.

If affirming that God will not violate the free choice of any human being in order to save that person is an "Arminian" view, then every major church father from the beginning, including Justin, Irenaeus, Athenagoras, Clement, Tertullian, Origen, Methodius, Cyril, Gregory, Jerome, Chrysostom, the early Augustine, Anselm, and Thomas Aquinas (whom Sproul greatly admires) were Arminians! (see appendix 1). Further, if Sproul's radical reformation view is correct, then even most Lutherans who follow Melanchthon, not Luther's *Bondage of the Will*, on this point are Arminians! What is more, then all moderate Calvinists, including W. G. T. Shedd, Lewis Sperry Chafer, John Walvoord, Charles Ryrie, Fred Howe, and many others are Arminians—even though

[28]This is an irrelevant "red herring" (diversion of the issue). He should have said "Moderate Calvinism," not "Dispensationalism."
[29]Sproul, *Willing to Believe*, 203.

all these people call themselves Calvinists (or "moderate" Calvinists) and believe in the same four points of Calvinism that Calvin believed (see chapter 4 and appendix 2).

SUMMING IT ALL UP

God's predestination and human free choice are a mystery, but not a contradiction. They go beyond reason, but not against reason. That is, they are not incongruous, but neither can we see exactly how they are complementary. We apprehend each as true, but we do not comprehend how both are true.

Of the three basic ways predetermination and free will may be related, two have serious problems. According to the classical theistic view of God held by all Calvinists and traditional Arminians, God is omniscient, eternal, independent, and indivisible in His being or essence. But such a Being cannot be dependent on anything for His knowledge. Hence, the Wesleyan-Arminian's (and Molinist's) view that God's predetermination of human acts is dependent on His knowledge of our free choices is not feasible.

Likewise, the extreme view of God predetermining things in spite of (or without regard to) His foreknowledge is not plausible. For God's foreknowledge and His foredetermination cannot be separated. God is one simple (indivisible) Being. In Him knowledge and foredetermination are identical. Hence, He had to predetermine in accordance with His foreknowledge. And He must have foreknown in accordance with His predetermination.[30]

There is no contradiction in God knowingly predetermining and predeterminately knowing from all eternity precisely what we would do with our free acts. For God *determined* that moral creatures would do things *freely*. He did not determine that they would be *forced* to perform *free* acts. What is forced is not free, and what is free is not forced. *IN BRIEF, WE ARE CHOSEN BUT FREE.*

---

[30]Even strong Calvinists (like R. C. Sproul), who vehemently oppose any concept of predestination based on foreknowledge, nonetheless admit that "God predestines us according to what pleases him" (*Chosen by God*, 157). Yet Sproul also acknowledges that it is faith in His completed work that pleases God (Heb. 11:6; cf. 10:14). If so, then the distinction between "according to" and "based on" should be understandable to extreme Calvinists.

CHAPTER FOUR

AVOIDING EXTREME CALVINISM

A DEFINITION OF EXTREME CALVINISM

An extreme Calvinist is someone who is more Calvinistic than John Calvin (1509–1564), the founder of Calvinism. Since it can be argued that John Calvin did not believe in limited atonement (that Christ died only for the elect; see appendix 2), then it would follow that those who do are extreme Calvinists.[1] Although the roots of many points of extreme Calvinism are traceable all the way back to the later period of St. Augustine's life (see appendix 3), its beginnings in the modern world are found in Theodore Beza (1519–1605), a disciple of John Calvin and a contributor to the Synods of Dort (1618–19), a Calvinistic confession in response to the followers of Jacobus Arminius (1560–1609) in the Arminian Remonstrance of 1610. Extreme Calvinists are identified with these teachings:

---

[1]Calvinists who believe Calvin held to unlimited atonement are called Amyraldians, following Moise Amyraut (or Moses Amyrald, [1595–1664]), a French Protestant pastor. Amyrald believed that God desires all to be saved on the condition that they believe. Hence, he maintained both an ideal universalism and an actual particularism. See Brian Armstrong, *Calvinism and the Amyraut Heresy* (Madison, Wis.: University of Wisconsin Press, 1969).

T—Total Depravity
U—Unconditional Election
L—Limited Atonement
I—Irresistible Grace
P—Perseverance of the Saints

It is our purpose in this chapter to measure the first two of these tenets of extreme Calvinism against the Scriptures. Since it is possible to hold these "Five Points" in a moderate sense (as the author does—see chapter 7), this chapter will serve not only as a direct critique of extreme Calvinism but also as an indirect defense of a more moderate Calvinism.

AVOIDING EXTREME CALVINISM'S VIEW OF TOTAL DEPRAVITY

Extreme Calvinism is distinguished by a particular understanding of the "Five Points," which more or less stand or fall together, particularly the first four. That is, they are an interdependent unity. If one point is accepted, then logically all should be embraced. Likewise, if one is rejected, then logically all should be.

What total depravity does not imply for extreme Calvinists

For extreme Calvinists, total depravity does not mean that human beings are as depraved as they could be. Nor does it mean that they cannot do any social or domestic good, for most humans are capable of much "horizontal" good to others as a result of God's "common grace" to all men. But they are incapable of any "vertical" or spiritual good and, according to extreme Calvinism, they are totally incapable of initiating, attaining, or ever receiving the gift of salvation without the grace of God.

What total depravity does imply for extreme Calvinists

Extreme Calvinists believe that a totally depraved person is spiritually dead. By "spiritual death" they mean the elimination of all human ability to understand or respond to God, not just a separation from God. Further, the effects of sin are intensive (destroying the ability to receive salvation), not extensive (corrupting the ability to receive salvation). While many extreme Calvinists would deny the implications, the following chart illustrates the differences:

Moderate Calvinist View	Extreme Calvinist View
Corruption of Good	Destruction of Good
Effects of Sin Are Extensive	Effects of Sin Are Intensive
Born With Propensity to Sin	Born With Necessity to Sin
Human Will Is Diminished	Human Will Is Destroyed

While extreme Calvinists admit that fallen humans have biological life, they deny they are alive in any sense in which they can respond to God; their natures are so totally corrupt that sin is an unavoidable necessity.[2] And whereas the faculty of will is present, nonetheless, the ability to choose to follow God is destroyed.

AN EVALUATION OF VERSES USED TO SUPPORT THE EXTREME CALVINISTS' VIEW OF TOTAL DEPRAVITY

There are many verses used by extreme Calvinists to support their position. We will closely examine them.

Ephesians 2:1

"As for you, you were dead in your transgressions and sins..." (cf. Col. 2:13). Extreme Calvinists note that "Dead men cannot make themselves come alive."[3] What they need is life, and a dead person cannot give life to himself. Dead persons cannot even so much as believe that someone else can raise them to life again.

Response

This extreme Calvinistic interpretation of what is meant by spiritual "death" is questionable. First of all, spiritual "death" in the Bible is a strong expression meaning that fallen beings are totally separated from God, not completely obliterated by Him. As Isaiah put it, "your iniquities have *separated* you from your God" (Isa. 59:2). In brief, it does not mean a total destruction of all ability to hear and respond to God, but a complete separation of the whole person from God.

Second, even though they are spiritually "dead," the unsaved persons can perceive the truth of God. In Romans, Paul declares

---

[2]Many extreme Calvinists use terms like "propensity," "inclination," and "bent" toward sin, but they really mean "necessity." This is clear in the following quote from Jonathan Edwards: "That *propensity* is truly esteemed to belong to the nature of any being, or to be inherent in it, that is the *necessary* consequence of its nature..." (Edwards, "Works," in *The Works of Jonathan Edwards* [Carlisle, Pa.: Banner of Truth, 1974], 1.145, emphasis added).

[3]See R. C. Sproul, *Chosen by God*, 114.

emphatically that God's truth is "clearly seen" by them so that they are "without excuse" (1:20). Adam and Eve were spiritually "dead" after they ate the forbidden fruit. Yet they could hear the voice of God and responded to Him (Gen. 3:10). And this was not merely a hearing of the tangible sounds. Their reaction reveals that they understood the meaning of the words.

Third, "dead" is only one of many figures of speech used to describe the fallen state. It is also depicted as "sickness," which does not imply the person had no ability to hear and respond to God (Matt. 9:12). In short, depravity involves the *corruption* of life but not its *destruction*. The image of God in fallen humans is effaced but not erased. Even unsaved people are said to be in God's image (Gen. 9:6). The image is marred but not eradicated by sin (cf. James 3:9).

Fourth, if spiritually "dead" amounts to a kind of spiritual annihilation, rather than separation, then the "second death" (Rev. 20:10) would be eternal annihilation, too—a doctrine rejected by extreme Calvinists. A spiritually dead person, then, is in need of spiritual life from God. But he does exist, and he can know and choose. His faculties that make up the image of God are not absent; they are simply incapable of initiating or attaining their own salvation. Like a drowning person, a fallen person can reach out and accept the lifeline even though he cannot make it to safety on his own.

Finally, in the parallel passage (Col. 2:12–13) Paul speaks of those "dead in your sins and in the uncircumcision of your sinful nature" being able to believe. For he said, you have been "raised with him through *your faith* in the power of God."

John 1:12–13

"Yet to all who received him, to those who believed in his name, he gave the right to become children of God—children born not of natural descent, *nor of human decision* or a husband's will, but born of God." According to the extreme Calvinist's interpretation of this passage, the new birth does not result from any human decision or free choice—it is from God.

Response

There are at least two serious mistakes in such an interpretation of this text. First, verse 12 makes it plain that the means by which this new birth is obtained is by "all who *receive* him [Christ]." This involves an act of free will. Second, this passage is

58

simply denying that there is any other source of the new birth other than God Himself. It is not "of" (Greek: *ek*, out of) human sources, whether parents, husband, or ourselves. No one can save us but God. God is the *source* by which the new birth is given (v. 13), but free will is the *means* by which it is "received" (v. 12). It is "by" grace but "through" (Greek: *dia*) faith that we are saved (Eph. 2:8).

Romans 9:16

"So then it is *not of him who wills*, nor of him who runs, but of God who shows mercy" (NKJV). To the strong Calvinists this seems unmistakable evidence that salvation "*does not . . . depend on man's desire* [will]" (NIV). R. C. Sproul is incautiously triumphant about this, claiming: "This one verse is absolutely fatal to Arminianism."[4]

Response

Again, the Greek idea "of" here can mean "out of" (cf. John 1:13). It is a reference to the *source* of salvation, not the *means* by which we receive it—this means it is a *free act* of our will in receiving it (John 1:12; Eph. 2:8, etc.). All forms of Calvinism and Arminianism believe that God is the one who initiated salvation, even before the world began (Eph. 1:4). Only God can be the source of *God's* saving "mercy." However, as the Bible indicates later in Romans 9 (v. 22) and elsewhere, we can reject God's mercy (2 Peter 3:9; Acts 7:51).

John 3:3, 6–7

"Jesus declared, 'I tell you the truth, no one can see the kingdom of God unless he is *born again.* . . . Flesh gives birth to flesh, but the Spirit gives birth to spirit. You should not be surprised at my saying, "You must be *born again.*" ' " Likewise, a number of other passages assert that man is so totally depraved that he must be born all over again spiritually (cf. 1 Peter 1:3, 23; 1 John 5:4). For extreme Calvinists, regeneration is the condition of faith, not the reverse. R. C. Sproul affirms that "A cardinal point of Reformed theology is the maxim: 'Regeneration precedes faith.' " He added, "We do not believe in order to be born again; we are born again in order that we may believe"[5] (see appendix 10).

Response

There is no disagreement that depraved humans need to be born anew, to be given a new "Self" (Col. 3:10) and made a "new

---

[4]Ibid., 151.
[5]Ibid., 72.

creation" (2 Cor. 5:17). The dispute is over whether this comes by an act of God apart from the recipient's free choice. On this point the text both here and elsewhere indicates that this new birth comes through an act of faith on the part of the recipient. According to this very passage, it is "whoever believes" that gets eternal life (John 3:16). And in 1 John 5:4 it is "everyone born of God overcomes the world. This is the victory that has overcome the world, even *our faith.*" Although prompted—not coerced—by grace, the act of faith is an act of the believer, not a gift from God only to the elect (see appendices 5 and 6).

John 6:65

Jesus said, " 'This is why I told you that no one can come to me unless the Father has enabled him.' " Sproul comments, "The passage teaches at least this much: It is not within fallen man's ability to come to Christ on his own, without some kind of divine assistance."[6]

Response

Moderate Calvinists and Arminians agree with this. As Sproul himself admits, the *real* question is: "Does God give the ability to come to Jesus to all men?"[7] The answer is that there is nothing here or anywhere else to say God limits His willingness to provide this ability to only some. Indeed, the Bible is clear that He is patient, "not wanting anyone to perish, but everyone to come to repentance" (2 Peter 3:9), and that He "wants all men to be saved and to come to a knowledge of the truth" (1 Tim. 2:4; see also Ezek. 18:32).

1 Corinthians 2:14

"But the natural man receiveth not the things of the Spirit of God: for they are foolishness unto him: neither can he know [them], because they are spiritually discerned" (KJV). This is used by extreme Calvinists to support the idea that unregenerate persons cannot even understand the Gospel or any spiritual truths of Scripture.

Response

This interpretation, however, fails to take note that the word "receiveth" (Greek: *dekomai*) means "to welcome." It simply affirms

---

[6]Ibid., 68.
[7]Ibid.

that while he does *perceive* the truth (Rom. 1:20), he does not *receive* it. There is no welcome in his heart for what he knows in his head. He has the truth, but he is holding it down or suppressing it (Rom. 1:18). It makes no sense to say that an unsaved person cannot understand the gospel before he is saved. On the contrary, the entire New Testament implies that he cannot be saved unless he understands and believes the gospel. ⌐ | Cor 15:3

Total depravity is to be understood in an *extensive*, rather than an *intensive*, manner. That is, sin extends to the whole person, "spirit, soul, and body" (1 Thess. 5:23), not just to part of the person. However, if depravity has destroyed man's ability to know good from evil and to choose the good over the evil, then it would have destroyed man's ability to sin. If total depravity were to be true in this intensive (read: extreme Calvinist) sense, it would destroy man's ability to be depraved at all. For a being with no moral faculties and no moral abilities is not a moral being at all; instead, it is amoral, and no moral expectation can be held over it.

But this isn't what Scripture teaches. In a parallel passage Paul speaks of unbelievers being "darkened in their understanding and separated from the life of God *because of* the ignorance that is in them *due to the hardening of their hearts*." This implies a free and deliberate act by which they have "*lost* all sensitivity" (Eph. 4:17–19). In other words, their fallen condition and eventual lostness are not only a result of being born that way but also because they have chosen to be that way.

Titus 1:15

Extreme Calvinists also cite Paul saying, "To the pure, all things are pure, but to those who are corrupted and do not believe, *nothing is pure*. In fact, both *their minds and consciences are corrupted.*" Here again, fallen humans seem incurably and unavoidably wicked.

Response

However, Paul makes it clear that their depraved condition is also a result of their free choice. For in the very next verse he speaks of their being "disobedient" (v. 16). Fallen humans are in darkness, but that is because they "love darkness rather than light" (John 3:19). Love is a choice. Thus they are condemned because they do not believe (John 3:18), not the reverse.

People are ultimately condemned for two reasons: First, they are born with a sinful nature that puts them on the road to hell; second, because they choose not to heed the warning signs along the road telling them to repent (Luke 13:3; Acts 17:30). That is, they sin inevitably (though not necessarily)[8] because they are born with a sinful nature, *and* they find themselves in a sinful condition where they are bound by sin because they have chosen to be in this condition. In the very text cited in support of the extreme Calvinists' view it declares that fallen men are "unbelieving" (Titus 1:15).

John 8:44

" 'You belong to your father, the devil, and you want to carry out your father's desire.' " From this text extreme Calvinists conclude that fallen humans cannot avoid sinning because they are by nature "the children of the devil" (1 John 3:10) who have "been taken captive by him to do his will" (2 Tim. 2:25–26 NKJV).

Response

It is true that unbelievers belong to the devil and that "the whole world lies under the sway of the wicked one" (1 John 5:19 NKJV). But it does not follow that we have no free choice in the matter. Jesus said, " 'I tell you the truth, *everyone who sins* is a slave to sin' " (John 8:34). In fact, in the very text cited to support the extreme Calvinist view, note that it says: " '*You want [will]* to carry out your father's [the devil's] desire' " (John 8:44). It is by their choice that they follow the devil.

Ezekiel 36:26

" 'I will give you a new heart and put a new spirit in you; I will remove from you your heart of stone and give you a heart of flesh.' " This is used to ground their belief that humans are so depraved that God has to give them a new heart before they can even respond to or believe in God.

Response

The extreme Calvinistic conclusion from this text does not follow for several reasons. First, in context the passage is speaking prophetically about "the house of Israel" returning to "their own land" in the last days (v. 17 NASB). And in a similar text it says plainly that their stony heart condition was a result of their own free choice. Ezekiel told them earlier: "Cast away all your trans-

---

[8]By "necessarily" here we mean coercively, unavoidably, or against one's will. One is never forced to sin. He could always have avoided it, if not in his own natural (God-given) powers, at least by God's special grace (cf. 1 Cor. 10:13).

gressions . . . and *make yourself a new heart and a new spirit*" (Ezek. 18:31 NASB). On another occasion God said through Jeremiah, " *'They turned their backs to me* and not their faces; though I taught them again and again, *they would not listen or respond* to discipline' " (Jer. 32:33). Rather, " *'They set up* their abominable idols in the house that bears my Name and defiled it' " (Jer. 32:34). But when they returned to God, then He said, " 'I will give them one heart and one way' " (v. 40 NASB).

Second, as many other passages indicate, Israel's return is contingent on their repentance. Moses wrote, "When all these blessings and curses I have set before you come upon you and *you take them to heart* wherever the LORD your God disperses you among the nations, and *when you and your children return to the* LORD your God and *obey him with all your heart* and with all your soul according to everything I command you today, *then the* LORD *your God will restore your fortunes* and have compassion on you and gather you again from all the nations where he scattered you" (Deut. 30:1–3). It is clear that their restoration was dependent first on their repentance. They have to change their minds first before God will change their hearts.

Finally, God said He would "give" this new heart to them. But such gifts must be received by an act of the will. The gift of salvation is received by faith. As Paul said, it is "by grace you have been saved, *through faith*" (Eph. 2:8–9). Salvation comes through faith; faith does not come through salvation.

Nowhere in the Bible is faith given only to some to believe (see appendix 5). Rather, all are called on by God to believe and to repent. Paul said, " 'In the past God overlooked such ignorance, but now *he commands all people everywhere to repent*' " (Acts 17:30). The Philippian jailer was told, as are all unbelievers (cf. Rom. 10:13; John 3:16): " *'Believe* in the Lord Jesus, and you will be saved . . .' " (Acts 16:31). The clear implication from these and all biblical passages speaking of how we receive salvation is that belief is something all people can and should do, not something that only some must wait to get from God before they can do.

Ephesians 2:3

"All of us also lived among them at one time, gratifying the cravings of our *sinful nature* and following its desires and thoughts. Like the rest, we were *by nature* objects of wrath." On the basis of this and like passages (cf. John 8:44), extreme Calvinists argue that we cannot avoid doing what we are by nature any more than pigs can stop acting like pigs or dogs like dogs. Sin is unavoidable.

Response

First of all, even if sin were unavoidable for a sinner, it is not unavoidable to be a sinner. There is a way out of sin. The sinner can believe and be saved (John 3:16; Acts 16:31); even in this very passage we are informed that salvation is received *"through faith"* (v. 8).

Furthermore, it is a mistake to view depravity as necessitating sin. Even Augustine, the forefather of modern Calvinism, said, "We are born with the propensity to sin and the necessity to die."[9] Notice that he did not say we are born with the necessity to sin, but only with the propensity or inclination to sin. Sin in general is inevitable, but each sin in particular is avoidable—by the grace of God. One can always become a believer, and for a believer there is always a way of escape from sin (1 Cor. 10:13).

Psalms 51:5

"Surely *I was sinful at birth*, sinful from the time my mother conceived me" (Ps. 51:5). From this the extreme Calvinists conclude that we cannot ever help sinning, since we are born that way and can't help it.

Response

It is true that we are born in sin (Job 15:14; Ps. 58:3) and that we inherit the inclination to sin from Adam. Indeed, we sinned in Adam (Rom. 5:12). Hence, we deceive ourselves if we say we have no sin nature (1 John 1:8). But it does not follow from this inborn *tendency* to sin that we have the *necessity* to sin. Among others, being born in sin means at least three things: (1) we are born with a propensity to sin; (2) we are born with the necessity of dying; (3) imputed to us was the legal guilt of Adam's sin (Rom. 5:12–21), a guilt that was removed by the work of Christ, the Last Adam (Rom. 5:18–19).

Even some of the strongest passages on human depravity speak of it also as a matter of human choice: *"We* all, like sheep, *have gone astray, each of us has turned to his own way;* and the LORD has laid on him the iniquity of us all" (Isa. 53:6); *"All of us have become* like one who is unclean, and all our righteous acts are like filthy rags; we all

---

[9]See St. Augustine, *City of God,* 14.1.

shrivel up like a leaf, and like the wind *our sins sweep us away*" (Isa. 64:6); *"All have turned away, they have together become worthless;* there is no one who does good, not even one" (Rom. 3:12).

Extreme Calvinists love quoting Romans 9 (see response earlier in this chapter) but often overlook the implications of verses 11–12: "Yet, *before the twins were born or had done anything good or bad*—in order that God's purpose in election might stand: not by works but by him who calls—she was told, 'The older will serve the younger.'" But this text makes it clear that even though we are born in sin, yet before birth no personal sins are committed. These are done only after one is old enough to know the difference between good and evil (Isa. 7:15). Jesus said, " 'If you were blind, you would not be guilty of sin; but now that you claim you can see, your guilt remains' " (John 9:41).

Romans 8:7–9

"The sinful mind is hostile to God. It does not submit to God's law, *nor can it do so*. Those controlled by *the sinful nature cannot please God*. You, however, are *controlled not by the sinful nature* but by the Spirit...." This appears to say that unsaved persons are not free not to sin. That is, sin follows necessarily from their very nature. We sin because we are sinners by nature, rather than being sinners because we sin.

Response

It is true that we are sinners by nature, but that old nature does not make sin *necessary* any more than a new nature makes good acts necessary. The old nature only makes sin *inevitable*, not unavoidable. Since we are free, sin is *not* necessary. Again, as Augustine said, we are born with the propensity to sin, not the necessity to sin. If sin were necessary, then we would not be responsible for it (see chapter 2), which the Bible declares we are (Rom. 3:19). Furthermore, Paul makes it clear in this section of Romans that our enslavement to sin is our free choice. He wrote, "Don't you know that *when you offer yourselves to someone to obey* him as slaves, you are slaves to the one whom you obey—whether you are slaves to sin, which leads to death, or to obedience, which leads to righteousness?" (Rom. 6:16). We are born with a bent to sin, but we still have a choice whether we will be its slave.

Romans 3:10–11

"There is no one righteous, not even one; there is no one who understands, no one who seeks God." Romans 10:20 adds, " 'I was found by those who did not seek me; I revealed myself to those who did not ask for me.'" Indeed, there are many verses that indicate that no one comes to God unless He draws them (cf. John 6:44, 65) and that it is *God* who seeks *us* (Luke 19:10).

Response

The moderate Calvinist (and Arminian) has no problem with such a rendering of these verses. It is God who *initiates* salvation. "Salvation is of the LORD" (Jonah 2:9 KJV). "We love Him because He first loved us" (1 John 4:19 NKJV). We seek Him, then, only because He has first sought us. However, as a result of the convicting work of the Holy Spirit on the whole "world" (John 16:8) and "the goodness of God" (Rom. 2:4 NKJV), some people are moved to repent. Likewise, as a result of God's grace some seek Him. Hebrews declares that "without faith it is impossible to please God, because anyone who comes to him must believe that he exists and that he rewards *those who earnestly seek him*" (11:6). God is found by those who seek Him, yet when they find Him they discover that He first sought them.

2 Corinthians 3:5

"Not that we are competent in ourselves to claim anything for ourselves, but our competence comes from God." Jesus adds, "'Apart from me you can do nothing'" (John 15:5). These and like verses are used by extreme Calvinists to show that we are so depraved that we are totally incapable of even responding to the gospel without His power.

Response

These verses prove only that we cannot *attain* salvation by our own will. They do not demonstrate that we cannot *receive* the gift of salvation. Further, moderate Calvinists do not deny that God's grace works on the unregenerate to move them to faith. It only denies that any such work is irresistible on the unwilling (see below), or that God gives faith only to the elect, without which no one can be saved (see appendix 5).

AVOIDING EXTREME CALVINISM'S VIEW OF UNCONDITIONAL ELECTION

The second premise of extreme Calvinism is unconditional election, by which is meant that there are absolutely no conditions for

God's electing some to salvation. There are no conditions, either for God's giving of salvation or for our receiving it.

Strangely, even some extreme Calvinists, like R. C. Sproul, seem to acknowledge this distinction, saying, "We must be careful to distinguish between conditions that are necessary for salvation and conditions that are necessary for election. . . ." He adds, "There are all sorts of conditions that must be met for someone to be saved. [A strange statement for one who believes salvation is by "faith alone"!] Chief among them is that we must have faith in Christ" (*Chosen by God*, 155).[10] However, when we understand that even faith to believe is an "unconditional gift to the elect," the so-called "condition" of faith turns out to be no real condition for man at all. It is a "condition" only in the sense that God has to place it there first before the justification will occur.

AN EVALUATION OF VERSES USED TO SUPPORT THE EXTREME CALVINISTS' VIEW OF UNCONDITIONAL ELECTION

Many texts are offered by extreme Calvinists to support their view that election is totally unconditional for either God or human beings. The following often appear.

Ephesians 1:5–11

God "predestined us to be adopted as his sons through Jesus Christ, *in accordance with his pleasure and will.*" Also, "he made known to us the mystery of *his will according to his good pleasure,* which he purposed in Christ. . . ." Again, "In him we were also chosen, having been *predestined* according to the plan of him who works out everything in conformity with *the purpose of his will* . . ." (1:5, 9, 11).

Response

Moderate Calvinists agree that there are no strings attached to the gift of salvation—it is unconditional. When election occurred—before the foundation of the world (Eph. 1:4)—the elect were not even created yet. God elected on His own, without any conditions that needed to be performed on the part of the elect.

---

[10]The catch is that even faith is a result of "irresistible regeneration." Surprisingly, Sproul even admits that "The Reformed view does, in a narrow sense, see obedience as a 'condition' (but never the ground) of justification. . . . The real necessary condition is the presence of real faith which will of necessity yield the fruit of obedience" (*Willing to Believe*, 179).

However, the question is not whether there are any conditions for God *giving* salvation; the question is whether there are any conditions for man *receiving* salvation. And here the Bible seems to be very emphatic that faith is the condition for receiving God's gift of salvation. We are "justified *by faith*" (Rom. 5:1 NASB). We must *"believe* on the Lord Jesus Christ" in order to be saved (Acts 16:31 NKJV). "Without faith it is impossible to please God, because anyone who comes to him *must believe* that he exists and that he rewards those who earnestly seek him" (Heb. 11:6).

Romans 8:28

"And we know that in all things God works for the good of those who love him, who have been *called according to his purpose.*" Here again, election is unconditional from God's standpoint. There is nothing outside God that prompts it.

Response

That these and like texts show the unconditional nature of election from God's point of view is not challenged. But the question is not whether election is unconditional from the vantage point of the *Giver* but whether there are any conditions for the *receiver.*

This and other Scriptures reveal that election is related to foreknowledge. Romans 8:29, the very next verse, says, "Those God foreknew he also predestined." And 1 Peter 1:2 proclaims that the elect "have been chosen *according to the foreknowledge of God* the Father." This affirms that God is the unconditional source of the election, and that election is done with full foreknowledge of all things. But we have demonstrated that the elect will freely choose to believe. Election is not *based on* or dependent on foreknowledge. Rather, it is merely *in accord with* it (see chapter 3).

An illustration is in order. Suppose a young man (whom we will call Jim) is contemplating marriage, and knows two young ladies (whom we will call Joan and Betty), either of whom would make a good wife for him. As a Christian, he has three basic choices: (1) to propose to neither of them; (2) to propose to Joan; or (3) to propose to Betty. Bear in mind that the young man is under no compulsion. There is nothing outside his own will that places demands on him to choose any one of the three options (or any other one).

Suppose further that the young man happens to know that if he proposes to Joan she will say yes and if he proposes to Betty she will say no. Suppose then, in accordance with this foreknowledge of how she will freely respond, that Jim chooses to propose to Joan.

Suppose even that he knew she would be reluctant at first but with persistent and loving persuasion she would eventually—freely—accept his offer. The decision on his part was entirely free, uncoerced, and not based on anything outside himself. But it was also a decision that was with full knowledge of the response and which respected the free choice of the person to whom he decided to propose. This is analogous to what the moderate Calvinists believe about God's unconditional election.

In contrast, let's hold the same illustration up against extreme Calvinists' belief. They would say that if Jim foreknew that both women would refuse his proposal for marriage unless coerced against their will to do so,[11] he would not have to show his love to either of them. Instead he could, for instance, decide to force Betty to marry him against her will. Would we not say that "forced love" is a contradiction in terms? And since Jim represents God in the illustration, would not this make God into someone who forces Himself on others in violation of their integrity? It seems to me that this is precisely what the extreme Calvinists are affirming (see section on "irresistible grace" in chapter 5).

Romans 8:29

"For those[12] God foreknew he also predestined.... And those he predestined, he also called; those he called, he also justified; those he justified, he also glorified." Many extreme Calvinists take "foreknown" to refer to the fact that God foreloved.[13] In this case, to foreknow and to choose or elect would be the same thing. They cite other passages in attempts to support this (e.g., Deut. 7:7–8; Jer. 1:5; Amos 3:2; Matt. 7:22–23). If so, then God's foreknowledge would not have any reference to foreknowing how the elect would respond. But this is not the case, as our response shows.

Response

First, even if this is true, it is irrelevant, since extreme Calvinists believe in God's infallible foreknowledge (cf. Isa. 46:10) regard-

---

[11]Extreme Calvinists insist they hold to the truth that man is free and uncoerced. They claim: "Man is free—one hundred percent free—free to do exactly what he wants. *God does not coerce a single one against his will.*" Yet Palmer adds shortly thereafter, "Incidentally, *the Christian has no free will either....* *Christ will not let him reject Him*" (see Edwin Palmer, *The Five Points of Calvinism*, 36, emphasis mine). Language is emptied of meaning when we speak of such things as being coerced to act freely.

[12]Paul is referring to "those" particular people (i.e., the elect) whom God foreknew in a special sense, not everyone whom He foreknows in His omniscience.

[13]See David N. Steele and Curtis C. Thomas, *The Five Points of Calvinism* (Phillipsburg, N.J.: Presbyterian & Reformed, 1963), 85f.

less of what these verses teach. And if God does foreknow infallibly, then He would still foreknow what people would freely believe, and He would still have to decide whether He would have to force them to believe in Him or else elect those He knew could be persuaded to freely accept His grace (see chapter 3).

Second, there is strong evidence to show that "foreknow" does not mean "choose" or "elect" in the Bible. For one thing, many verses use the same root word (Greek: *ginosko*) for knowledge of persons where there is no personal relationship: *Matt. 25:24*—" 'I knew that you are a hard man, harvesting where you have not sown and gathering where you have not scattered seed' "; *John 2:24*—"But Jesus would not entrust Himself to them, for he knew all men"; *John 5:42*—" 'I know you. I know that you do not have the love of God in your hearts' " (cf. John 1:47; Ps. 139:1–2, 6).

Further, "know" does not usually mean "choose" in either the Old or New Testament. Of the 770 times the Hebrew word "know" (*yada*) is used in the Hebrew Old Testament, the Greek Old Testament (the Septuagint) translates it by the Greek word *ginosko* about five hundred times. And in the New Testament this word is used about two hundred twenty times, the vast majority of which do not mean to choose.[14] What is more, even the few texts used by extreme Calvinists (e.g., Hos. 13:5; Gen. 18:17–19; Jer. 1:5–6; Amos 2:10–12; 3:1–4;) are doubtful,[15] since they show that a relationship is involved—not merely a choice but also a relationship set up by a choice. Otherwise, why would God ask them to "walk together" (Amos 3:1–4) after saying He "knew" them (cf. Hos. 13:5)?[16]

In addition, "foreknow" (Greek: *proginosko*) is used in the New Testament in reference to advanced knowledge of events: "Therefore, dear friends, since you *already know* this [in advance], be on your guard so that you may not be carried away by the error of lawless men and fall from your secure position" (2 Peter 3:17; cf. Acts 2:23; 1 Peter 1:18–20). Thus, the extreme Calvinist's equating of foreknowing and foreloving does not follow.

Finally, the word "chosen" by God is used of persons who are not the elect. Judas, for example, was "chosen" by Christ but not

---

[14]There is possibly only one case where "know" and "love" are equated in the New Testament (1 Cor. 8:1–4). But even here "know" is a better translation. See Roger T. Forster and V. Paul Marston, *God's Strategy in Human History* (Wheaton, Ill.: Tyndale House Publishers, 1974), 188–189.

[15]See Forster and Marston, 182–87.

[16]Ibid., 186–87. The Hebrew word "know" (*yada*) is translated in this instance by the Greek word *epistamai* in the Septuagint, meaning to "understand fully." Here, too, it means knowledge, not merely choice, though God's choice is in the light of His knowledge.

one of the elect: "Jesus replied, 'Have I not chosen you, the Twelve? Yet one of you is a devil!' " (John 6:70). Israel was chosen as a nation, but not every individual in Israel will be saved (see Rom. 9:7, 27–29).

Furthermore, even if one could demonstrate that sometimes "foreknowledge" means "to forechoose" (as it could in Romans 11:2), this does not demonstrate the extreme Calvinist's view of unconditional election. For the question still remains as to whether God ordained an act of free choice as a means of receiving His unconditional grace.

1 Corinthians 1:27–29

"But *God chose* the foolish things of the world to shame the wise; *God chose* the weak things of the world to shame the strong. *He chose* the lowly things of this world and the despised things . . . *so that no one may boast before him.*" Extreme Calvinists argue that if salvation in any way depended on us, then we could boast. But since we cannot boast, then salvation in no way depends on us— even on our faith.

Response

First, neither this nor any other passage of Scripture affirms that faith is not a necessary condition for receiving God's gift of salvation. Indeed, many passages say that faith is a condition for receiving salvation (see John 3:16; Acts 16:31; Rom. 5:1). Second, it is a mistake to believe that the exercise of faith or trust in God's complete provision for our salvation is a ground for boasting. As a condition for salvation, faith is opposed to works and works are opposed to faith. For "to the man who does not work but trusts God who justifies the wicked, his faith is credited as righteousness" (Rom. 4:5). "*Where, then, is boasting? It is excluded. On what principle?* On that of observing the law? No, but *on that of faith*" (Rom. 3:27). Salvation, then, can be an unconditional gift from God, even though receiving it is conditioned on an act of faith on our part.

Matthew 11:27

" 'All things have been committed to me by my Father. No one knows the Son except the Father, and *no one knows the Father except the Son and those to whom the Son chooses to reveal him.*' " It seems apparent from this that only those Jesus *chooses* (known as "the elect") will know the Father in a personal way.

Response

This is certainly true, and it is acknowledged by those who oppose extreme Calvinism. The question, though, is whether one has to be willing to receive this revelation before he will come to know God personally. The answer here is in the context, the same being true for other references. In this very passage Jesus invites His listeners to "come unto Me" and "take my yoke upon you" (vv. 28–29 KJV). Elsewhere, He chides unbelievers for not being willing: " 'O Jerusalem, Jerusalem, you who kill the prophets and stone those sent to you, how often I have longed to gather your children together, as a hen gathers her chicks under her wings, but *you were not willing* " (Matt. 23:37). God chooses only to reveal Himself personally to the *willing*. Jesus said, " 'If anyone *chooses to do God's will*, he will find out whether my teaching comes from God or whether I speak on my own' " (John 7:17). It is noteworthy also that it does *not* say that Jesus wishes only to reveal the Father to some. Indeed, God desires all to be saved (Matt. 23:37; 2 Peter 3:9).

John 15:16

" '*You did not choose me, but I chose you* and appointed you to go and bear fruit—fruit that will last.' " It seems evident that Jesus claimed that we were chosen by Him, not the reverse. Hence, our election is unconditional.

Response

The context here favors it being a reference to Jesus' choice of the Twelve to be His disciples, not God's choice of the elect to eternal salvation. After all, Jesus is speaking to the eleven apostles (John 15:8; 16:17). In addition, the word "chosen" by God is used of persons who are not the elect. Judas, for example, was "chosen" by Christ but was not one of the elect: "Jesus replied, 'Have I not chosen you, the Twelve? Yet one of you is a devil!' " (John 6:70).[17]

2 Thessalonians 2:13

"But we ought always to thank God for you, brothers loved by the Lord, because *from the beginning God chose you to be saved*

---

[17]Even if this means eternal election, there is no debate with the fact that our election is unconditional from God's standpoint. However, neither this nor any other text affirms that there is no condition for receiving salvation. It is clear, of course, that God chose us before we chose to accept him. And our decision to accept His offer of salvation is not the basis for His choice of us. We did not choose Him—either first or as the basis of His choice of us. We merely responded to His gracious offer of salvation based solely on His unconditional grace. But we do have a choice in receiving this unconditional gift of salvation, for "all who *received* him, to those who believed in his name, he gave the right to become children of God" (John 1:12).

through the sanctifying work of the Spirit and through belief in the truth."

Response

As with many other passages, there is no debate with the extreme Calvinists that the elect are chosen unconditionally by God. But they neglect to note that these very verses they quote declare that this salvation came to us *"through belief in the truth."* In short, we were chosen *but free*—which is directly contrary to the conclusion of the extreme Calvinists (see chapter 2 and appendix 5).

In summary, the error of extreme Calvinism regarding "unconditional election" is the failure to adhere to an election that is unconditional from the standpoint of the Giver (God), but has one condition for the receiver—faith.[18] This, in turn, is based on the mistaken notion that faith is a gift only to the elect (see appendix 6), who have no choice in receiving it.

SOME CONCLUDING THOUGHTS

Extreme Calvinism, as represented by the traditional "Five Points," has been demonstrated to lack biblical support for the first two of these points: total depravity and unconditional election. In contrast, the moderate Calvinist view of these points (see chapter 7 and appendices 5 and 7) is in full accord with Scripture. To complete our study we turn now to the last three points of traditional "Five-Point" Calvinism: limited atonement, irresistible grace, and the perseverance of the saints.

Another objection to freewill is as follows:
When we get to heaven, we will no longer sin, thus, are we not forced to do good? Our choice to sin will be eradicated will it not? And thus if that be possible then, it is possible now.

The difference is is that choice is not simply deciding between good and evil, but deciding between one alternative to the other. In heaven, we will still have choice and free will, but the alternative of sin will not exist. We will only do good because that is the only moral option available.

---

[18]Some extreme Calvinists admit that faith is a condition for receiving salvation (see Sproul, *Willing to Believe*, 133). However, they hasten to say that faith is a *result* of "irresistible regeneration."

What they mean is that faith is not a condition that unregenerate humans must exercise before they can receive the gift of salvation. Sproul acknowledges that this is "the most crucial point of the debate between Dispensationalism (moderate Calvinism) and Reformed Theology (extreme Calvinism)" (see Sproul, *Willing to Believe*, 198).

CHAPTER FIVE

AVOIDING EXTREME CALVINISM (CONTINUED)

In the preceding chapter we examined the first two letters of the "Five-Point" T-U-L-I-P of strong Calvinism: Total Depravity and Unconditional Election. We continue here in chapter 5 with the last three: Limited Atonement, Irresistible Grace, and the Perseverance of the Saints.

AVOIDING EXTREME CALVINISM'S VIEW OF LIMITED ATONEMENT

Extreme Calvinists argue that limited atonement is supported by the fact that the objects of Christ's death are always believers, not unbelievers. They further contend that if Christ paid the price for the salvation of all unbelievers, then all would be saved. In other words, they argue that rejection of limited atonement leads to universalism (the belief that everyone will be saved), which of course is contrary to Scripture (e.g., see Matt. 25:41; 2 Thess. 1:7–9; Rev. 20:10–15).

AN EVALUATION OF VERSES USED TO SUPPORT THE EXTREME CALVINISTS' VIEW OF LIMITED ATONEMENT

Many verses are offered by these Calvinists to support their view that Christ did not die for all mankind but only for the elect. The following are the main texts used.

Matthew 1:21

This text affirms that " 'She [the Virgin Mary] will give birth to a son, and you are to give him the name Jesus, because he will save his people from their sins' "(Matt. 1:21). Along with this are several other verses used to imply that Jesus only died for believers: " 'Greater love has no one than this, that he lay down his life for his friends' " (John 15:13); " 'I lay down my life for the sheep' " (John 10:15); " 'Be shepherds of the church of God, which he bought with his own blood' " (Acts 20:28); "Christ loved the church and gave Himself up for her" (Eph. 5:25); "who gave Himself for us to redeem us from all wickedness and to purify for Himself a people that are his very own, eager to do what is good" (Titus 2:14); "He who did not spare His own Son, but delivered Him up for us all, how shall He not with Him also freely give us all things? Who shall bring a charge against God's elect? It is God who justifies" (Rom. 8:32–33 NKJV).

Response

First of all, it should be observed that there is a logical fallacy in arguing that (1) because Christ died for believers (2) He did not also die for unbelievers.

Second, to put it another way, while the text declares that (1) Christ died for those in the church, it does not say that (2) Christ died for *only* those in the church. For example, for me to say that I love my friend Carl does not mean that I do not love my neighbor Larry. The fact that I have affirmed my love for Carl in no way posits that I do not also love Larry.

Finally, the New Testament plainly states that God does love all and that Christ did die for all: " 'For God so loved the world that he gave his one and only Son' "(John 3:16); "He is the atoning sacrifice for our sins, and not only for ours but also for the sins of the whole world" (1 John 2:2); "[He] wants all men to be saved and to come to a knowledge of the truth" (1 Tim. 2:4). There are numerous other verses that say the same thing (see appendix 6).

Ephesians 5:25

"Husbands, love your wives, *just as Christ loved the church* and gave Himself up for her." The assertion in this case is that the focus of Christ's love is only the church, not unbelievers. The text does not say that Christ loved and died for the "world" but only His bride, the church.

Response

There are good reasons why the fact that Christ loves the church does not mean He did not love the world as well. For one thing, the fact that I love my wife does not logically mean that I lack love for other persons. It simply puts special focus on my love for someone who is special in my life.[1]

Second, Christ's wife—the church—is a body of all persons who accept Christ (John 1:12) and are baptized by the Holy Spirit into one body (1 Cor. 12:13). The door of the true church is open to all who will enter in and be part of this special group that experiences His special love. For "God so loved the world" (John 3:16) and wants all to partake of the relationship Christ has to His bride. Thus, "the Spirit and the bride say, 'Come!' And let him who hears say, 'Come!' *Whoever* is thirsty, let him come; and *whoever* wishes, let him take the free gift of the water of life" (Rev. 22:17).

Ephesians 1:4

"For he *chose us* in him before the creation of the world to be holy and blameless in his sight." The Bible also asserts that Christ was "the Lamb slain from the foundation of the world" (Rev. 13:8 NKJV). From this it is argued that Christ the Lamb was only slain for the elect. To die for anyone else than the elect would be a waste, for only the elect will be saved. God knew and chose before the world began exactly who the elect were.

Response

The fact that only believers were chosen in Christ before time began does not mean that Christ did not die for all human beings. God knew exactly who would believe, since He knows all things beforehand (Isa. 46:10; Rom. 8:29). Peter says believers "have been

---

[1]This and other verses reveal a special (unique) love of Christ for His church, which is what all Calvinists believe in distinction from most Arminians. What separates the moderate Calvinist from the extreme Calvinist is that the former affirms and the latter denies that Christ died for the non-elect and desires them to be a part of His bride as well, so that they too can experience this special love.

chosen according to the foreknowledge of God the Father" (1 Peter 1:2). Paul affirms that "those God foreknew he also predestined" (Rom. 8:29). The Atonement is limited in its application, but it is not limited in its extent. Certainly this passage does not say it is limited in scope, and many other passages (see below) tell us that it is not (see appendix 6).

1 Corinthians 15:3

"For what I received I passed on to you as of first importance: that Christ died for *our sins* according to the Scriptures" (cf. John 10:11; Rom. 4:25; 2 Cor. 5:21). The point being made by extreme Calvinists is that when the Bible says Christ died for someone, it identifies that group as believers by phrases like "we," "our," or "for us."

Response

Few teachings are more evident in the New Testament than that God loves all people, that Christ died for the sins of all human beings (cf. 1 Tim. 2:4–6; 1 John 2:2; 2 Peter 2:1), and that God desires all persons to be saved (see appendix 6). That only believers are mentioned in some passages as the object of Christ's death does not prove the Atonement is limited in its extent for several reasons.

First, when the Bible uses terms like "we," "our," or "us" of the Atonement it speaks only of those to whom it has been *applied,* not for all those for whom it was *provided.* In doing so it does not thereby limit the Atonement in its possible application to all people. It speaks, rather, of some to whom it has been already applied.

Second, the fact that Jesus loves His bride and died for her (Eph. 5:25) does not mean that God does not love the whole world and does not desire all to be part of His bride, the church. Indeed, as the verses below will show, " 'God so loved the world that he gave his one and only son' " (John 3:16). And Jesus desired all His Jewish kinsmen to be saved (Matt. 23:37), as did Paul (Rom. 9:1–2; 10:1–2).

Third, this reasoning overlooks the fact that there are many passages declaring that Jesus died for more than the elect (e.g., see John 3:16; Rom. 5:6; 2 Cor. 5:19), as we discuss in detail elsewhere (again, see appendix 6).

John 5:21

" 'For just as the Father raises the dead and gives them life, even so *the Son gives life to whom he is pleased to give it.'* " This verse is sometimes used by extreme Calvinists in an attempt to prove limited atonement whereby Christ gives spiritual life only to the elect.[2]

Response

First of all, if this interpretation were true it would contradict the clear teaching of other texts in John (John 3:16) and elsewhere (1 John 2:2; 2 Peter 2:1). And all true Calvinists, following Calvin, believe the Bible is the Word of God and does not contradict itself. Second, the use of "just as" in this text indicates the Son is doing the same thing as the Father, and the Father "raises the dead." So it is not a reference to salvation but to resurrection of the dead. Finally, the resurrection in this very chapter of John refers to "all who are in the graves" (5:28), both saved and unsaved (v. 29). Hence, the resurrection life given is not limited to the elect: both saved and unsaved are resurrected.

John 17:9

" 'I pray for *them* [the disciples]. *I am not praying for the world,* but for those you have given me, for they are yours.' " The "them" is plainly a reference to His disciples (v. 6). Extreme Calvinists point out that Jesus explicitly denied praying for the "world" of unbelievers. If true, this would be support that the Atonement is limited to the elect, the only ones for whom Christ prayed. It is argued that this fits with a limited view of the Atonement.

Response

Several important things should be noted in response to this. First, the fact that Christ only prayed for the elect in this passage does not in itself prove that He never prayed for the non-elect at any time. If, as extreme Calvinists admit, Jesus as a man could have had negative answers to His prayers,[3] then He could have prayed for some people who were not elect, even if it is not recorded in Scripture. Many things Jesus did are not recorded (cf. John 21:25).

Second, Christ prayed for non-elect persons. His prayer, " 'Father, forgive them for they know not what they do' " (Luke 23:34 KJV) undoubtedly included people who were not elect.[4] Further,

---

[2] See Steele and Thomas, *The Five Points of Calvinism,* 51.

[3] Even extreme Calvinists believe that Jesus as a man could have had unanswered prayers (see John Gill, *The Cause of God and Truth* [London: n.p., 1814], new ed., 1.87–88; cf. 2.77).

[4] There is no evidence that one thief on the cross, all the Roman soldiers, or the mockers present ever were saved.

78

Jesus indirectly prayed for the world by asking us to "'pray the Lord of the harvest to send out laborers into His harvest' " (Luke 10:2 NKJV), yet knowing that not all would be saved (Matt. 13:28–30). In fact, He wept for unbelievers (Matt. 23:37) and prayed that unbelievers would be saved (John 11:42).

Third, even if Jesus had not prayed for the non-elect, still other passages of the New Testament reveal that the apostle Paul did, and he exhorts us to do the same. He cried out, "Brothers, my heart's desire and prayer to God for the Israelites is that they may be saved" (Rom. 10:1), even though he knew only a remnant would be saved (Rom. 11:1–5). He adds elsewhere, "I urge, then, first of all, that requests, prayers, intercession and thanksgiving be made *for everyone*" (not just the elect; 1 Tim. 2:1).

Fourth, even if it could be demonstrated that Christ did not pray for the non-elect, it would not mean He does not love them and did not die for their sins. A special prayer for those who would become believers is understandable (John 17:20). But this no more proves He does not love the world than my saying "I pray daily for my children" proves I do not love all the children of the world. My children have a special place in my prayers, just as Christ's disciples had a special place in His prayers. The important thing is that Jesus wanted everyone to be His children (Matt. 23:37; 1 Tim. 2:4–6; 2 Peter 3:9). The alternative is predestination for hell. However, Matt says hell was prepared for the devil and his angels. The fact that it *Romans 5:15* was intended to include unsaved shows man was not predestined for hell. Matt.25:41

"For if the many died by the trespass of the one man, how much more did God's grace and the gift that came by the grace of the one man, Jesus Christ, overflow to *the many*!" Also, "For just as through the disobedience of the one man the many were made sinners, so also through the obedience of the one man *the many* will be made righteous" (Rom. 5:19). Extreme Calvinists insist that in both cases the benefit of Christ's death is only to "the many" [the elect] but not to "all" (cf. Heb. 9:28).

Response

In response to this argument for limited atonement, it is noteworthy that "many" in Romans 5 is used in contrast with "one" (Adam or Christ), not in contrast to "all." In fact, the "many" is interchangeable with "all." This is evident from several things: (1) The term "all" is used in this same passage (vv. 12, 18) as interchangeable with "many"; (2) Once, the two terms refer to the same thing: in verse 15 "many died" refers to the same thing as verse 12 where "all died" as a result of Adam's sin; (3) The contrast is between "one" and "all" (v. 18), just as in the next verse it is between "one" and "many" (v. 19); and (4) If "many" means only "some" as in "limited atonement," then only some people, not all, are condemned because of Adam's sin. For instance, Romans 5:19 declares that "just as through the disobedience of the one man the *many* were made sinners, so also through the obedience of the one man the *many* will be made righteous." Yet all true Calvinists believe in the universality of sin. By the same logic with the same word in the same verse they should believe in the universal extent of the Atonement.

Mark 10:45 (cf. also Matt. 26:28)

" 'For even the Son of Man did not come to be served, but to serve, and to give his life as *a ransom for many.*' " This and many other New Testament passages teach substitutionary atonement (1 Cor. 15:3; 2 Cor. 5:21; 1 Peter 2:22; 3:18). But extreme Calvinists insist that logic demands that if Christ died for all, then all would be saved. For if Christ was substituted for their sin, then He paid for it and they are free. But the Bible teaches that all will not be saved (cf. Matt. 25:40–41; 2 Thess. 1:7–9; Rev. 20:10–15). Therefore, they argue that Christ could not have died for the sins of all mankind.

Response

First, this conclusion is not really an exposition of these passages—which say nothing about a limited atonement. Rather, it is a speculative inference. Second, the inference is not logically necessary. That a benefactor buys a gift and freely offers it to someone does not mean that person *must* receive it. Likewise, that Christ paid for our sins does not mean we *must* accept the forgiveness of sins bought by His blood.

Third, the word "many" is again used to mean "all." It is "many" in contrast to "few," not "many" in contrast to "all." As just mentioned, "many" and "all" are also used interchangeably (see Rom. 5:12–19). This is supported by usage of the term in both the Old and New Testaments. The most widely accepted authority on the Greek New Testament concludes that *polloi* (many) has the inclusive meaning of "all" in the crucial redemptive passages.[5] Jesus

---

[5]See Gerhard Friedrich, ed., *Theological Dictionary of the New Testament*, vol. VI, trans. and ed. Geoffrey W. Bromiley (Grand Rapids, Mich.; Wm. B. Eerdmans Publishing Co., 1964–76), 536–45.

said "many" (all) are called but "few" are chosen (Matt. 20:16 NKJV).

Finally, that Christ's death made everyone *savable* does not thereby mean that everyone is *saved*. His death on the Cross made salvation *possible* for all men but not *actual*—it is not actual until they receive it by faith. This should not be difficult for an extreme Calvinist to understand. For even though the elect were *chosen* in Christ, the Lamb slain before the creation of the world (Rev. 13:8; Eph. 1:4), nonetheless, they were not actually *saved* until God regenerated and justified them. Before the moment in time when they were regenerated, the elect were not saved actually but only potentially. Salvation, then, can be *provided* for all without it being *applied* to all. There is enough Bread of Life put on the table by Christ for the whole world, even though only the elect partake of it. The Water of Life is there for "whoever" (all) to drink (John 4:14), even though many refuse to do so.

John 1:9

"The true light that gives light to every man was coming into the world." Some Calvinists reason that this supports limited atonement, since "world" and "every man" cannot refer to the whole human race. If they did, then everyone would be saved. But since other Scriptures clearly repudiate universalism (cf. Matt. 25:41; Rev. 20:10–15), then it must refer to the elect scattered around the world.

Response

There are several reasons this does not refer only to the elect but to the fallen world as a whole. First, this usage is consistent with the generic use of the word "world" throughout John's writings (cf. John 3:16–18; 1 John 2:1–2, 15–17). Second, this interpretation is supported by the context (vv. 10–11) where John refers to Jesus not being recognized or received by the world in general. Third, that the Light (Christ) has been manifested in the "world" does not mean He was accepted by all the world. Indeed, the very next verses indicate He was not. For "He was in the world, and though the world was made through him, the world did not recognize him. He came to that which was his own, but his own did not receive him" (John 1:10–11).

Romans 9:11–13

"Yet, before the twins were born or had done anything good or bad—in order that God's purpose in election might stand: not by works but by him who calls—she was told, 'The older will serve the younger.' Just as it is written: 'Jacob I loved, but Esau I hated.' " This is a favorite passage of extreme Calvinists, especially those who believe in double-predestination. For it appears to say that God not only loves just the elect, but also that He even hates the non-elect (appendix 7).

Response

Few scriptural texts are more misused by extreme Calvinists than this one.[6] First of all, God is not speaking here about the *individual* Jacob but about the *nation* of Jacob (Israel). In Genesis when the prediction was made (25:23 NKJV), Rebekah was told, " 'Two *nations* are in your womb, two *peoples* shall be separated from your body.... And the older shall serve the younger.' " So the reference here is not to *individual* election but to the *corporate* election of a nation—the chosen nation of Israel.[7]

Second, regardless of the corporate election of Israel as a nation, each individual had to accept the Messiah in order to be saved. Paul said, "I could wish that I myself were cursed and cut off from Christ for the sake of *my brothers, those of my own race, the people of Israel*" (Rom. 9:3–4). He added, "Brothers, my heart's desire and prayer to God for the Israelites is that they may be saved" (Rom. 10:1). Even though of the end times he says later that "all Israel will be saved" (Rom. 11:26), he is referring to Israel at that time. And clearly at present there is only "*a remnant*" (11:5). So even though Israel as a nation was elect, nonetheless, each individual had to accept God's grace by "faith" in order to be saved (11:20).

Third, God's "love" for Jacob and "hate" for Esau is not speaking of those men before they were born, but long after they lived. The citation in Romans 9:13 is not from Genesis when they were alive (c. 2000 B.C.) but from Malachi 1:2–3 (c. 400 B.C.), long after they died! The evil deeds done by the Edomites to the Israelites are well documented in the Old Testament (e.g., Num. 20). And it is for

<hr>

[6]R. C. Sproul is a case in point (for instance, see *Chosen by God*, 148–50).

[7]Even Piper, who holds that the Romans 9 passage is speaking of *individual* election to eternal salvation admits of modern scholars that "the list of those who see no individual predestination to eternal life or death is impressive." Indeed, "Sanday and Headlam (*Romans*, 245), for example, take the position that 'the absolute election of Jacob ... has reference simply to the election of one to higher privileges, as head of the chosen race, than the other. It has nothing to do with their eternal salvation. In the original to which St. Paul is referring, Esau is simply a synonym for Edom.' Similarly, G. Schrenk (*TDNT*, IV, 179) says on Rom. 9:12, 'The reference here is not to salvation, but to position and historical task, cf. the quotation from Gen. 25:23 in v. 12: "The elder shall serve the younger." ' " (John Piper, *The Justification of God*, 2d ed. [Grand Rapids, Mich.: Baker Book House, 1993], 57).

these that God is said to have hated them as a country. Here again, this did not mean that no individuals from that country would be saved. In fact, there were believers from both Edom (Amos 9:12) and the neighboring country of Moab (Ruth 1), just as there will be people in heaven from every tribe, kindred, nation, and tongue (Rev. 7:9).[8]

Fourth, the Hebrew word for "hated" really means "loved less." Indication of this comes from the life of Jacob himself. For the Bible says Jacob "loved also Rachel *more than* Leah.... The Lord saw that *Leah was hated*" (Gen. 29:30–31). "The former implies strong positive attachment and the latter, not positive hatred, but merely a less love."[9]

The same is true in the New Testament, as when Jesus said " 'If anyone comes to me and does not *hate his father and mother* . . . he cannot be my disciple' " (Luke 14:26). A parallel idea is expressed in Matthew 10:37: " 'Anyone who *loves* his father or mother *more than* me is not worthy of me.' " So even one of the strongest verses used by extreme Calvinists does not prove that God hates the nonelect or even that He does not love them. It simply means that God's love for those who receive salvation looks so much greater than His love for those who reject it that the latter looks like hatred by comparison.

A couple of illustrations make the point. The same loving stroke that makes a kitten purr seems like hatred if she turns the opposite direction and finds her fur being rubbed the wrong way. Likewise, the person standing under the Niagara Falls of God's love with his cup upside down may complain that his cup is empty. Whereas, another with his cup right side up may appear to be receiving more loving treatment. In reality, God's expressed love is the same for both believers and unbelievers. He is simply patiently waiting for one to repent (i.e., turn the "cup" of his life right side up). The *expressed* love is the same for both believer and unbeliever; the *received* love is greater for the believer.[10]

---

[8]John Piper, widely held by extreme Calvinists to have the best treatment on Romans 9, makes this mistake. Piper claims that "the divine decision to 'hate' Esau was made 'before they were born or had done anything good *or evil* (9:11).' " But, as shown on the previous page, the reference here is not to something said in Genesis about the *individuals* Jacob and Esau *before they were born.* What Genesis 25 says is simply that the older would serve the younger. What is said in Malachi 1:2–3 about the *nations* of Jacob and Esau (Edom) is not only centuries after their progenitors had died, but it is also in regard to what the nation of Edom had done to the chosen *nation* of Israel (ibid., 175).

[9]See Forster and Marston, *God's Strategy in Human History*, 60.

[10]1 John 4:16 affirms that "God is love," and love can constrain in a moral sense (2 Cor. 5:14), but it cannot compel moral choices in a physical sense. In this sense, love always operates persua-

1 Corinthians 15:22

"For as in Adam all die, so in Christ all will be made alive." Some extreme Calvinists claim that "all" must mean only the elect here. Palmer wrote, "Although it is clear that every person in the world died in Adam (Rom. 5:12), *it is equally clear that everybody in the world has not died in Christ.* There are many people who have not been crucified in Christ. They hate Him."[11] Thus, strange as it may seem, "*all* will be made alive" is supposed by extreme Calvinists to support limited atonement.

Response

There are at least three reasons why this text *does not* uphold limited atonement. First, in this verse "all" means "all." "All" does not mean "some." This is the pattern when "all" is used in the context of salvation in the New Testament. Second, there is a tight logical connection between the two "alls" in the passage. And it is admitted that the first "all" means literally all fallen human beings. Third, as with John 5:21, this text *is not* speaking about salvation at all; it refers to the resurrection of all men. It affirms that by virtue of Christ's resurrection "all will be made alive," that is, they will be resurrected. What this text is saying is that not all are resurrected to *salvation*; some are raised to *condemnation* (John 5:21–29).

That 1 Corinthians 15:22 is speaking of the resurrection, not salvation, could not be more evident from the context. It is introduced by these words: "But Christ has indeed been *raised from the dead*, the firstfruits of those who have fallen asleep. For since death came through a man, *the resurrection of the dead* comes also through a man" (vv. 20–21). Indeed, the entire chapter is on the physical resurrection from the dead.

1 Peter 3:18

"For *Christ died for sins* once for all, the righteous for the unrighteous, to bring you to God." And, "He Himself bore our sins in his body on the tree, so that we might die to sins and live for righteousness; by his wounds you have been healed" (1 Peter 2:24).

---

sively but never coercively.

Numerous verses in Scripture teach *unlimited* atonement. God so loved "the world" (John 3:16); Christ's death is the satisfaction for the sins of "the whole world" (1 John 2:2); His blood "bought" the redemption of even apostates (2 Peter 2:1); Christ died "for all" (2 Cor. 5:14); and He reconciled "the world" to God (v. 19). These and other passages are discussed in detail elsewhere (see appendix 6).

[11]Palmer, *The Five Points of Calvinism*, 53.

These and many other Scriptures (cf. 2 Cor. 5:21) imply a substitutionary atonement (cf. Isa. 53). But many limited atonement advocates insist that if Christ was substituted for all, then all will be saved. And since, of course, all Calvinists believe only some, not all, will be saved, then it follows that for extreme Calvinists Christ must have died for only the elect.[12] They often point to John McCleod Campbell's work, *The Nature of the Atonement* (1856), as a demonstration of the incompatibility of universal atonement and substitutionary atonement.[13]

Response

The first thing to note is that this objection is a form of special pleading, based on a different view of substitution. Of course, if substitution is automatic, then everyone for whom Christ is substituted will automatically be saved. But substitution need not be automatic; a penalty can be paid without it automatically taking effect. For instance, the money can be given to pay a friend's debt without the person being willing to receive it. Those, like myself, who accept the substitutionary atonement but reject limited atonement simply believe that Christ's payment for the sins of all mankind did not automatically save them; it simply made them savable. It did not automatically apply the saving grace of God into a person's life. It simply satisfied (propitiated) God on their behalf (1 John 2:2), awaiting their faith to receive God's unconditional gift of salvation, which was made possible by Christ's atonement.[14]

THE EXTREME CALVINISTS' GOD IS NOT REALLY ALL-LOVING

The stark truth of the matter is that the God of extreme Calvinism is not all-loving. Limited atonement necessarily means God has only limited love. In a redemptive sense, He loves only the elect. He does not really love all sinners and desire them to be saved. Everyone He desires to be saved, gets saved, and that is only the elect. R. C. Sproul, a popular proponent of limited atonement, understands the dilemma: "It is the non-elect that are the problem. If some are not elected unto salvation then it would seem that God

---

[12]See R. K. McGregor Wright, *No Place for Sovereignty* (Downers Grove, Ill.: InterVarsity Press, 1996), 149.

[13]However, it should be pointed out that McCleod rejected limited atonement.

[14]For an excellent treatment of this whole matter see Robert Lightner, *The Death Christ Died* (Grand Rapids, Mich.: Kregel, 1998).

is not all that loving toward them." In fact, God is not really loving at all toward them with regard to their salvation. If He were, then they would be part of the elect, for according to extreme Calvinists, whomever God really wants to be saved will be saved. R. C. Sproul's response to "the problem," though, is a bit shocking. He argues that to say God should have so loved the world, as He did the elect, is to assume that "God is obligated to be gracious to sinners. . . . God may owe people justice, but never mercy."[15]

But how can this be? Both justice and mercy (or love) are attributes of an unchangeable and infinite God. God by His very nature manifests to all His creatures what flows from all His attributes.[16] So, whereas there is *nothing in the sinner* to merit God's love, nonetheless, *there is something in God* that prompts Him to love all sinners, namely, God is all-loving (omnibenevolent).[17] *Hence, extreme Calvinism is in practice a denial of the omnibenevolence of God.*[18]

It does not help matters to say that God has given "an 'opportunity' to all men to be saved if they want to." For Sproul admits, "Calvinism assumes that without the intervention of God no one will ever want Christ. Left to themselves, no one will ever choose Christ."[19] Yet the extreme Calvinists' God, who can give this desire to all, deliberately refuses to give it to any but a few elect. There is something seriously wrong with this picture!

Charles Spurgeon was a strong Calvinist himself, yet his confession is instructive with regard to limited atonement: "We do not know why God has purposed to save some and not others. . . . We cannot say why his love to all men is not the same as his love to the elect."[20] Indeed, even to say God desires all to be saved is inconsistent with limited atonement. How can God desire contrary to His own eternal and unchangeable decree? And if God loves only the elect, then He is not omnibenevolent. *God cannot be all-loving if He does not love all.*

---

[15]Sproul, *Chosen by God*, 33–34.

[16]This applies also to His holiness, which hates *sin* in *all* persons.

[17]Jonathan Edwards attempts to avoid this painful logic by making salvation an arbitrary act of mercy rather than something flowing from God's essential nature of love (see *Jonathan Edwards: Representative Selections*, 119). However, this is an unsuccessful maneuver for several reasons. First, the Old Testament word translated "mercy" (KJV) means "compassionate love" (see NIV). Second, love is of the very essence of God (1 John 4:16) who cannot change (Mal. 3:6; Heb. 1:11; 6:19; James 1:17). Third, even one of Edwards' disciples, R. C. Sproul, admits that God is necessarily good and yet free at the same time (*Willing to Believe*, 111).

[18]R. C. Sproul apparently does not see the inconsistency here. He admits that "it is 'necessary' for God to be good" and that "God can do nothing but good" (*Willing to Believe*, 111), yet at the same time he contends that redemptively God chooses to love only some persons (the elect).

[19]Ibid., 34.

[20]Cited by Iain Murray in *Spurgeon v. Hyper-Calvinism: The Battle for Gospel Preaching*, 117.

The root problem here is a philosophical one. Extreme Calvinists hold a voluntaristic view of God's attribute of love: God can will to love whomever He chooses and not love (or hate) those He wishes. But if this is so, then God is neither essentially loving nor all-loving. In extreme Calvinism, an action is right (whether loving or not) simply because God wills it. But this is both a denial of God's unchanging nature and an ultimate slur on the character of God (see appendix 12 for a more detailed discussion).

Extreme Calvinistic voluntarism reduces God's "essence" to an arbitrary will. Consider John Piper's revealing statement: "To put it more precisely, *it is the glory of God and his essential nature mainly to dispense mercy (but also wrath, Ex. 34:7) on whomever he pleases apart from any constraint originating outside his own will. This is the essence of what it means to be God. This is his name.*"[21]

But this is clearly *not* God's name. His name is the eternal, unchanging "I AM" (Ex. 3:14; cf. Mal. 3:6). Name stands for character or essence in Scripture. God's name is not His will—certainly not an arbitrary one that is not rooted in and bound by His unchangeable essence.

AVOIDING EXTREME CALVINISM'S VIEW OF IRRESISTIBLE GRACE

Another essential belief of extreme Calvinism is irresistible grace, though some seem embarrassed by the term and use softer words like "effectual grace."

AN EVALUATION OF VERSES USED TO SUPPORT THE EXTREME CALVINISTS' VIEW OF IRRESISTIBLE GRACE

Many passages in the Bible are employed to support the idea of "irresistible grace." These deserve careful scrutiny. Among them are the following.

Romans 9:15

" 'I will have mercy on whom I have mercy, and I will have compassion on whom I have compassion.' " Also, " '*I [God] will harden Pharaoh's heart*, and . . . he will not listen to you' " (Ex. 7:3–4). This is used to bolster the idea that Pharaoh had no real choice in the matter

---

[21]Piper, *The Justification of God*, 88–89 (italics his).

(cf. John 12:36ff). Allegedly, when God moved on his heart to accomplish His purpose, Pharaoh could not resist.

Response

God did not harden Pharaoh's heart contrary to Pharaoh's own free choice. The Scriptures make it very clear that Pharaoh hardened his own heart. They declare that Pharaoh's heart "grew hard" (Ex. 7:13; cf. 7:14, 22), that Pharaoh "hardened his heart" (Ex. 8:15), and that "Pharaoh's heart grew hard" the more God worked on it (8:19 NKJV). Again, when God sent the plague of the flies, "Pharaoh hardened his heart at this time also" (8:32 NKJV). This same phrase, or like phrases, is repeated over and over (cf. 9:7, 34–35). While it is true that God predicted in advance that it would happen (Ex. 4:21), nonetheless the fact is that Pharaoh hardened his own heart first (7:13; 8:15, etc.), and then God only hardened it later (cf. 9:12; 10:1, 20, 27).[22] Further, it was God's *mercy* that occasioned the hardening of Pharaoh's heart. For each time he pleaded with Moses to lift the plague, he was further confirmed in his sin by adding to his guilt and by making it easier for him to reject God the next time.

What is more, the Hebrew word "hardened" (*chazaq*) can and often does mean to "strengthen" (Judg. 3:12; 16:28) or even to "encourage" (cf. Deut. 1:38; 3:28).[23] Taken in this sense, it would not carry any sinister connotations but would simply state that God made Pharaoh strong to carry through with his (Pharaoh's) will against Israel.

However, even if the word is taken with the strong meaning of hardening, the sense in which God hardened Pharaoh's heart could be likened to the way the sun hardens clay and also melts wax. If Pharaoh had been receptive to God's warnings, his heart would not have been "hardened" by God. When God gave Pharaoh a reprieve from the plagues, he took advantage of the situation. "But when Pharaoh saw that there was relief, he hardened his heart and did not heed them [Moses and Aaron], as the LORD had said" (Ex. 8:15). So there is a sense in which God hardens hearts, and a sense in which He does not.[24] This same reasoning applies to other texts

---

[22]John Piper stands the order and thought of the text on its head, claiming implausibly that "it is just as probable that 'the hardening of man by God appears as self-hardening' " (Piper, *The Justification of God*, 163). This is an almost classic example of reading one's theology into the text as opposed to reading the text.

[23]See Forster and Marston, *God's Strategy in Human History*, 158–59.

[24]Even some strong Calvinists like R. C. Sproul agree that God is not hardening Pharaoh's heart actively, but only passively in the sense of giving him up (cf. Rom. 1:24ff.) to his own sinful desires (*Chosen by God*, 144–46).

that speak of God hardening a person in their unbelief (cf. John 12:37ff.).

Finally, parallel passages by Paul support the idea that it is man doing the initial hardening, not God. Romans 2:5 asserts, "But because of your stubbornness and your unrepentant heart, you are storing up wrath against yourself for the day of God's wrath, when his righteous judgment will be revealed."

Romans 9:19

"One of you will say to me: 'Then why does God still blame us? For *who resists his will?*' " This seems to imply that God's power in salvation is literally irresistible regardless of what one wills.

Response

In response, it should be pointed out first that the phrase "who resists his will?" is not an affirmation by the biblical author but a question posed in the mouth of an objector. Note the introductory phrase, "One of you will say to me." A similar objector is introduced in Romans 3:8: "Why not say—'let us do evil that good may result?' " So the idea that one cannot resist God's will may be no more part of Paul's teaching than the view that we should do evil so good may come.

Furthermore, Paul clearly rejects the objector's stance in the very next verse, saying, "But who are you, O man, to talk back to [i.e., resist] God?" (Rom. 9:20). His answer implies that the objector can and is resisting God by raising this very question. But more importantly, the direct implication is that if it is irresistible, then we should not be blamed.

In addition, in Romans 11:19–20 when Paul *agrees* with the objector he writes, "well said" (NKJV). No such statement is added here in Romans 9.[25]

Another point to remember is that things that eventually seem "irresistible" were not so to begin with. For example, sin only becomes unavoidable when one freely rejects what is right and his conscience becomes hardened or seared (cf. 1 Tim. 4:2). Likewise, righteousness becomes only irresistible when we freely yield to God's grace. Thus, grace is only irresistible to the willing, not to the unwilling. As John Walvoord insightfully puts it, "Efficacious

---

[25]Even John Piper, who believes in irresistible grace on the unwilling, admits that many scholars hold that Paul rejects the objector's statement (Piper, *The Justification of God*, 189–90).

grace never operates in a heart that is still rebellious, and no one is ever saved against his will."[26]

Irresistible grace operates the way falling in love does. If one willingly responds to the love of another, eventually they reach a point where that love is overwhelming. But that is the way they willed it to be. Even if Paul agreed with the objector that God's work is irresistible, it would not support the hard line of extreme Calvinism, since God uses irresistible saving grace only on the willing, not the unwilling.

Finally, even if one could show that God is working here (1) irresistibly, (2) on individuals, (3) for eternal salvation—all of which are doubtful—it would not follow necessarily that He works irresistibly *on the unwilling.* Indeed, as we have seen, God does not force free creatures to love Him. Forced love is both morally and logically absurd.

Romans 9:21

"Does not the potter have the right to make out of the same lump of clay some pottery for noble purposes and some for common use?" Or, as the King James Version translates it, "Hath not the potter power over the clay, of the same lump to make one vessel unto honour, and another unto dishonour?" The image this conjures up in a Western mind is often a deterministic, if not fatalistic, one where they have no choice but are overpowered by God.

Response

However, a Hebrew mind would not think this way, knowing the parable of the potter from Jeremiah 18. For in this context the basic lump of clay will either be built up or torn down by God, *depending on Israel's moral response to God.* For the prophet says emphatically, "If that nation I warned *repents* of its evil, then I will relent and not inflict on it the disaster I had planned" (18:8). Thus, the unrepentant element of Israel becomes a "vessel for dishonour" and the repentant group a "vessel for honour" (see comments on Romans 9:22 below).

Further, there is a different use of prepositions in "vessel *unto* honour" versus a "vessel *of* wrath" (Rom. 9:22). A vessel *of* wrath is one that has received wrath from God, just as a vessel of mercy has received mercy from God. But a vessel *unto* honor is one that gives

---

[26]Walvoord, *The Holy Spirit: A Comprehensive Study of the Person and Work of the Holy Spirit* (Grand Rapids, Mich.: Zondervan, 1991), 124.

honor to God. So a repentant Israel will, like a beautiful vessel unto [for] honor, bring honor to its Maker. But like a vessel of dishonor (literally, "no-honor"), an unrepentant Israel will not bring honor to God, but will rather be an object of His wrath.

Romans 9:22

"What if God, choosing to show his wrath and make his power known, bore with great patience the *objects [vessels] of his wrath—prepared for destruction?*" Does this not indicate that God has predestined the lost to damnation? Many strong Calvinists believe that it does. The Puritan predestinarian William Ames wrote, "There are two kinds of predestination, election and rejection or [*reprobatio*]." He added, "Reprobation is the predestination of certain men so that the glory of God's justice may be shown in them, Rom. 9:22; 2 Thess. 2:12; Jude 4."[27]

Response

As indicated above, this passage implies that the "vessels of wrath" are objects of wrath because they refuse to repent. They did not willingly bring honor to God, so they became objects of God's wrath. This is evident from the fact that they are "endured [by God] with much longsuffering" (Rom. 9:22 NKJV). This suggests that God was patiently waiting for their repentance. As Peter said, "The Lord is ... longsuffering to us-ward, not willing that any should perish, but that all should come to repentance" (2 Peter 3:9 KJV).

Furthermore, taking Paul as the best commentator on his own writings, earlier in Romans he noted that the wrath of God comes on the wicked because of their own willful disobedience. He wrote, "But *because of your stubbornness and your unrepentant heart,* you are storing up wrath against yourself for the day of God's wrath, when his righteous judgment will be revealed" (Rom. 2:5). There is absolutely no reason to believe, as the extreme Calvinists do, either here or anywhere else in Scripture, that God predestines certain persons to eternal hell apart from their own free choice.

Luke 14:23

In a parable Jesus said, "Then the master told his servant, 'Go out to the roads and country lanes and *make [compel] them come* in, so that my house will be full' " (Luke 14:23). This is a strong word

---

[27]Ames, *The Marrow of Theology*, 154.

meaning "force" and applies directly through the parable to coercing people into the kingdom of God. Most hardcore Calvinists from the time of the later Augustine (see appendix 3) have taken this to mean God uses coercive power on the unwilling to get them saved.

Response

Inside the New Testament, the word "compel" (Greek: *anagkadzo*) has a range of meanings. It is sometimes used in a *physical sense* of being "forced" against the will (cf. Acts 26:11; Gal. 2:3, 14; 6:12). But on other occasions it has a *moral sense.* "Jesus *constrained* his disciples to get into a ship" (in Matt. 14:22 KJV). There is no indication of any physical coercion in this case. Although another Greek word is used, the idea is the same when Paul speaks of being "compelled" by the love of Christ (2 Cor. 5:14). In fact, not counting Luke 14:23, of the other eight times the word "compel" is used in the New Testament, at least four of them are in the moral sense where one is not forced against his will (cf. Matt. 14:22; Mark 6:45; Acts 28:19; 2 Cor. 12:11).

Outside the New Testament this word means "to compel someone in all the varying degrees from friendly pressure to forceful compulsion."[28] Not only is there no necessity here of taking this in the sense of irresistible grace against one's will, but everything we know about free choice (see chapter 2 and appendices 1 and 5) is that what is done freely is not done by "constraint" or "compulsion" (cf. 1 Cor. 7:37; 1 Peter 5:2).

John 6:44

" 'No one can come to me *unless the Father who sent me draws him,* and I will raise him up at the last day.' " According to extreme Calvinists, this speaks of an irresistible drawing by God.[29] They note that the word "draw" (Greek: *elkuo*) means to "drag" (Acts 16:19; James 2:6).

Response

In order to understand the issue properly, a number of things must be taken into consideration. First of all, like any word with a range of meaning, the given meaning of this Greek word must be determined by the context in which it is used. Sometimes in the New Testament it does mean to drag a person or object (cf. John

---

[28]See Friedrich, *Theological Dictionary of the New Testament,* 1:345.
[29]See Sproul, *Chosen by God,* 69–70.

18:10; 21:6, 11; Acts 16:19). At other times it does not (cf. John 12:32; see also below). Standard Greek Lexicons allow for the meaning "draw" as well as "drag."[30] Likewise, the Greek translation of the Old Testament (the Septuagint) uses it in both senses. Deuteronomy 21:3–4 employs it in the sense of "drag" and Jeremiah 38:3 to "draw" out of love.[31]

Second, John 12:32 makes it plain that the word "draw" cannot mean "irresistible grace" on the elect for one simple reason: Jesus said, " 'But I, when I am lifted up from the earth, will draw *all men* to myself' " (John 12:32). No true Calvinist believes that all men will be saved.

Third, the word "all" cannot mean only *some* men in John 12:32. Earlier (John 2:24–25) when Jesus said He knew "all" men sin, it was clear that He was not just speaking of the elect. Why then should "all" mean "some" in John 12:32? If He meant "some," He could easily have said so.

Finally, their being drawn by God was conditioned on their faith. The context of their being "drawn" (6:37) was "he who believes" (6:35) or "everyone who believes in Him" (6:40). Those who believe are enabled by God to be drawn to Him. Jesus adds, " 'This is why I told you that no one can come to me unless the Father has enabled him' " (John 6:65). A little later He says, " 'If anyone *chooses* to do God's will, he will find out whether my teaching comes from God or whether I speak on my own' " (John 7:17). From this it is evident that their understanding of Jesus' teaching and being drawn to the Father resulted from their own *free choice*.

James 1:18

"*He chose to give us birth* through the word of truth, that we might be a kind of firstfruits of all he created." It is clear that God was the one who chose for us to be born, not ourselves (cf. John 1:13).

Response

Here again, there is no question that God is the *source* of salvation. Had He not chosen to save, then no one would be saved. But the question remains as to the *means* by which we *receive* that sal-

---

[30]See William F. Arndt and F. Wilbur Gingrich, *A Greek-English Lexicon of the New Testament and Other Early Christian Literature* (Chicago: The University of Chicago Press, 1957), 251; Henry George Lidell and Robert Scott, *A Greek-English Lexicon* (Oxford: At the Clarendon Press, 1968), 216; and Friedrich, *Theological Dictionary of the New Testament*, 2.503.

[31]This reference is Jeremiah 38:3 in the LXX.

vation. That is, does God save us *apart* from our free choice or *through* it? Nothing in this text, or any other for that matter, declares that God chooses to save us against our will. Just the contrary is true (see chapter 2). For "by grace" are we saved *"through faith"* (Eph. 2:8–9). Our salvation is "through the word" (Rom. 10:17; James 1:18), but the Bible declares that the Word must be received by faith (Acts 2:41; Heb. 4:1–2) to be effectual (see appendix 10).

John 3:27

" 'A man can receive *only what is given him from heaven.*' " Extreme Calvinists use this to prove that God's grace is irresistible.[32]

Response

However, this does not say anything about God's work of salvation being irresistible. In fact, it says we are to "receive" it. This implies a free act of the will that can either accept or reject God's offer. Indeed, there are specific cases where God's grace is rejected, as the following passages demonstrate.

GRACE IS NOT IRRESISTIBLE ON THE UNWILLING

Those who insist that God's will cannot be resisted confuse what God wills *unconditionally* with what He wills *conditionally.* God wills the salvation of all persons conditionally—conditioned on their repentance (2 Peter 3:9). Hence, God's will in this sense can be resisted by an unrepentant heart. Of course, God's will to save those who believe (i.e., the elect) is unconditional. So this is not a repudiation of unconditional election. Election is unconditional from the standpoint of the Giver (God), but it is conditional from the standpoint of the receiver. And since God foreknows for sure who will receive it, the result is certain. Thus, in this sense God's grace on the elect *is* irresistible.

Furthermore, there are very clear passages affirming that the Holy Spirit can be resisted. This applies to both God's will (Greek: *thelo*, wish, desire) and His plan (Greek: *boulomai*, counsel, plan). Consider the following Scriptures.

Luke 7:30 declares, "The Pharisees and experts in the law *rejected God's purpose* [will][33] for themselves, because they had not been bap-

---

[32]See Steele and Thomas, *The Five Points of Calvinism,* 55.
[33]The Greek word for "purpose" (*boulan*) can mean counsel, decision, or will (see William F. Arndt and F. Wilbur Gingrich, *A Greek-English Lexicon of the New Testament,* 145).

tized by John." Acts 7:51 affirms, "You stiff-necked people, with un-circumcised hearts and ears! You are just like your fathers: You always *resist the Holy Spirit*!" Even John Calvin commented on this text, saying that Luke is speaking of their "desperate inflexibility" when "they are said to be *resisting the Spirit.*"[34] But how can God's work on them be irresistible when it was actually resisted?

Also, Matthew 23:37 affirms emphatically that Jesus desired to bring the Jews who rejected Him into the fold but could not because they would not. He cried, "O Jerusalem, Jerusalem, you who kill the prophets and stone those sent to you, how often I have longed to gather your children together, as a hen gathers her chicks under her wings, *but you were not willing.*" God's grace is not irresistible on those who are unwilling.

Finally, there are many other texts indicating that man can defy the will of God.[35] This is true of both unbelievers (cf. Matt. 12:50; 7:21; John 7:17; 1 John 2:17) and believers (1 Thess. 4:3). Of course, in one sense eventually and ultimately God's will prevails in that He sovereignly wills that those who reject His offer of salvation will be lost. In this sense, God's overruling will is being done through their will to reject Him. But with regard to His will that all men be saved (1 Tim. 2:4; 2 Peter 3:9), it is clear that it can be resisted. In short, it is God's ultimate and sovereign will that we have free will to resist His will that all be saved.

C. S. Lewis has some very insightful comments in this connection. In *Screwtape Letters* he wrote, "the Irresistible and the Indisputable are the two weapons which the very nature of His [God's] scheme forbids Him to use. Merely to override a human will ... would be for Him useless. He cannot ravish. He can only woo."[36] In *The Great Divorce* Lewis adds, "There are only two kinds of people in the end: those who say to God, 'Thy will be done,' and those to whom God says, in the end, 'Thy will be done.' All that are in Hell, choose it. Without that selfchoice there could be no Hell."[37]

---

[34]*Calvin's Commentaries: The Acts of the Apostles*, 1:213, emphasis mine.
[35]Most Calvinists distinguish different dimensions of God's will, such as (1) God's *prescriptive* will (e.g., "Be perfect"); (2) His *permissive* will (which allows sin); and (3) His *providential* or over-ruling will (which brings good out of evil). God's will is often resisted in the sense of (1), since we are always disobeying His commands. But His permissive (2) and providential (3) wills cannot be resisted, for He never allows more than what He permits, and He always accomplishes His ultimate purposes (Isa. 55:11). The command (or call) to be saved is a command that He allows to be resisted (2 Peter 3:9; Matt. 23:37).
[36]*Screwtape Letters*, 128.
[37]Lewis, *The Great Divorce*, 69.

GRACE IS IRRESISTIBLE ONLY ON THE WILLING

R. C. Sproul, an ardent Calvinist himself, reminds us that "the dreadful error of hyper-Calvinists is that it involves God coercing sin."[38] What he does not seem to appreciate is that *it is also a dreadful error to coerce good*. Forced freedom, whether of good or evil, is contrary to the nature of God as love and contrary to the God-given nature of human beings as free. Forced freedom is a contradiction in terms.

Short of coercion, Calvinists disagree about the degree of persuasion God places upon a person with the degree of sovereignty one is willing to attribute to God (see chapter 1). Extreme "Calvinists" from the later Augustine (see appendix 3) to R. C. Sproul do not blink at the use of the terms "compel" or "coerce" of God's grace. St. Augustine wrote, "Let them [the Donatists] recognize in his [Paul's] case Christ first *compelling*, and afterward teaching; first striking, and afterward consoling."[39] He also said, "The Lord Himself bids the guests in the first instance to be invited to His great supper; and afterward *compelled*."[40] Sproul adds, "If God has no right of *coercion*, then he has no right of governing his creation."[41]

Moderate Calvinists like me are willing to affirm that God can be as persuasive as He desires to be, *short of coercion*. In theological terms, this means God can use irresistible grace on the willing. But this kind of divine persuasion will be like that of a courtship. God will woo and court so persuasively that those willing to respond will be overwhelmed by His love.

AN UNSUCCESSFUL MANEUVER

Some extreme Calvinists use a kind of smoke-and-mirror tactic to avoid the harsh implications of their view. They claim that God does no violence toward a rebellious will; He simply gives a new one. In R. C. Sproul's words, "If God gives us a desire for Christ we will act according to that desire." This sounds reasonable enough until the implied words are included: "If God gives us a[n irresistible] desire for Christ we will [irresistibly] act according to that

---

[38]Sproul, *Chosen by God*, 143.
[39]St. Augustine, "On the Correction of the Donatists," in *A Select Library of the Nicene and Post-Nicene Fathers of the Christian Church*, ed. Philip Schaff (Grand Rapids, Mich.: Wm. B. Eerdmans Publishing Co., 1956), 6.22–23, emphasis mine.
[40]Ibid., 6.22, emphasis mine.
[41]*Chosen by God*, 42, emphasis mine.

desire." Now it can be seen that extreme Calvinists are using word magic in an attempt to hide the fact that they believe God forces the unwilling against their will.

What extreme Calvinists want to do is to avoid the repugnant image of a reluctant candidate being forced into the fold or captured into the kingdom.[42] Therefore, they argue that "Once that desire is planted, those who come to Christ do not come kicking and screaming against their wills. They come because they want to come."[43] Of course, here again it is the implied but missing words that shine a whole new light on the picture. What Sproul really means is this: "Once that desire is [irresistibly] planted, those who come to Christ do not come kicking and screaming against their wills." In other words, once someone is dragged against his will, then he will act willingly. But no matter how well the act of "irresistible grace" is hidden by euphemistic language, it is still a morally repugnant concept.

The problem with the idea of "irresistible grace" in extreme Calvinism, according to this analogy, is that there is *no informed consent* for the treatment. Or, better yet, the patients are dragged kicking and screaming into the operating room, but once they are given a head transplant, they (not surprisingly) feel like an entirely different person!

Again, noted defender of irresistible grace R. C. Sproul states the problem well: "The sinner in hell must be asking, 'God, if you really loved me, why didn't you coerce me to believe? I would rather have had my free will violated than to be here in this eternal place of torment.'" He adds, "If we grant that God can save men by violating their wills, why then does he not violate everybody's will and bring them all to salvation?" Then, Sproul confesses, "The only answer I can give to this question is that I don't know. *I have no idea why God saves some but not all.*" He then adds, "I don't doubt for a moment that God has the power to save all."[44]

If this is the case, then Sproul must doubt that God has the love to save all. That is to say, the extreme Calvinists' God is all-powerful, but He is not all-loving! And in coercing the elect into

---

[42]Ibid., 123.
[43]Ibid.
[44]Ibid., 36–37, emphasis mine.

the kingdom, the supposedly irresistible "grace" of regeneration[45] negates God's infinite goodness.

However, a theological rose by any other name is still a theological rose. The truth is that extreme Calvinists believe that God uses irresistible force to change a person from not loving Christ to loving Christ. Hence, irresistible love is forced love. And forced "love" is not love at all.

EXTREME CALVINISM POSITS A COERCIVE GOD

Everyone who believes God is all-powerful admits that God could, if He wished, force people to do things against their will. The real question is not *could* but *would*—that is, *would* an all-loving Being force free creatures to do things against their will? The extreme Calvinists say yes. Virtually all the great church fathers including the early Augustine up to the time of Luther said no (see appendix 1). And even Lutherans follow Melanchthon, not Luther's *Bondage of the Will*, in rejecting this compulsive view.

AVOIDING EXTREME CALVINISM'S VIEW OF THE PERSEVERANCE OF THE SAINTS

The final letter in the Calvinist's T-U-L-I-P is "P" for "Perseverance of the Saints." For Calvinists, this means all of those who are regenerated will persevere to the end. They will all make it to heaven.

All Calvinists believe in perseverance

All Calvinists believe that all the elect will persevere in their faith and be saved. That is, all the regenerated are elect, and all the elect will be in heaven.[46] In popular language, Calvinists of all varieties believe "once saved, always saved." They hasten to point out, however, that "the perseverance of the saints depends on the per-

---

[45]Sproul speaks reluctantly of "the irresistible character of regenerating grace," but tries to soften its compulsive nature by insisting there is no external compulsion. He cites Calvin, saying, "The Lord draws men by their own wills," but then admits these are *wills "which he [God] Himself has produced"* (*Willing to Believe*, 113, emphasis mine). But if God produced the will by irresistible force, then it is theological double-talk to say that we do it willingly (pp. 112–13). This irresistible act of regeneration is compared to an act of resurrection on a passive and dead body. What could be more compulsive?

[46]However, Augustine and his followers up to the Reformation believed that some of the regenerate are not elect and would not persevere (see Augustine, *City of God*, 22). In this sense they were like later Arminians.

severance of God." Or, more properly, it depends on "the preservation of God."[47]

In the words of the *Westminster Confession of Faith* (chapter 17, 1), perseverance means: "They whom God hath accepted in his Beloved, effectually called and sanctified by his Spirit, can neither totally nor finally fall away from the state of grace; but shall certainly persevere therein to the end, and be eternally saved."

EXTREME VS. MODERATE CALVINISM ON PERSEVERANCE

There is not always a discernable difference between extreme and moderate Calvinists on the matter of perseverance. However, at least some extreme Calvinists seem to imply that none of the elect will die in sin, while the moderate Calvinist holds that no elect person will be lost, even if he dies in sin.

Another way to explain the difference is that moderate Calvinists believe in both temporal assurance on earth and eternal security in heaven for the elect, whereas some extreme Calvinists appear to believe only in the latter, since one cannot be really sure that he is one of the elect until he perseveres to the end. The elect are secure, but according to the extreme Calvinist no professing Christian can be absolutely sure that he is one of the elect until he meets the Lord. There is such a thing as "false assurance"; Calvin even speaks of a "false work of grace."[48] And Sproul asserts that "we may think that we have faith when in fact we have no faith."[49]

A. A. Hodge said, *"Perseverance in holiness,* therefore, in opposition to all weakness and temptations, is the *only sure evidence* of the genuineness of past experience, of the validity of our confidence as to our future salvation." While there can be a "temporary withdrawal of restraining grace" while an elect person is "allowed to backslide for a time," nonetheless, *"in every such case* they are graciously restored."[50] This seems to imply that if someone backslides and does not turn around before he meets his Maker, then that is proof that he was not truly saved. If so, then no matter what evidence one may have manifested in his life for many years before this, he could not have had true assurance that he was saved. This

---

[47]Palmer, *The Five Points of Calvinism,* 69–70.
[48]Calvin, *Institutes of the Christian Religion,* 3.2.
[49]*Chosen by God,* 165–66.
[50]A. A. Hodge, *Outlines of Theology* (Grand Rapids, Mich.: Wm. B. Eerdmans Publishing Co., 1949), 544–45.

reminds us that there is such a thing as "false assurance." Further, Hodge adds, "we can decrease it. We can even lose it altogether, at least for a season."[51] The bottom line for these extreme Calvinists is that no one can be sure he is one of the elect until he gets to heaven.

However, in a seeming inconsistency they go on to speak about present assurance.[52] Since extreme Calvinists often speak as though they can be sure of salvation before death—even providing criteria for knowing whether we are saved,[53] we will not belabor the point here.

Nonetheless, strong similarity between the two Calvinists' views, as opposed to Arminianism, is that salvation of the believer is eternally secure from the very first moment of salvation. Verses used to support this contention are discussed later (see chapter 7).

SOME CONCLUDING THOUGHTS

A careful examination of Scripture reveals that extreme Calvinists, particularly on the first four points, are unsupported by the many texts they employ. When properly understood in their contexts, these passages do not support their interpretation of the "Five Points" of extreme Calvinism as expressed in the traditional T-U-L-I-P, with the possible exception of the last point as held by some. We turn, then, to examine extreme Arminianism and its dangers.

[51]Ibid., 164, 166.
[52]The great Puritan theologian William Ames (1576–1633) wrote of perseverance: "This certainty about the thing itself, which is called a certainty of the object, is made fast for all true believers. But the perceiving of it, which is called a certainty of the subject, is not always enjoyed by all." However, "it may be acquired by any without special revelation and it should be sought by all" (*The Marrow of Theology*). R. C. Sproul claims "that it is still not only possible for us to have a genuine assurance of our salvation, but that it is our duty to seek such assurance" (*Chosen by God*, 167–68).
[53]Sproul, *Chosen by God*, 170–71.

CHAPTER SIX

AVOIDING EXTREME ARMINIANISM

Like a pendulum, theological movements tend to go to one extreme or the other. In the last chapter we examined the extreme Calvinists' view, which sacrifices human free will at the expense of divine sovereignty. In this chapter we will examine the extreme Arminian view, which sacrifices God's sovereignty on the altar of man's free choice. But before we discuss extreme Arminians, it is necessary to sketch briefly what is meant by "Arminianism."

WHAT IS ARMINIANISM?

Arminianism is the theology of the followers of Jacobus [James] Arminius (1560–1609), a Dutch Reformed theologian whose views were expressed in the *Remonstrance* (1610), formally set forth a year after his death. Since the *Remonstrance* comprises five often misunderstood points, we cite them in their own words:

(1) God elects on the basis of His "eternal, unchangeable purpose" only "those who, through the grace of the Holy Ghost, shall believe on this His Son Jesus." He also wills "to leave the incorrigible and

unbelieving in sin and under wrath";[1]

(2) Christ "died for all men and for every man, so that he has obtained for them all . . . redemption and the forgiveness of sins; yet that no one actually enjoys this forgiveness of sins except the believer. . . ."[2]

(3) "That man has not saving grace of himself, nor of the energy of his free will . . . can of and by himself neither think, will, nor do any thing that is truly good (such as saving faith eminently is); but that it is needful that he be born again of God in Christ. . . ."[3]

(4) "That this grace of God is the beginning, continuance, and accomplishment of all good, even to this extent, that the regenerate man himself, without prevenient or assisting, awakening, following, and co-operative grace, can neither think, will, nor do good. . . ." It adds, "But as respects the mode of the operation of this grace, it is not irresistible. . . ."[4]

(5) "That those who are incorporated into Christ by a true faith . . . have thereby full power to . . . win the victory . . . but whether they are capable . . . of becoming devoid of grace, that must be more particularly determined out of the Holy Scriptures, before we ourselves can teach it with the full persuasion of our minds."[5]

Arminius's views were formally condemned at the Calvinists' Synod of Dort (1618–19), and many of his followers were banished and persecuted. The condemnation by the extreme Calvinists followed the proclamation of the five points of the *Remonstrance* and served as the basis of the famous "Five Points" of the T-U-L-I-P (see chapters 4 and 5). It was not until 1795 that there was official toleration for views of the Arminians.

A modified version of the Arminian position was carried on in the teachings of the Englishmen John Wesley (1703–1791), Charles

---

[1]More fully, Article 1 of the Arminian *Remonstrance* states: "That God, by an eternal unchangeable purpose in Jesus Christ his Son, before the foundation of the world, hath determined, out of the fallen, sinful race of men, to save in Christ, for Christ's sake, and through Christ, those who, through the grace of the Holy Ghost, shall believe on this his Son Jesus, and shall persevere in this faith and obedience of faith, through this grace, even to the end; and, on the other hand, to leave the incorrigible and unbelieving in sin and under wrath . . ." (Philip Schaff, *The Creeds of Christendom* (Grand Rapids, Mich.: Baker Book House, 1983), 3.545.

It is noteworthy that there is no mention here, or in the other four articles, of being elect on the basis of their foreseen faith, as extreme Calvinists allege. Arminius did, however, mistakenly believe that God owed sinners something because of His justice (Arminius, "Works," in *The Writings of James Arminius*, vol. 1, 2.497–98). The truth is that it was God's love, not His justice, that prompted Him to provide salvation for all men.
[2]Ibid., 2.546.
[3]Ibid., 2.546–547.
[4]Ibid., 2.547.
[5]Ibid., 2.549.

Wesley (1707–1788), and their friend John William Fletcher (1729–1785). Subsequently, this was continued in Methodism, Pentecostalism, the Holiness Movement, and the Charismatic Movement. (However, George Whitfield's Calvinistic teachings have also been held by many in the Wesleyan tradition.) The greatest Wesleyan-Arminian theologian at the turn of the nineteenth century was Richard Watson (1737–1816; see his *Theological Institutes* [T. Mason and G. Lane, 1936]).

AVOIDING EXTREME ARMINIANISM[6]

In recent years a serious extreme has emerged in Arminian circles that is self-labeled "Free Will Theism" or the "Openness of God" view.[7] Actually, it shares some similarities with "Process Theology"[8] and is more appropriately called the New Theism or Neotheism.[9]

THE NEW KID ON THE BLOCK

Neotheists have carried Arminianism to a dangerous extreme. They have "created" a new view that is neither identical to the traditional theism of Calvin and Arminius, nor is it the same as the radical liberal God of the Process Theology, which borrows from such thinkers as Alfred North Whitehead, Charles Hartshorne, Shubert Ogden, and John Cobb. Several proponents of this form of Arminianism, including Clark Pinnock, Richard Rice, John Sanders, William Hasker, and David Basinger, have collaborated on a volume titled *The Openness of God*.[10] Other Christian thinkers who share

---

[6]Some of the things listed under "extreme Armininianism" are really what scholars call "Pelagianism" or even "Process Theology," and should not be identified with traditional Arminianism.

[7]See Clark Pinnock, et al., *The Openness of God* (Downers Grove, Ill.: InterVarsity Press, 1994).

[8]Clark Pinnock, "Between Classical and Process Theism" in *Process Theology*, ed. Ronald Nash (Grand Rapids, Mich.: Baker Book House, 1987); William Hasker, *God, Time, and Knowledge* (Ithaca, N.Y.: Cornell University Press, 1989); David and Randall Basinger eds., *Predestination and Free Will* (Downers Grove, Ill.: InterVarsity, 1986).

[9]Neotheists list five characteristics of their position: 1. "God not only created this world *ex nihilo* but can (and at times does) intervene unilaterally in earthly affairs"; 2. "God chose to create us with incompatibilistic (libertarian) freedom—freedom over which He cannot exercise total control"; 3. "God so values freedom—the moral integrity of free creatures and a world in which such integrity is possible—that He does not normally override such freedom, even if He sees that it is producing undesirable results"; 4. "God always desires our highest good, both individually and corporately, and thus is affected by what happens in our lives"; and 5. "God does not possess exhaustive knowledge of exactly how we will utilize our freedom, although He may very well at times be able to predict with great accuracy the choices we will freely make" (Pinnock, *Openness of God*, 156).

[10]Ibid.

similar views or who have expressed sympathy for this position include Greg Boyd, Stephen Davis, Thomas Morris, and Richard Swinburne.[11]

As noted elsewhere,[12] Neotheism has exalted free will at the expense of divine sovereignty. Since the Bible affirms both sovereignty and free choice (see chapters 1 and 2), Neotheism is an extreme to be avoided.

A DENIAL OF GOD'S TRADITIONAL ATTRIBUTES

As discussed in chapter 2, the traditional Christian view of God held by the early church fathers (see appendix 1), expressed in the great confessions and creeds of the Christian church and embraced by the Reformers, including Luther, Calvin, Zwingli, and later Arminius—firmly upheld the traditional attributes of God. Among other things, these included that God is transcendent (beyond the universe), immanent (within the universe), Creator *ex nihilo* (out of nothing), and can cause supernatural events (miracles). In addition, these attributes include that God knows all things (has omniscience), God is before all things (has eternality), God never changes (has immutability), and God is in complete control of all things (has sovereignty). But it is precisely these attributes of traditional Christian theology (including Calvinist and Arminian) that are denied by those extreme Arminians who embrace Neotheism.

A DENIAL OF GOD'S FOREKNOWLEDGE OF FREE EVENTS

While Neotheists claim to believe in omniscience, they make a serious qualification that negates the historical position that God infallibly knows all things, including all future events.

---

[11]Those who have written books include Richard Rice, *God's Foreknowledge and Man's Free Will* (Minneapolis: Bethany House Publishers, 1985); Ronald Nash, ed., *Process Theology* (Grand Rapids, Mich.: Baker Book House, 1987); Greg Boyd, *Trinity and Process* (New York: Peter Lang, 1992) and *Letters from a Skeptic* (Wheaton, Ill.: Victor, 1994); J. R. Lucas, *The Freedom of the Will* (Oxford: Clarendon Press, 1970) and *The Future: An Essay on God, Temporality and Truth* (London: Basil Blackwell, 1989); and Peter Geach, *Providence and Evil* (Cambridge: Cambridge University Press, 1977). Richard Swinburne's *The Coherence of Theism* (Oxford: Clarendon Press, 1977) and Thomas V. Morris's *Our Idea of God: An Introduction to Philosophical Theology* (Downers Grove, Ill.: InterVarsity, 1991) are close to the view. A. N. Prior, Richard Purtill, et al., have written articles defending Neotheism. Others who show sympathy to the view include Stephen T. Davis, *Logic and the Nature of God* (Grand Rapids, Mich.: Wm. B. Eerdmans Publishing Co., 1983) and Linda Zagzebski, *The Dilemma of Freedom and Foreknowledge* (Oxford: Oxford University Press, 1991).

[12]See Norman L. Geisler, *Creating God in the Image of Man?* (Minneapolis: Bethany House Publishers, 1997).

It is unbiblical to deny God's foreknowledge

The extreme Arminian's argument against God knowing future free acts is unbiblical. Since much of the future involves free human actions, this would place any revelation from God regarding the future in serious jeopardy. But the Bible is filled with such predictions about the future.

God knows all things

The Bible declares that God knows all things, including our future free choices. He is omniscient. The psalmist declared, "Great is our Lord, and mighty in power: His understanding is infinite" (Ps. 147:5 NKJV). God says through Isaiah that He knows the end from the beginning (Isa. 46:10). And according to the psalmist, God knows the very secrets of our heart (Ps. 139:1–6). Indeed, "Nothing in all creation is hidden from God's sight. Everything is uncovered and laid bare before the eyes of him to whom we must give account" (Heb. 4:13).

God knows who the elect are

Further, God knows who the elect are. They were chosen in Christ before the foundation of the world (Eph. 1:4). God not only knows who is going to heaven (Rom. 8:29; 1 Peter 1:2); He also knows who is not (cf. Rev. 20:10–15).

In addition, God knew from eternity that Christ would die for our sins (1 Peter 1:18–20; Rev. 13:8). Yet this involved Christ's free choice (John 10:17–18).

God knows who the non-elect are

God knew and predicted that Judas would betray Christ (Acts 1:20) and that he would be lost forever (John 17:12). He also knew eternally and infallibly predicted that the Beast and False Prophet would be cast into the lake of fire (Rev. 19:20). He also names some who are among the elect before they ever get to heaven. Paul includes himself among those whom God knew and chose before the foundation of the world (Eph. 1:4). But if, as Neotheists claim, God cannot know future free acts, then this would not be possible.

God predicted numerous human events

Since virtually all human events involve free choices, it follows that nearly every supernatural prediction in the Bible involved God's infallible foreknowledge of what human beings would freely choose. The late Professor Barton Payne, in his comprehensive catalogue of prophecies, lists 1,817 predictions in the Bible (1,239 in the OT and 578 in the NT). Payne lists 191 biblical prophecies with reference to

Christ.[13] Some of these specified the town (Bethlehem) in which Christ would be born (Mic. 5:2) and the time He would die (Dan. 9:26 ff.), namely, around A.D. 33. Daniel predicted the succession of the great world kingdoms of Babylon, Medo-Persia, Greece, and Rome (Dan. 2, 7), including his account of the exploits of Antiochus Epiphanes (Dan. 11) in amazing detail. Isaiah 44:28 (cf. 45:1) predicted by name Cyrus, king of Persia, a century and a half before he was born. Isaiah (11:11; cf. Deut. 28:1f.) predicted the return of Israel to her land centuries in advance. Ezekiel (44:2) predicted the closing of the Golden Gate on the east side of Jerusalem until the time of the Messiah. Ezekiel (26:3–14) also foresaw the destruction of Tyre, which was centuries later literally fulfilled by Nebuchadnezzar and then Alexander the Great. Jeremiah (49:16–17) prophesied the doom of Edom (Petra), which remains as a tourist site in Jordan to this day. There were numerous other biblical prophecies made hundreds of years in advance that have been literally fulfilled, including the unlikely desert flourishing (Ezek. 36:33–35) and the increase of knowledge and education in the last days (Dan. 12:4). Not a single biblical prophecy has ever failed.[14] None of this would have been possible without God's infallible foreknowledge of future free acts.

Furthermore, God knows who will be lost and who will be saved (Matt. 25:40–41). He knows the order of events in the last days and has laid it out in the book of Revelation (see chapters 6–19). There are literally hundreds of events known and predicted by God in advance, and these clearly reveal His infallible foreknowledge of the future.

It is unreasonable to deny God's foreknowledge

Not only is it unbiblical to deny God's knowledge of future free events, it is also unreasonable. The following arguments support this conclusion:

The alleged impossibility of knowing free acts in advance

Extreme Arminians (Neotheists) deny that God has infallible knowledge of future free acts on the alleged grounds that God cannot know in advance what we will freely choose to do. Their reasoning goes like this:

(1) Whatever is infallibly known in advance must be determined.

---

[13]See J. Barton Payne, *Encyclopedia of Biblical Prophecy* (London: Hodder & Stoughton, 1973), 674–75; 665–70.
[14]See Norman L. Geisler, "Prophecy as Proof of the Bible," in *Baker's Encyclopedia of Christian Apologetics* (Grand Rapids, Mich.: Baker Book House, 1999), 611–18.

(2) A freely chosen event cannot be determined by another.

(3) Therefore, what is infallibly foreknown cannot be freely chosen.

However, this reasoning is unsound. The second premise is false. For, as already shown (in chapter 3), there is no contradiction between God knowing for sure (has determined) what will freely occur in the future (is freely chosen). Just because someone could have chosen another way does not mean that God did not know for sure which way he would choose.

The alleged impossibility of knowing future events

Neotheists have offered another argument against God having infallible knowledge of future free acts. It goes like this:

(1) The future has not yet actually occurred.

(2) Truth is what corresponds to what actually is.

(3) Therefore, it is impossible to know something is true before it actually occurs.

There are at least two major problems with this reasoning. First, it is possible that God knows from eternity that an event that is *future to us* would one day occur (and then be true). In this case, it would not be true in advance before it occurred, but it would be true that God knew in advance that it would one day occur and then be actually true.

Second, no such problem exists for a God who is eternal, that is, beyond time—and the Bible and good reason inform us that God is (see the following page). Hence, *nothing is future to God.* If God is beyond time, then all time is spread before Him in one eternal *now.* He sees the way a man on the top of the hill sees the whole train at once, while the man in the tunnel below sees only one car going by at a time, noticing neither the one already past nor the one yet to come.[15] God is not standing on one day of the calendar of time, looking back at the days past and forward to the days to come. Rather, He is looking down on the whole calendar, *seeing all the days at once* (cf. 2 Tim. 1:9; Titus 1:2).

The inconsistency of denying God's infinite knowledge

Extreme Arminians (Neotheists) admit that God is infinite, yet they deny His knowledge is infinite. But this is inconsistent, for

---

[15]Another way to put it is this: (1) What is infallibly foreknown cannot be otherwise; (2) What is free can be otherwise; (3) Therefore, what is infallibly foreknown cannot be free. In this form, there is an equivocation on the second premise. Premise (1) means that it cannot *actually* come to pass contrary to the way God foreknew it would. But in premise (2) it means that it was *possible* that we had not chosen this way. If we had chosen otherwise, then an all-knowing, eternal God would have known for certain that it would be *that* way. Hence, there is no contradiction.

God's knowledge is identical with His essence, since He is admitted to be a necessary Being (that is, one that cannot cease to exist). And a necessary Being is what it is necessarily. That is, nothing is accidental to the being (existence) of a necessary Being. Whatever God "has," that He *is*—essentially.

So if God "has" knowledge, then He *is* knowledge in His entire being. But His entire *Being* is infinite. Therefore, God must be infinite in His knowledge (Ps. 147:5). And if infinite in knowledge, then He must know everything that is possible to know.[16] That is, He must know everything that is not impossible. But the future is not impossible, since it will one day be actual. Therefore, God must be able to know the future. In brief, God can know the potential as well as the actual. And the future is potential. Therefore, God can know the future (Isa. 46:10).

A DENIAL OF GOD'S IMMUTABILITY (UNCHANGEABILITY)

Another important attribute extreme Arminians reject is God's immutability. This, too, is both unbiblical and unreasonable.

It is unbiblical to deny God's immutability

Scripture affirms from beginning to end that God is unchangeable. Moses declared that "God is not a man, that he should lie, nor a son of man, that he should change his mind. Does he speak and then not act? Does he promise and not fulfill?" (Num. 23:19). The book of First Samuel adds, " 'He who is the Glory of Israel does not lie or change his mind; for he is not a man, that he should change his mind' " (15:29). Speaking of the perishable universe, the psalmist asserted, "They will perish, but you remain; they will all wear out like a garment. Like clothing you will change them and they will be discarded. But you remain the same, and your years will never end" (Ps. 102:26–27). The prophet Malachi cited God, proclaiming, " 'I the LORD do not change. So you, O descendants of Jacob, are not destroyed' " (3:6). The writer of Hebrews declares that "it is impossible for God to lie" (6:18). He adds, "Jesus Christ is the same yesterday and today and for ever" (Heb. 13:8). The apostle Paul told Timothy that "if we are faithless, he [God] will remain faithful, for he cannot disown Himself" (2 Tim. 2:13). And

---

[16]The only thing an omniscient Being cannot know is what is impossible, like a square circle. For example, God cannot know that what is true is false, or that what is good is evil.

James writes that "Every good and perfect gift is from above, coming down from the Father of the heavenly lights, who does not change like shifting shadows" (1:17). That is to say, God does not even change in the slightest. In fact, as Hebrews affirms, it is impossible for God to change.

It is unreasonable to deny God's immutability

Everything that changes has a cause. Change is a movement from a state of potentiality *for* that change *to* the actual change itself. But no potentiality can actualize itself, any more than steel can make itself into a skyscraper. Therefore, there must be some "actualizer" outside the change to account for it. The whole universe *is* changing.[17] Therefore, the whole universe needs a Cause beyond it that is not changing (i.e., God). God is the Unchanging Cause of all that changes.

Furthermore, God cannot change since He is Pure Actuality. He is the "I AM" (Ex. 3:14), the self-existent one. He has no potentiality not to be, since He is (as even Neotheists admit) a necessary Being. But a necessary Being by nature cannot *not* exist. He must exist, and cannot go into nonexistence. Yet if a Necessary Being has no potentiality not to exist, then He cannot change. For to change demands a potential for the change. Therefore, God must be unchangeable in His being.

This, of course, does not mean that God cannot enter into changing relationships. But it is not God who changes when the relationship changes, any more than the pillar changes when the man moves from one side of it to the other. The man may change in relation to the pillar, but the pillar does not change. Likewise, the universe changes in relation to God, but God does not change (cf. Heb. 1:10–12).

An objection to God's unchangeability answered

Extreme Arminians (Neotheists) object that the Bible often speaks of God as changing. He changes in answer to prayer (e.g., see Ex. 32). He changed His mind about having made the world (Gen. 6:6). He changed His mind when Nineveh repented (Jonah 3:10). However, there are many reasons for concluding that *none of these Scriptures prove that God's nature actually changes.*

---

[17]According to the second law of Thermodynamics, the entire universe is running down, that is, running out of useable energy (again, see Ps. 102:26–27). And it is this visible, perishable universe that points to an invisible, imperishable God behind it (see Rom. 1:19–20; cf. Acts 17:24–29).

First of all, if God really did change, it would be contradictory to all the Scriptures just cited. And the Bible does not contradict itself.[18]

Second, as just noted, God cannot change. If He did, then He would not be God—there would be something more ultimate than He is that is the unchanging basis for His change and all other change.

Third, the Bible often uses anthropomorphism (speaking of God in human terms). Speaking of God as changing is an anthropomorphism. For example, the Scriptures speak of God as having eyes (Heb. 4:13), arms (Num. 11:23), and even feathers (Ps. 91). Yet extreme Arminians do not take these literally!

Fourth, it is not God who actually changes but man. When riding our bikes into the wind, we say, "the wind is against us." And when we turn around and ride in the other direction, we say "the wind is for us." In actual fact, the wind did not change; we did. Likewise, when a sinner repents, God does not change; the sinner does. For God's justice demands that He has an unchanging hatred toward evil, and His love demands that He have an unchanging mercy toward those who forsake their sin. So when the sinner repents, he simply moves from the action of God that flows from His unchanging attribute of justice to that which flows from His unchanging attribute of love. *God does not change.*

A DENIAL OF GOD'S ETERNALITY

Extreme Arminians also deny God's eternality. While acknowledging that God has no beginning, they deny that He is beyond time or nontemporal. This, too, is without biblical or rational justification.

It is unbiblical to deny God's eternality

All orthodox Christians believe the universe had a beginning (Gen. 1:1; John 1:3; Col. 1:16). But time began with the space/time universe. Only God existed prior to time. God is "before all things" (Col. 1:17). The psalmist said, "From everlasting to everlasting, Thou art God" (Ps. 90:2 KJV). Often the Bible speaks of God as being there "before the foundation of the world" (John 17:24 KJV; cf. Matt. 13:35; 25:34).

---

[18]For evidence that the Bible is not self-contradictory, see Norman L. Geisler and Thomas A. Howe, *When Critics Ask* (Grand Rapids, Mich.: Baker Book House, 1992), especially chapter 1.

But if God was before all time, then He is eternal. God was there *"before the beginning of time"* (2 Tim. 1:9). In fact, God brought time into existence when He "framed the *ages*" (Heb. 1:2, Rotherham translation). God "alone has immortality" (1 Tim. 6:16 NKJV), an immortality without beginning or end. He is literally the First and the Last (Rev. 1:11 NKJV).

It is unreasonable to deny God's eternality

In spite of the clear teaching of Scripture and of the great fathers of the Christian Church, extreme Arminians teach that God is temporal, that He is in time.

But none of the arguments Neotheists have given for a temporal God are convincing. Instead, there are powerful arguments demonstrating that God must be nontemporal, that is, eternal.

Whatever is in time, changes

Whatever is in time is changing, for time is a measurement of temporal change. Time is a computation according to a before and an after. But only what changes has a before and an after. Therefore, whatever is temporal in its being must change. But as shown above, God cannot change. As a result, it follows that God cannot be temporal.

Whatever is in time had a beginning

As is demonstrated by the Kalam Argument for God's existence,[19] there cannot be an eternal number of moments passing in succession one after the other, for an infinite number of moments cannot be traversed (only a limited number can be traversed). So if there were an infinite number of moments before the present moment, then the present moment would never have arrived. But the present moment *has* arrived. Therefore, there cannot have been an infinite number of moments before the present one, but only a finite (limited) number. Hence, whatever is in time had a beginning. But even Neotheists admit that God had no beginning. If so, then He cannot be temporal or in time.

Whatever created time cannot be in time

Extreme Arminians (Neotheists) acknowledge that God created the entire spatio-temporal universe out of nothing. But time is an essential part of the cosmos. If so, then God must have created time. But if time is something that is of the essence of creation, then

---

[19]See William Lane Craig, *The Kalam Cosmological Argument* (Macmillan, 1979).

it cannot be an attribute of the uncreated—that is, of God. God is, as the Bible says, "before the beginning of time" (2 Tim. 1:9; Titus 1:2).

Whatever is temporal is also spatial and material

According to the contemporary concept of space, time, and matter, whatever is temporal is also spatial. And whatever is spatial is also material. But God is not immaterial (John 4:24). Therefore, if God is in time, then He is also spatial and material. Neotheists reject this conclusion. But if space and matter are denied of God, then time must also be denied.

Another result of Neotheistic logic is that God could not think any faster than the speed of light—the fastest thing in the space/time universe. If God's thoughts do not encompass the universe simultaneously, then there is no way He can be in control of it. He cannot even think it all at once, let alone be in complete control of it.

A DENIAL OF GOD'S SOVEREIGNTY

As was demonstrated in chapter 1, the Bible emphatically affirms the sovereignty of God. Likewise, there are good arguments from the attributes of God to show that God is in complete control of the entire created universe.[20]

It is unbiblical to deny God's sovereignty

To summarize, God is "before all things" (Col. 1:17). He is also *"before the beginning of time"* (2 Tim. 1:9). Further, "Through him [Christ] all things were made; without him nothing was made that has been made" (John 1:3). "For by him all things were created: things in heaven and on earth, visible and invisible" (Col. 1:16). And God is "sustaining all things by his powerful word" (Heb. 1:3). Paul adds, "He is before all things, *and in him all things hold together"* (Col. 1:17).

And, as has been clearly demonstrated, the God of the Bible knows all things. The psalmist declares, "His understanding is infinite" (Ps. 147:5 NKJV). He knows the end from the beginning (Isa. 46:10), even the very secrets of our heart (Ps. 139:1–6). "Everything is uncovered and laid bare before the eyes of him to whom we must give account" (Heb. 4:13).

---

[20]See chapter 1.

We have already seen also that God can do all things. He is all-powerful. "Nothing is impossible with God" (Luke 1:37). God is omnipotent.

A God who is before all things, upholds all things, knows all things, and can do all things is also in control of all things. This complete control of all things is called the sovereignty of God. The Bible affirms God's sovereignty in many ways. First, God is in sovereign control of His creation. Yahweh is called "the Great King" (Ps. 48:2). His reign is eternal: "The LORD is enthroned as King forever" (Ps. 29:10). And He is king over all the earth: "The LORD is King for ever and ever; the nations will perish from his land" (Ps. 10:16). Nothing happens apart from God's will. Job confessed to God: " 'I know that you can do all things; no plan of yours can be thwarted' " (Job 42:2). The psalmist adds, "Our God is in heaven; he does whatever pleases him" (Ps. 115:3). Again, "The LORD does whatever pleases him, in the heavens and on the earth, in the seas and all their depths" (Ps. 135:6).

Solomon declared that "The king's heart is in the hand of the LORD; he directs it like a watercourse wherever he pleases" (Prov. 21:1). God is the Sovereign over all sovereigns. He is "King of kings and Lord of lords" (Rev. 19:16).

God is in charge of all human events. He ordains the course of history before it occurs (Dan. 2, 7), and He "is sovereign over the kingdoms of men" (Dan. 4:17).

God not only rules in the visible realm but also in the invisible domain. He is "over all creation" including "visible and invisible, whether thrones or dominions or principalities or powers" (Col. 1:15–16 NKJV). The angels come before His throne to get their orders to obey (1 Kings 22; Job 1:6; 2:1). They are positioned before the throne of God and never stop praising Him (Rev. 4:8).

God's sovereign domain includes not only the good angels but also the evil ones (Phil. 2:10; cf. 1 Kings 22:19–22). Satan, too, is under God's sovereign hand (Job 1:6; 2:1; cf. Rev. 12:12; 20:2).

God is in sovereign control of everything we choose, even our own salvation (Eph. 1:11; cf. Eph 1:4; Rom. 8:29–30; Acts 2:23). If God is sovereign, then He is in control of the whole universe. And if He is in control of the whole universe, then extreme Arminianism is wrong.

It is unreasonable to deny God's sovereignty

God's sovereignty flows from His attributes of omniscience and omnipotence, as well as the fact that He freely created and sustains all things. Anyone who knows all, can do all, and on whose will the very existence of all things depends *can* exercise sovereign control over everything. This follows logically from these attributes. Since we have already given the good reasons why God possesses these attributes, we have thereby also provided the solid reasons for His *ability* to sovereignly control the entire created universe.

Of course, the degree to which God exercises this sovereignty will be limited by two things: (1) He cannot do what is impossible to do; and (2) He will do only what He wills to do, not everything He is capable of doing. God is capable of creating more than He did; He is able to do more miracles than He has done, and He has the power to annihilate beings He has not chosen to annihilate. Just how God uses the unlimited power He has will be determined by His will in accordance with His absolutely perfect nature. Often, this will be inscrutable to finite creatures. As Paul declares, "Oh, the depth of the riches of the wisdom and knowledge of God! How unsearchable his judgments, and his paths beyond tracing out!" (Rom. 11:33). And as Moses informs us, "The secret things belong to the LORD our God, but the things revealed belong to us and to our children" (Deut. 29:29).

SOME CONCLUDING THOUGHTS

In chapters 4 and 5 we examined the extreme Calvinist view, which sacrifices human free will at the expense of divine sovereignty. In chapter 6 we have scrutinized the extreme Arminians, who sacrifice God's sovereignty on the altar of man's free choice. Both are unnecessary extremes and as such entail theological dangers to be avoided. We turn, then, to explore a more moderate position.

CHAPTER SEVEN

A PLEA FOR MODERATION

By this point, the observant reader is no doubt asking, "What's left? If extreme Calvinism and extreme Arminianism are to be avoided, then which view is correct?" Well, there are at least two major views remaining: moderate Calvinism and moderate Arminianism. Both are opposed to extreme Calvinism and extreme Arminianism.

EXTREME VS. MODERATE CALVINISM

The chart on page 116 summarizes the primary differences between what is here called extreme Calvinism and moderate Calvinism. Even extreme Calvinists admit that "All the Five Points of Calvinism [as they understand them] hang or fall together" (Palmer, 69). What they do not say is that there is a moderate way to understand these Five Points, in which they also stand or fall together.

The Five Points	Extreme Calvinism	Moderate Calvinism
Total Depravity	Intensive (destructive)[1]	Extensive (corruptive)
Unconditional Election	No condition for God or man	No condition for God; One condition for man (faith)
Limited Atonement	Limited in extent (only for elect)	Limited in result (but for all men)
Irresistible Grace	In compulsive sense (against man's will)	In persuasive sense (in accordance with man's will)
Perseverance of the Saints	No saint will die in sin[2]	No saint will ever be lost (even if he dies in sin)

A defense of moderate Calvinism is found in chapters 4 and 5 ("Avoiding Extreme Calvinism") in two ways: *explicitly* by a critique of extreme Calvinism and *implicitly* in the implied alternative. Further criticisms of the extreme Calvinist view are recorded in appendices 1–9.

A MODERATE CALVINIST'S UNDERSTANDING OF T-U-L-I-P

We have already evaluated the extreme Calvinists' understanding of T-U-L-I-P (in chapters 4 and 5). Here we simply note how a moderate Calvinist understands these five Calvinistic doctrines.

T—Total depravity is amply supported by Scripture in the moderate Calvinist sense. All the Scriptures used by extreme Calvinists are accepted by moderate Calvinists; the only difference is that moderates insist that being "dead" in sin does not mean that unsaved people cannot understand and receive the truth of the gospel as the Spirit of God works on their hearts. That is, it does not in effect *erase* the image of God (but only *effaces* it).

U—Unconditional election is also held by moderate Calvinists. It is unconditional from the standpoint of the Giver, even though

---

[1]Some extreme Calvinists deny that they believe the image of God is "destroyed" in fallen humans—at least formally. But *logically* this is what their view demands and practically this is what they hold.

[2]Not all extreme Calvinists hold this, though some do and others are inconsistent on the point.

there is one condition for the receiver—faith.[3]

L—Even limited atonement is affirmed by moderate Calvinists in the sense that it is limited in its application. That is, although redemption was purchased for all and is available to all, nonetheless, it will only be applied to those whom God chose from all eternity—the elect.

I—Irresistible grace is held by moderate Calvinists. Irresistible grace is exercised on all who are willing, as was stated in chapter 5. That is, anyone who is receptive to God's work in his heart will be overwhelmed by His grace.

P—Perseverance of the saints, too, is an essential part of moderate Calvinism. It affirms that all regenerate (justified) people eventually will be saved. This is supported by numerous Scriptures.

A DEFENSE OF ETERNAL SECURITY

Moderate Calvinists, such as I am, differ with Arminians on many points. One crucial point has to do with whether or not "once saved, always saved" is accurate. That is, whether or not it is possible to lose one's salvation. It is my conviction that the Bible favors the Calvinist's position of eternal security—that a truly saved person can never lose his/her salvation.

The New Testament is replete with verses which teach that salvation can never be lost or rejected.[4] Among them the following stand out.

John 5:24

" 'I tell you the truth, whoever hears my word and believes him who sent me *has eternal life and will not be condemned;* he has crossed over from death to life.' " Those who truly believe can be certain now that they will be in heaven. Eternal life is a present possession the moment one believes.

John 6:39–40

" 'And this is the will of him who sent me, that *I shall lose none of all that he has given me,* but raise them up at the last day. For my Father's will is that *everyone who looks to the Son and believes in him*

---

[3]This does not mean the sinner does something to become one of the elect. God alone does that on the basis of grace alone (this is evident in the verses used to support God's sovereignty in chapter 1). It means only that the elect must believe in Christ to receive this gift of salvation.
[4]Some believers, such as Lutherans, believe salvation cannot be "lost" but it can be "rejected" (by apostasy). The net result is the same, though—once they had it; now they don't.

shall have eternal life, and I will raise him up at the last day.'" Clearly Christ will lose "none" of His children.

John 10:27–28

"'My sheep listen to my voice; I know them, and they follow me. *I give them eternal life, and they shall never perish;* no one can snatch them out of my hand. *My Father, who has given them to me, is greater than all; no one can snatch them out of my Father's hand.'"*

What makes our salvation sure is not only God's infinite love, but also His omnipotence. "No one," not even ourselves, can pry us out of His hand.

John 17:12

Speaking of His disciples, Jesus prayed to the Father: "'While I was with them, I protected them and kept them safe by that name you gave me. *None has been lost* except the one doomed to destruction so that Scripture would be fulfilled.'" Jesus' prayer also included believers not yet born (see v. 20).

We are assured here by Jesus' efficacious prayer that all true believers will be saved. Only those doomed to destruction by their own unwillingness to repent (cf. 2 Peter 3:9) will be lost.

Hebrews 10:14

"By one sacrifice *he has made perfect forever* those who are being made holy." According to this passage, the one sacrifice of Christ on the cross secured forever the salvation of the elect. Since this was secured at the Cross, before we were ever born, it follows that any true believer is assured now that he will be in heaven.

Romans 8:16

Paul said, *"The Spirit Himself testifies with our spirit that we are God's children."* This is a present witness of our ultimate state: We know now that we are God's sons. And God's sons can no more be condemned than God's Son in whom they are accepted (Eph. 1:4). And since, according to all Calvinists, salvation cannot be lost, it follows that extreme Calvinists must admit that regardless of whether a believer falls into sin or not he will be in heaven. For he does not get there by his own righteousness but by Christ's righteousness imputed to him (see 2 Cor. 5:21; Titus 3:5–7).

Romans 8:29–30

"For *those* God foreknew he also predestined. . . . And *those* he predestined, he also called; *those* he called, he also justified; *those* he justified, he also glorified." This golden chain is unbroken. The same persons who were predestined were called, justified, and eventually glorified (made it to heaven). In order to avoid eternal security, the word "some" would have to be inserted into the text, but it is not there. *All* who are justified will eventually be glorified.[5]

Romans 8:37–39

"*Who shall separate us from the love of Christ?* Shall trouble or hardship or persecution or famine or nakedness or danger or sword? As it is written. . . . No, in all these things we are more than conquerors through him who loved us. For *I am convinced that neither death nor life, neither angels nor demons,* neither the present nor the future, nor any powers, neither height nor depth, *nor anything else in all creation, will be able to separate us from the love of God that is in Christ Jesus our Lord.*" This passage needs little comment, merely contemplation. It is difficult to conceive of language that is more inclusive. There is literally no one and nothing that can separate a believer from Christ!

Ephesians 1:13–14

"And you also were included in Christ when you heard the word of truth, the gospel of your salvation. *Having believed, you were marked in him with a seal,* the promised Holy Spirit, who is a deposit *guaranteeing our inheritance* until the redemption of those who are God's possession—to the praise of his glory." That is, as soon as one believes, he is marked by the presence of the Holy Spirit as one of whom God guarantees His ultimate salvation.

Philippians 1:6

"*Being confident* of this, that he [God] who began a good work in you will carry it on to completion until the day of Christ Jesus." Paul expressed confidence that the God who initiated the saving process in our lives would finish it. That is, all the regenerate will make it to heaven.

2 Timothy 1:12

Paul proclaims: "*I know whom I have believed, and am convinced that he is able to guard what I have entrusted to him for that day.*" Since our salvation does not depend on our faithfulness but on God's

---

[5]Contrary to the belief of some extreme Calvinists, this does not prove atonement is limited in its extent but only in its application. The "call" here refers to the effectual call of the elect, not the general call, offer, or command for all to be saved (Acts 17:30; 2 Peter 3:9).

(2 Tim. 2:13), our perseverance is assured by Him. Hence, we can "know" presently that we are heaven bound by His grace.

2 Timothy 2:13

"*If we are faithless, he will remain faithful, for he cannot disown Himself.*" Even if our faith falters, His faithfulness does not. In order for us to lose our salvation God would have to "disown Himself." He would have to cease being God.

1 Peter 1:5

Peter adds, "Through faith *[we] are shielded by God's power until the coming of the salvation* that is ready to be revealed in the last time." By placing our faith in His faithfulness we are assured now that God's power will keep us to the end.

1 John 5:13

John declares: "I write these things to you who believe in the name of the Son of God so *that you may know that you have eternal life.*" Throughout this book, the apostle lists ways we can "know" now that we are one of God's elect, namely, if we obey His commandments (2:3); keep His Word (2:5); walk as He did (2:5); love the brethren (3:14); love in deed, not only word (3:18); have the Holy Spirit within us (3:24); love one another (4:12); and not continue in sin (5:18; cf. 3:9). In short, if we have the presence of the Spirit in our hearts and manifest the fruit of His Spirit in our lives (cf. Gal. 5:22–23), then we can be assured that we are one of the elect. We do not have to wait until we meet Christ to know that we belong to Him.

Jude 24–25

"To *him who is able to keep you from falling* and to present you before his glorious presence without fault and with great joy—to the only God our Savior be glory, majesty, power and authority, through Jesus Christ our Lord, before all ages, now and forevermore!" Whatever warnings the Bible may give about our falling,[6] we are assured that a true believer will experience no fall that will involve the loss of heaven. For an all-powerful God is able "to keep us from falling."

---

[6]Calvinists of various varieties interpret the warning passages differently. Some, following Calvin, take them as hypothetical, not actual. Others, like the author, consider them to be actual but to be warnings about losing our *rewards* (1 Cor. 3:15), not our *salvation.* See Jodie Dillow, *The Reign of the Servant King* (Hayesville, N.C.: Schoettle Publishing Co., 1992).

ANSWERING OBJECTIONS RAISED BY ARMINIANS

Arminians object to the use of the above verses to prove "Once saved, always saved." Several reasons are offered by them to support their conclusion.

THE PROMISE OF SALVATION IS CONDITIONAL

One reason given is the argument that all these promises are conditioned—conditioned on the believer continuing in the faith. Colossians 1:23 is often used in connection with this: *"if you continue in your faith,* established and firm, not moved from the hope held out in the gospel."* In his defense of Arminianism, Robert Shank argues that there are some eighty-five "New Testament Passages Establishing the Doctrine of Conditional Security."[7] He stresses texts that speak of "continuing," "abiding," "holding fast," etc. For example, 1 Corinthians 15:2 says, "By this gospel you are saved, *if you hold firmly* to the word I preached to you."

But Calvinists respond by observing that neither this nor any other text asserts that a true believer will ever lose his faith. Rather, a proof that they are truly believers is that they will continue in the faith. John says, "No one who is born of God will continue to sin, because God's seed remains in him; he cannot go on sinning, because he has been born of God" (1 John 3:9). He adds, "They went out from us, but they did not really belong to us. For if they had belonged to us, they would have remained with us; but their going showed that none of them belonged to us" (1 John 2:19). However weakened by sin, true believers endure in their faith to the end. This demonstrates that the promise of salvation is not conditional.

BELIEF IS A CONTINUAL PROCESS

Also, Arminians argue that the Bible uses "belief" in the present tense, not as a once-for-all completed act when we were first saved. For example, the famous verses in the gospel of John that promise eternal life for believing, do so while speaking of belief as a continual process. Hence, they can be translated, for example, "For God so loved the world that he gave his one and only Son, that *whoever continues to believe in him* shall not perish but have eternal life" (John 3:16).

---

[7]Robert Shank, *Life in the Son* (Minneapolis: Bethany House Publishers, 1989), 334–37.

In response to this, there are several very important things to point out. First of all, not all references to belief that brings salvation are in the present tense. Some are in the aorist tense in the Greek and indicate a completed action. For instance, Romans 13:11 declares, "The hour has come for you to wake up from your slumber, because our salvation is nearer now than *when we first believed.*" Second, continued belief can be a condition of ultimate salvation without necessitating that salvation can be lost. God knows in advance that all who begin to believe will continue by His grace to persevere to the end. In short, God is able to keep us by His power (1 Peter 1:5; Phil. 1:6). Third, since salvation is in three stages, it is no surprise that belief in the present is stressed in the Bible. We were saved from the *penalty* of sin (justification) in the past; we are being saved from the *power* of sin in the present (sanctification); and we will be saved from the *presence* of sin in the future (glorification). But even though we must "work out [our] own salvation" in the present (Phil. 2:12), it is God "who works in" us both "to will and to act according to his good purpose" (Phil. 2:13). Fourth, nowhere does God's Word say that those who are truly believers will lose their salvation (see next page). It only says that those who believe should and will continue to believe to their eventual salvation. Finally, it is not our works of righteousness or lack thereof (Titus 3:5–7) that get us to heaven, but Christ's righteousness, which is imputed to us the moment we believe (cf. 2 Cor. 5:21; John 5:24).

SYMMETRICAL NATURE OF FAITH

The next Arminian argument is one from the nature of faith. Arminians contend that if we can exercise faith to "get in" Christ then we can use the same faith to "get out" of Christ. Just like getting on and off a bus headed for heaven, we can exercise our free choice at either end. Not to be able to do this, they insist, would mean that once we get saved, then we are no longer free. Freedom is symmetrical; if you have the freedom to get saved, then you also have the freedom to get lost again.

In response to this argument, it is important to observe a few things. First of all, this rationale is not *biblically based*; it is *speculative* and should be treated as such. Second, it is not logically necessary to accept this reasoning, even on a purely rational basis. Some decisions in life are one-way with no possibility of reversing them: suicide, for example. Saying "oops" after jumping off a cliff will not reverse the consequences of the decision. Third, by this same logic the Arminian would have to argue that we can be lost even after we get to heaven. Otherwise, he would have to deny we are free in heaven. But if we are still free in heaven and yet cannot be lost, then why is it logically impossible for us to be free on earth and yet never lose our salvation? In both cases the biblical answer is that God's omnipotent power is able to keep us from falling—in accordance with our free choice.

VERSES USED BY ARMINIANS TO SHOW ONE CAN LOSE HIS SALVATION

Many verses are used by Arminians to show that a believer can lose his salvation. Space does not permit a detailed explanation of all of them,[8] but they fall into two broad categories, both of which will now be refuted.

PROFESSING BUT NOT POSSESSING BELIEVERS

First, there are the verses that deal with professing believers who apparently never had saving faith. These include the following:

Matthew 7:22–23

Jesus said, " 'Many will say to me on that day, "Lord, Lord, did we not prophesy in your name, and in your name drive out demons and perform many miracles?" Then I will tell them plainly, *"I never knew you.* Away from me, you evildoers!" ' "

Response

In spite of their profession and even miraculous signs done in His name, it is clear from the emphasized words *"I never knew you"* that those referred to were never saved.

2 Peter 2:22

This verse also speaks of *professing* (but not *possessing*) Christians who were never truly converted; who denied "the sovereign Lord who bought them" (v. 1); who had "known the way of righteousness" (v. 21). Yet they had not followed it, but like a "dog" (not a lamb) showed that they were really "slaves of corruption" (v. 19 NASB) and not a "new creation" (2 Cor. 5:17) of God.

---

[8]See Augustus Hopkins Strong, *Systematic Theology* (Old Tappan, N.J.: Fleming H. Revell Company, 1907), 882–86, for a complete listing of such verses. And consult Charles Stanley, *Eternal Security* (Nashville, Tenn.: Thomas Nelson, 1990) for a discussion of the most important verses Arminians use to support their claim that we can lose our salvation.

Revelation 3:5

"He who overcomes will, like them, be dressed in white. *I will never blot out his name from the book of life,* but will acknowledge his name before my Father and his angels."

Response

Two things are noteworthy about this text. First, it is a promise to those "dressed in white," which is a description of saints (Rev. 7:14), and therefore an inference that they will never lose their salvation. Second, it does not say that God *will* ever blot anyone's name from the book of life.

Revelation 22:19

"And if anyone takes words away from this book of prophecy, God will take away from him his share in the tree of life[9] and in the holy city, which are described in this book."

Response

This appears to be a warning to unbelievers, not believers. They never made it to the holy city because they are "outside" the heavenly gates (v. 15) and are described as "unjust" (v. 11 NKJV).

TRUE BELIEVERS LOSE REWARDS, NOT SALVATION

The second group of verses used by Arminians refers to those who are truly saved but are only losing their rewards, not their salvation. Several sample texts include the following.[10]

1 Corinthians 3:11–15

"For no one can lay any foundation other than the one already laid, which is Jesus Christ. If any man builds on this foundation using gold, silver, costly stones, wood, hay or straw, his work will

---

[9]The rendering "book of life" (KJV) does not follow the best manuscript tradition. Even so, the verse possesses no insurmountable problem for eternal security. It easily could be another way to designate unbelievers by noting that they have no place in the Book of Life.

[10]Some passages do not refer to losing either salvation or rewards, but to something else. Matthew 10:22 is a case in point: " 'All men will hate you because of me, but *he who stands firm to the end will be saved.*' " The context of this reference (cf. vv. 17, 23) and a similar passage indicate (in Matt. 24:15–44) that He is probably speaking about the believers who live through the Great Tribulation to come (see *Bible Knowledge Commentary: New Testament Edition,* 42). If so, then it means those who live through the Tribulation will go into the coming earthly kingdom of Christ. Even if it refers to salvation, it merely shows that the elect will persevere unto salvation.

be shown for what it is, because the Day will bring it to light. It will be revealed with fire, and the fire will test the quality of each man's work. If what he has built survives, he will receive his reward. If it is burned up, *he will suffer loss* [of reward]; *he himself will be saved*, but only as one escaping through the flames."

Response

Even through David's gross sins of murder and adultery, he did not lose his salvation. Rather, he prayed in his sin, "Create in me a pure heart.... Restore to me the *joy* of your salvation and grant me a willing spirit, to sustain me" (Ps. 51:10, 12). He had not lost his salvation but only the *joy* of it. Believers in sin are not happy. They are sons under the discipline of the Lord (Heb. 12:5–11; cf. 1 Cor. 11:28–32). The loss is of reward, not salvation.

1 Corinthians 9:27

"I beat my body and make it my slave so that after I have preached to others, *I myself will not be disqualified for the prize*."

Response

Paul is speaking here of loss of reward, not of salvation (cf. 1 Cor. 3:15; 2 Cor. 5:10). For he speaks of it as a "prize" to be won, not a "gift" to be received (Rom. 6:23). In any event, warnings to persevere are not inconsistent with an assurance of salvation any more than exhortations to "work out [our] own salvation" (Phil. 2:12) are contradictory to "God working in us" (Phil. 2:13) to accomplish it.

Hebrews 6:4–6

"*It is impossible* for those who have once been enlightened, who have tasted the heavenly gift, who have shared in the Holy Spirit, who have tasted the goodness of the word of God and the powers of the coming age, *if they fall away, to be brought back to repentance*, because to their loss they are crucifying the Son of God all over again and subjecting him to public disgrace."

Response

There are several problems with taking this to refer to believers who can lose salvation. The passage declares emphatically that "it is impossible to renew them again to repentance" (Heb. 6:6 NASB), and few Arminians believe that once a person has backslidden it is impossible for him to be "saved again." But while the description of the spiritual status of those spoken of in this passage differs from other ways of expressing it in the New Testament, some of the phrases are very difficult to take any other way than that the person was saved. For example, (1) these had experienced "repentance" (Heb. 6:6), which is the condition of the acceptance of salvation (Acts 17:30); (2) they were "enlightened" and had "tasted the heavenly gift" (Heb. 6:4); (3) they were "partakers of the Holy Spirit" (v. 4 NKJV); (4) they had "tasted the good word of God" (v. 5 NKJV); and (5) had tasted the "powers of the age to come" (v. 5 NKJV).

Of course, if they were believers, then the question arises as to their status after they had "fallen away" (v. 6 NASB). In response, it should first be noted that the word for "fall away" (*parapesontas*) does not indicate a one-way action as would be true of apostasy (Greek: *apostasia*); rather, it is the word for "drift," indicating that the status of the individuals is not hopeless. Second, the very fact is that it is "impossible" for them to repent again indicates the once-for-all nature of repentance. In other words, they don't need to repent again since they did it once, and that is all that is necessary for "eternal redemption" (Heb. 9:12). Third, the text seems to indicate that there is no more need for "drifters" (backsliders) to repent again and get saved all over any more than there is for Christ to die again on the Cross (Heb. 6:6). Fourth, the writer of Hebrews calls those he is warning "beloved" (Heb. 6:9 NASB), a term hardly appropriate for unbelievers. Finally, the phrase "persuaded of better things" of them indicates they were believers.

Hebrews 10:26–29

"If we deliberately keep on sinning after we have received the knowledge of the truth, no sacrifice for sins is left, but only a fearful expectation of judgment and of raging fire that will consume the enemies of God. Anyone who rejected the law of Moses died without mercy on the testimony of two or three witnesses. How much more severely do you think a man deserves to be punished who has trampled the Son of God under foot, who has treated as an unholy thing the blood of the covenant that sanctified him, and who has insulted the Spirit of grace?"

Response

As strong as this sounds, like the other warning passages in Hebrews (see comments on Heb. 6:4–6 above), this, too, appears not to be a warning about loss of salvation but about loss of rewards. This conclusion is supported by several considerations. First, the persons involved are described clearly as *"brethren"* (v. 19 NKJV), and *"His [God's] people"* (v. 30), and believers who have a "High Priest" (Christ, v. 21 NKJV), and a "confession of . . . hope" given only to the "faithful" (v. 23 NKJV). Second, the text is not speaking of salvation but of a *"great reward"* (v. 35 NKJV). Third, those mentioned have "a better and enduring possession . . . in heaven" (v. 34). Fourth, they have been "illuminated" by God (v. 32) and have possessed the "knowledge of the truth" (v. 26), phrases that fit with believers. Fifth, they have suffered with and have had compassion for the author of the book as believers (vv. 33–34). Sixth, they are described as those who can do the "will of God" (v. 36), something only believers can do (John 9:31). Seventh, the reference to those who "insulted the Spirit of grace" implies they were believers who had that Spirit to insult. Eighth, the "certain fearful expectation of judgment" fits the description of the believers coming before the judgment seat of Christ (2 Cor. 5:10), where their works will be tried by fire and they could suffer loss of reward: "His work will be shown for what it is, because the Day will bring it to light. *It will be revealed with fire,* and the fire will test the quality of each man's work. If what he has built survives, he will receive his *reward*" (1 Cor. 3:13–14). Finally, the illustration used of those who died under the law of Moses (Heb. 10:28) speaks of physical death for disobedience, not of eternal death or separation from God. Paul speaks of physical death of believers for sin in 1 Corinthians 11:30 (cf. 1 John 5:16).

Galatians 5:4

"You who are trying to be justified by law have been alienated from Christ; *you have fallen away from grace.*"

Response

This verse speaks of true believers who, again, are called "brethren" (6:1) and who had placed their "faith" in Christ (3:2 NKJV) for their "justification" (3:5, 11). They had "begun in the Spirit" (3:3 NKJV) but were now "fallen . . . from grace" (5:4) *as a means of their sanctification* and had gone back to the keeping of the law (3:5), which only brings one into bondage (3:10). They had not lost their salvation but only their true sanctification, which also comes by grace, not by the law.

2 Timothy 2:17–18

"Their teaching will spread like gangrene. Among them are Hymenaeus and Philetus, who have wandered away from the truth.

They say that the resurrection has already taken place, and *they destroy the faith of some.*"

Response

There are several reasons why this text does not indicate a loss of salvation. First, it does not say their *salvation* was destroyed but only their *faith* in a future resurrection. Second, only a few verses earlier is one of the strongest of all verses on eternal security, which affirms that even "if we are faithless, he will remain faithful, for he cannot disown Himself" (v. 13). Third, the context focuses on belief in the resurrection. Hence, it may refer only to loss of belief in the resurrection as a future event. Fourth, even if it refers to the loss of faith in general, it is not the genuine faith (1 Tim. 1:5) that endures but a formal faith (2 Tim. 3:5), which even demons have (James 2:19), and is not sufficient for salvation (cf. James 2:14ff.).

2 Timothy 4:7

"I have fought the good fight, *I have finished the race, I have kept the faith.*"

Response

Paul speaks of keeping the faith, but he does not say that those who do not keep the faith will not be saved. In fact, he says in the very next verse that the result of his keeping the faith is not *salvation* but a *reward*—"the crown of righteousness" (v. 8). Those who are not faithful as Paul will not receive such a crown. As he says elsewhere, "He will suffer loss; [yet] he himself will be saved, but only as one escaping through the flames" (1 Cor. 3:15). And as John affirms, "They went out from us, but *they did not really belong to us.* For if they had belonged to us, they would have remained with us; but their going showed that none of them belonged to us" (1 John 2:19).

TRUE BELIEVERS MANIFEST EVIDENCE OF THEIR FAITH

A true believer in Christ cannot lose his/her salvation, but neither should one take it for granted that he is saved. There are many Scriptures exhorting us to examine ourselves to make sure we are true believers.

2 Corinthians 13:5

"*Examine yourselves to see whether you are in the faith;* test yourselves. Do you not realize that Christ Jesus is in you—unless, of course, you fail the test?"

2 Peter 1:10

"Therefore, my brothers, be all the more eager to *make your calling and election sure*. For if you do these things, you will never fall." From *God's* standpoint our election is sure. It was ordained before the foundation of the world (Eph. 1:4–5, 11). Yet *we* are exhorted to make sure that we are one of the elect. This can be known in many ways, as the numerous verses on assurance of salvation indicate, such as the witness of the Spirit (Rom. 8:16), the fruit of the Spirit in our lives (Gal. 5:22–23), and love for the brethren (1 John 4:7).

Philippians 2:13

"Therefore, my dear friends, as you have always obeyed—not only in my presence, but now much more in my absence—continue to *work out your salvation* with fear and trembling." It is important to note that Paul is speaking to believers. They already have the first stage of salvation (justification). Second, while it is true that we are asked to work out our salvation (i.e., sanctification), notice that Paul immediately adds: "for *it is God who works in you* to will and to act according to his good purpose" (v. 13). And what God is working is His own sovereign will ("good pleasure"), which was determined "before the foundation of the world" (Eph. 1:4–5, 11). Again, both are true.

Jude 21

"*Keep yourselves in God's love* as you wait for the mercy of our Lord Jesus Christ to bring you to eternal life." It is true that we should "keep [ourselves]," but it is also true that God keeps us in His love. As we are working *out* our own salvation, God is working it *in* and through us (Phil. 2:12–13).

1 Corinthians 13:7

"It [*love*] always protects, always trusts, always hopes, *always perseveres*." True love does always persevere. But this does not mean that we cannot know if we have the true love of God in our hearts. Indeed, the Bible declares that we can (Rom. 5:5; cf. Rom. 8:16). John said, "We *know that we have passed from death to life*, because we love our brothers" (1 John 3:14).

THE ROOTS OF MODERATE CALVINISM

We have been defending a moderate form of Calvinism. This view is not new. Its roots are found in the early writings of St.

Augustine. As indicated previously (and also in appendix 3), St. Augustine's earlier view was a more moderate form of what I have called extreme Calvinism. In our opinion, had Augustine not been thrown off track by his view of baptismal regeneration and the coercion of heretics to believe (during the Donatist controversy), extreme Calvinists would find no substantial support in the whole history of the Christian church up to the Reformation.

THE BOTTOM LINE

Moderate Calvinists and moderate Arminians, who represent the vast majority of Christendom, have much in common against the extremes in the opposing two views. Indeed, John Wesley himself (a moderate Arminian) said he was only a "hair's breadth from Calvin." And as is later demonstrated in appendix 2, Calvin himself rejected some things held in later extreme Calvinism (e.g., limited atonement).

Of course, there are some significant differences between moderate Calvinists and moderate Arminians, but they do not negate the similarities. One of those differences was discussed above, namely, whether "once saved, always saved" is accurate. But even here, in actual practice, the similarities are greater than many think. The vast majority of proponents of both views hold that if a professing Christian turns away from Christ and lives in continual sin that this is evidence that he is not saved. The difference is that the moderate Calvinists claim that he was never saved to begin with, and the moderate Arminians believe that he was. And both believe that the unrepentant who continue in sin are not true believers. As 1 John 3:9 said, "No one who is born of God will continue to sin, because God's seed remains in him; he cannot go on sinning, because he has been born of God." To illustrate, a pig and a lamb can fall in the same mud puddle. But when they do, the pig wants to stay there and the lamb wants to get out!

CHAPTER EIGHT

WHAT DIFFERENCE DOES IT MAKE?

A WORD TO THE WISE

By this point many readers are no doubt saying, "So what?" or "What difference does it make?" In reality, what practical difference *does* it make whether one is an extreme Calvinist, an extreme Arminian, or something in between?

Frankly, the answer to this question is that it makes a world of difference what we believe. Belief affects behavior, and so ideas have consequences. Good ideas lead to good consequences, and bad ideas have bad consequences. A person who believes the railroad crossing signal is stuck when, in truth, a train is coming, may soon be dead! Anyone who believes the ice on the lake is solid when, in fact, it is thin, may be about to drown! Likewise, false doctrine will lead to false deeds. To repeat the limerick, "Johnny was a good boy, but Johnny is no more. For what he believed was H_2O was H_2SO_4 (sulfuric acid)!"

SOME PRACTICAL CONSEQUENCES OF EXTREME CALVINISM

Extreme views of any kind often have serious consequences. This is true of both Calvinists and Arminians. First, let's take a look at what difference extreme Calvinism can and often does make in one's practical spiritual life.

Failing to take personal responsibility for our actions

Logically speaking, if "free choice" is doing what we can't help doing because by nature we simply do those kinds of things, then why should I take responsibility for my actions? If not "the devil made me do it," then it will be "God made me do it." Extreme Calvinism leads logically (if not practically) to personal irresponsibility: if our actions are good actions, they are such only because God has programmed us to do good; if evil, then we cannot help it, because we are sinners by nature and God has not given us the desire to do good.

Again, if I am really not the cause of my actions, then why should *I* take responsibility for them? Why should I take either credit or blame for them? After all, the extreme Calvinist believes that *ought* does not imply *can.* Responsibility does not imply the ability to respond. But if this is so, then why should I feel responsible? Why should I care when it is completely out of my hands one way or the other?

Even many strong Calvinists have acknowledged the extreme to which hyper-Calvinists (see appendix 7) took the doctrine of divine sovereignty. Iain Murray wrote, "They did not renounce the [Calvinistic] Confession of 1689, but they overlaid it with an incrustation of something that approached Antinomianism, and ate out the life of the churches and of the gospel as preached by many ministers." He adds, "*Divine sovereignty was maintained and taught, not only in exaggerated proportions but to the practical exclusion of moral responsibility.*"[1]

Hear the voice of a passionate but less extreme Calvinist, Charles H. Spurgeon, speaking against some hyper-Calvinists: "My heart bleeds for many a family where Antinomian doctrine has gained sway. I could tell many a sad story of families dead in sin, whose consciences are seared as with a hot iron, by the fatal preaching to which they listen." He adds, "I have known convictions stifled and desires quenched by the soul-destroying system which takes manhood from him and makes him no more responsible than an ox."[2]

---

[1] Cited by Iain Murray, *Spurgeon v. Hyper-Calvinism: The Battle for Gospel Preaching,* 126–27.
[2] Ibid., 155.

Blaming God for evil

Not only does extreme Calvinism tend to undermine personal responsibility but it logically lays the blame squarely on God for the origin of evil. Two personal illustrations make the point. Many years ago when the late John Gerstner and I taught together at the same institution, I invited him into one of my classes to discuss free will. Being what I have called an extreme Calvinist, he defended Jonathan Edwards' view that the human will is moved by the strongest desire. I will never forget how he responded when I pushed the logic all the way back to Lucifer. I was stunned to hear an otherwise very rational man respond to my question "Who gave Lucifer the desire to rebel against God?" by throwing up his hands and crying, "Mystery, mystery, a great mystery!" I answered, "No, it is not a great mystery; it is a grave contradiction." And this is because, on the premises of extreme Calvinism, only God could have given Lucifer the desire to rebel against God, since there is no self-determined free choice and Lucifer had no evil nature. But if this is so, then logically it must have been God who gave him the desire to sin. In short, God caused a rebellion against God! Perish the thought!

The second example is also tragic. A well-known conference speaker was explaining how he was unable to come to grips with the tragic death of his son. Leaning on his strong Calvinistic background, he gradually came to the conclusion: *"God* killed my son!" He triumphantly informed us that "then, and only then, did I get peace about the matter." A sovereign God killed his son, and therein he found ground for a great spiritual victory, he assured us. I thought to myself, "I wonder what he would say if his daughter had been raped?" Would he not be able to come to grips with the matter until he concluded victoriously that "God raped my daughter!" God forbid! Some views do not need to be refuted; they simply need to be stated.

When this same logic is applied to why people go to hell, the tragedy is even more evident. Actually, there is no real difference on this point between the extreme Calvinists and fatalistic Islam in which Allah says, in the holy book (the Qur'an), "If We [majestic plural] had so willed, We could certainly have brought Every soul its true guidance; But the Word from Me Will come true. 'I will Fill Hell with jinn and men all together' " (Sura 32:13). As the famous Persian poet Omar Khayyam put it,

> Tis all a chequer-board of night and days
> Where destiny with men for pieces plays;
> Hither and thither moves and mates and slays,
> And one by one back in the closet lays.

Lest the reader think this is an unfair caricature of extreme Calvinism in Muslim terms, listen to the words of the famous Puritan Calvinist William Ames: "[Predestination] depends upon no cause, reason, or outward condition, but proceeds purely from the will of him [God] who predestines." Further, "there are two kinds of predestination, election and rejection or reprobation.... The first act of election is to will the glory of his grace in the salvation of some men...." Likewise, "Reprobation is the predestination of certain men so that the glory of God's justice may be shown in them."[3]

True, some Calvinists reject this "double-predestination" in favor of God simply "passing over" the non-elect, but even they must admit that the result is the same: since God did not give them the desire to be saved "they are condemned to eternal misery."[4] The question still remains as to why God did not give the desire to all persons to be saved rather than selecting a mere few. Not a few persons raised in this tradition have asked themselves, "What difference does it make? If I am not one of the elect, then there is nothing I can do about it." To say the least, this can have a devastating effect on one's own salvation, to say nothing of one's enthusiasm to reach others for Christ (see 139).

Laying the ground for universalism

The $64,000 question for the extreme Calvinists is this: *If God can save anyone to whom He gives the desire to be saved, then why does He not give the desire to all people?* The answer can only be that God does not really will that all be saved. It does not suffice to claim that God's justice rightly condemns those who do not believe, since even faith is a gift from God that He could give to all if He wanted to do so.

Nor is it sufficient to claim that God justly condemns all sinners, because God is not only completely just but is also all-loving (1 John 4:16). Why, then, does His love not prompt Him to save all? It is this very reasoning, when combined with the truth of Scripture that God "is not willing that any should perish" (2 Peter 3:9), that leads logically to universalism. For if God can save all without

---

[3]Ames, *The Marrow of Theology*, 153–55.
[4]Hodge, *Outlines of Theology*, 222.

violating their free choice, and if God is all-loving, then there is no reason why all will not be saved. After all, according to extreme Calvinists, God's love is irresistible. Hence, such love focused on all men would inevitably bring all to salvation.

Undermining trust in the love of God

The blunt and honest answer of extreme Calvinism to this dilemma, in the face of the unavoidable logic leading to universalism, is to deny that God is all loving. In short—redemptively at least—God loves only the elect. This fits with the extreme Calvinist's belief in limited atonement (see chapter 5). For if God loves only the elect, then why should Christ have died for more than the elect?

But any diminution of God's love will sooner or later eat away at one's confidence in God's benevolence. And when it does, it can have a devastating effect on one's life. Indeed, this has been the occasion for disbelief and even atheism for many.[5]

A partially loving God is less than ultimately good. And what is less than ultimately good is not worthy of worship, since worship is attributing worth-ship to the object of worship. But if the extreme Calvinists' view of "God" is not the Ultimate Good, then it does not represent God at all. The God of the Bible is infinitely loving, that is, omnibenevolent. He wills the good of all creation (Acts 14:17; 17:25), and He desires the salvation of all souls (Ezek. 18:23, 30–32; Hos. 11:1–5, 8–9; John 3:16; 1 Tim. 2:4; 2 Peter 3:9).

At first blush, one is impressed with a God that supposedly loves him more than others and has elected him to eternal salvation. But upon further reflection, he cannot help but wonder why, if this God is so loving, He does not so love the world. When this thought sets in, the "amazing love" at first experienced by the elect turns to "partial love," and finally to a recognition that God actually hates the non-elect. In the words of extreme Calvinist William Ames, God "is said to hate them [the non-elect], Rom. 9:13. This hatred is negative or privative, because it denies election. But it has a positive content, for God has willed that some should not have eternal life."[6]

This doubt is implicit in the confession of some of the most pious persons. Indeed, were it not for their deep piety, it is doubtful

---

[5]Charles Darwin called hell a "damnable doctrine" (Charles Darwin, *The Autobiography of Charles Darwin*, ed. Nora Darwin Barlow [New York: W. W. Norton & Co., 1993], 87). And renowned agnostic Bertrand Russell said, "I do not myself feel that any person who is really profoundly humane can believe in everlasting punishment" (Bertrand Russell, *Why I Am Not a Christian* [New York: Simon and Schuster, 1957], 12).

[6]Ames, *The Marrow of Theology*, 156 (emphasis mine).

they could long maintain such a belief. Strong Calvinist Charles Spurgeon admitted, "We do not know why God has purposed to save some and not others. . . . We cannot say why his love to all men is not the same as his love to the elect."[7] If one allows this to gnaw at his mind long enough, it can turn him from being a particularist into being a universalist—from one unfortunate belief to another.

Undermining the motivation for evangelism

Many years ago a young man went to his spiritual mentor and informed him that he would like to be a missionary to the heathen. His hyper-Calvinistic advisor told him that if God wanted to save the world, He could do it without him. Fortunately, the young man did not heed his mentor's advice. His name was William Carey, famous missionary to India.[8]

God only knows for sure how many other extreme Calvinists feel the same. As a matter of fact, if their view is correct, then we need not get excited about missions for several reasons. First of all, God does not love the whole world in a redemptive sense, but only the elect. Second, Christ only died for the elect, not the world. Third, no one has the faith to believe unless God gives it to him. Fourth, God has willed to give faith only to a select few, "the frozen chosen." Fifth, when God's power works on the hearts of the unbelievers He wants to save, there is absolutely nothing they can do to refuse it. God's power is irresistible (see chapter 5). If all these were true—thank God they are not—it would be understandably hard to muster up much enthusiasm for missions or evangelism.

Charles Spurgeon pointedly remarked of hyper-Calvinists in his day: "But there are some people so selfish that, provided they go to heaven, it is enough they are in the covenant. They are dear enough people of God. . . ." But "They say it is equal whether God ordains a man's life or death. They would sit still to hear men damned. . . . They seem to have no feeling for anyone but themselves. They have dried the heart out of them by some cunning sleight of hand."[9]

John Gill, who according to some was the originator of hyper-Calvinism, is a practical example of the destructive influence on missions and evangelism. Spurgeon noted that "During the pastorate of my venerated predecessor, Dr. Gill, this Church, instead of increasing, gradually decreased. . . . But mark this, from the day when Fuller, Carey, Sutcliffe, and others, met together to send out

---

[7]Murray, *Spurgeon v. Hyper-Calvinism: The Battle for Gospel Preaching*, 112.
[8]See Mike Haykin, *One Heart and One Soul* (Phillipsburg, N.J.: Evangelical Press, n.d.), 195.
[9]Cited by Iain Murray in *Spurgeon v. Hyper-Calvinism: The Battle for Gospel Preaching*, 112.

missionaries to India, the sun began to dawn of a gracious revival which is not over yet."[10] Of Gill, Spurgeon added bluntly: "The system of theology with which many identify his [Gill's] name has chilled many churches to their very soul, for it has led them to omit the free invitations of the gospel, and to deny that it is the duty of sinners to believe in Jesus."[11]

Iain Murray adds, "In this connection it is noteworthy that just as renewed understanding of the free offer of the gospel led to the age of overseas missions in England, so it did also—by different means—in Scotland." Robert Moffat, a result of that revival, wrote, "Much depends on us who have received the ministry of reconciliation, assured that God our Saviour willeth the salvation of all."[12] The truth is, if it were to come down to one incorrect belief over another, the belief that God desires all to be saved is more consistent with *universal* atonement than with *limited* atonement.

Undermining the motivation for intercessory prayer

Not only does extreme Calvinism erode the basis for evangelism, it also tends to destroy the perceived need for intercessory prayer. While prayer cannot change the nature of God (see chapter 1), it can be used by God to implement His will to change people and things. Joshua prayed, and the sun stood still (Josh. 10). Elijah prayed, and the heavens were shut up for three and a half years (1 Kings 17–18; James 5:17). Moses prayed, and God's judgment on Israel was stayed (Num. 14). While prayer is not a means to get our will done in heaven, it is a means by which God gets His will done on earth. Things do change because we pray, for a sovereign God has ordained to use prayer as a means to the end of accomplishing these things. But if God will do these things even if we do not pray, then there is no need for prayer. What we believe about how God's sovereignty relates to our free will does make a difference in how—and how much—we pray.

A NATURAL REACTION

By this time many readers are no doubt saying, "Well, I know many Calvinists who are missionaries, zealous evangelists, and deeply dedicated prayer warriors." None of these alleged conse-

---

[10]Ibid., 120.
[11]Ibid., 127.
[12]Ibid., 120–21.

quences apply to them. For that we praise God. But for many reasons, this does not mean the above points are invalid.

First of all, not all Calvinists are extreme Calvinists. Many are more moderate (see chapter 7) and these criticisms do not apply to them.

Second, not all extreme Calvinists consistently live out their beliefs. Thankfully, sometimes people are better in their conduct than in their creed. It is a fact that life itself tends to round off the extreme ends of our views, whether Calvinistic or Arminian.

Third, the above consequences are logical results of the extreme Calvinists' view, whether or not they come to fruition in the lives of an individual extreme Calvinist or not. If they were consistent with their extreme views, these extreme actions would tend to manifest themselves in their lives. And this is a valid criticism of their view.

SOME PRACTICAL CONSEQUENCES OF EXTREME ARMINIANISM

Calvinists have no monopoly on extremes. Extreme Arminianism is a source of much harm as well.

Undermining confidence in the Bible

According to the extreme Arminians (Neotheists), God does not have infallible knowledge of future free choices. Yet almost all predictive prophecy involves future free choices. This being the case, for extreme Arminians, all the predictive prophecies in the Bible are fallible. But it is a fundamental view of evangelical Christians that the Bible is the infallible Word of God (see John 10:35; Matt. 5:17–18). Therefore, extreme Arminianism undermines confidence in the Bible—it cannot be trusted as the Word of God.

There are nearly two hundred predictions in the Bible about the coming of Christ. Virtually all of these involve the divine ability to foresee free choices. For example, the Old Testament predicted where Jesus would be born, namely, in Bethlehem (Mic. 5:2). This is true of numerous other predictions, including when Jesus would die (Dan. 9:25–27), how He would die (Isa. 53), and that He would rise from the dead (Ps. 16:10; cf. Acts 2:30–31). If the extreme Arminian is right, these can be nothing but good guesses on God's part. They could all be wrong, and no doubt some are. In any event, we cannot trust the Bible to speak infallibly. Our confidence in Scripture is undermined.

Another example, if God does not know for sure future free acts, is that He does not know that the Beast and False Prophet will be in the lake of fire. But the Bible says they will be there (Rev. 19:20; 20:10). Hence, either this prophecy could be false or else extreme Arminianism is not correct. Or, if extreme Arminianism is true, then this prediction may be false.

In response to this criticism, extreme Arminians argue God has infallible knowledge of necessary events and, on occasion, when necessary, He overrules free choice to accomplish His overall purposes.[13] This answer, however, does not make it for several reasons. First of all, the vast majority (if not all) of human events involve free choices that, according to extreme Arminianism, God cannot know infallibly.

Second, overruling human free choice is precisely what they object to in the strong Calvinist position. If God can and does overrule free choice on some occasions, then why not on others—especially those where the eternal destiny of the individual is concerned.

Third, of all the predictions made in the Bible about Christ and other events, there are no undisputed cases where the prophecy was wrong. But surely if God were merely guessing on all occasions, then He would be wrong on some.

Finally, the extreme Arminian view undermines the divine authority of Scripture—it leaves us with a fallible Bible. But the Bible itself says we can accept God's Word unconditionally. It says this explicitly in the context of affirming that He knows "the end from the beginning" (Isa. 46:10). Paul writes, "If we are faithless, he will remain faithful, for he cannot disown Himself" (2 Tim. 2:13). Again, he reminds us that "God's gifts and his call are irrevocable" (Rom. 11:29). Hence, with regard to these unconditional promises, "It does not, therefore, depend on man's desire or effort, but on God's mercy" (Rom. 9:16).

Destroying the ability to test a false prophet

Extreme Arminians object to the foregoing criticism by insisting that biblical prophecy is conditional. All predictions have an implied "if"—*if* things go as God has guessed they will. If so, then no predictions claim to be infallible, since they did not categorically predict anything.

While this response would avoid the charge of fallibility, none-

---

[13]See Pinnock, *The Openness of God*, chapter 6.

theless, it opens itself to other very serious charges. First of all, if all prophecy is conditional, then there could not be any way to know a false prophecy. But the Old Testament lays down tests for false prophets, one of which is whether or not the prediction comes to pass. For "if what a prophet proclaims in the name of the LORD does not take place or come true, that is a message the LORD has not spoken. That prophet has spoken presumptuously" (Deut. 18:22). If the extreme Arminians are correct, then this test would not be valid.

Further, the predictions about Christ cannot be conditional. The Bible tells us that His death was preordained before the foundation of the world (Acts 2:23; Rev. 13:8; cf. Eph. 1:4). In fact, it was absolutely necessary for our salvation (Acts 4:12; 1 Tim. 2:5; Heb. 9:22).

Finally, there is no evidence in the Bible that messianic prophecy is conditional. Conditional terms such as "if" are neither used nor implied in these passages. It is *eisegesis* (reading meaning into them) and not *exegesis* (reading the meaning from them) to say they are conditional.

Undermining the infallibility of the Bible

Not only does the extreme Arminian's denial that God knows future free acts diminish (or deny) God's omniscience and omnipotence, but it also entails a denial of the infallibility and inerrancy of the Bible, in which some extreme Arminians (e.g., Clark Pinnock) claim to believe. For if all prophecies are conditional, then we can never be sure they will come to pass. Yet the Bible affirms that they will. But for these Arminians, such pronouncements are not infallible, and they may be in error. Indeed, on the premise that God is only guessing, it is reasonable to assume that some *are* wrong. It is begging the issue to assume that it just so happened that all of His guesses turned out to be right.

Undermining hope in an ultimate victory over evil

Since extreme Arminians (Neotheists) insist that God does not know the future for sure and that He does not intervene against freedom except on rare occasions, it seems to follow that there is no guarantee of ultimate victory over evil. For how can He be sure that anyone will be saved without tampering with their freedom, which contradicts the extreme Arminian (libertarian) view of free will?

And positing the eternal annihilation of all who choose evil does not solve the Neotheist's dilemma. For this is the ultimate violation of free choice—the total destruction of it! This is to say nothing of the fact that both Scripture (Luke 16:19ff.; Rev. 19:20; 20:10) and centuries of orthodox Christian teaching stand against this aberrant doctrine.[14]

What is more, this view is contrary to the Bible, which predicts that Satan will be defeated, evil will be vanquished, and many will be saved (Rev. 20). But since, according to the extreme Arminian, this is a moral question that involves (libertarian) free will, it follows that God could not know this infallibly. However, the Bible does inform us that evil will be defeated (Rev. 21–22). But if this is so, neither God nor the Bible can be completely infallible and inerrant. Yet some extreme Arminians, such as Clark Pinnock, claim that it is. This is inconsistent.

Undermining trust in God's promises

It is clear that not all God's promises in the Bible are to everyone. Some are only to some people (e.g., Gen. 4:15). Others are only to a certain group of people (e.g., Gen. 13:14–17). Some are only for a limited time (e.g., Eph. 6:3). Many promises are conditioned on human behavior. They have a stated or implied "if" in them. The Mosaic Covenant is of this type. God said to Israel, " 'Now *if you obey me* fully and keep my covenant, then out of all nations you will be my treasured possession' " (Ex. 19:5–6). Other promises, however, are unconditional. Such was the land promise to Abraham and his offspring. This is clear from the facts that (1) no conditions were attached to it; (2) Abraham's agreement was not solicited; (3) it was initiated while Abraham was in a deep sleep (Gen. 15:12); (4) the covenant was enacted unilaterally by God who passed through the split sacrifice (Gen. 15:17–18); and (5) God reaffirmed this promise even when Israel was unfaithful (2 Chron. 21:7). Now, such unconditional promises, which involve free choices of creatures, would not be possible unless God knew for certain all future free choices.

Extreme Arminians offer 1 Kings 2:1–4 as an example of how a seemingly unconditional promise is really conditional. God promised David of his son Solomon: " 'My love will never be taken away from him, as I took it away from Saul, whom I removed from before you' " (2 Sam. 7:15–16). Yet later God seemed to take this back,

---

[14]See N. L. Geisler, "Annihilationism" in *Baker's Encyclopedia of Christian Apologetics* (Grand Rapids, Mich.: Baker Book House, 1999).

making it conditional on whether he (and his descendants) would "walk faithfully before me" (1 Kings 2:1–4). Thus, they argue that all seemingly unconditional promises are really conditional.

However, this argument fails for many reasons. First of all, it is a non sequitur, since the conclusion is much broader than the premises. Even if this were an example of an implied conditional, it would not mean that all promises are conditional. Second, it overlooks the many cases in Scripture (see above) where there are unconditional promises (cf. Rom. 11:29). These are counter-examples that refute the contention that all God's promises are conditional. Third, it is inconsistent with the extreme Arminian view of God. They insist that God is an ontologically independent Being. But God's knowledge is part of His essence or being. How then can God's knowledge be dependent on anything else?[15]

Finally, the argument is based on a failure to see that the two texts refer to two different things. In 2 Samuel God was speaking to David about never taking the kingdom away from his son Solomon. This promise was fulfilled, for in spite of Solomon's sins (1 Kings 11:1–2) the kingdom was not taken from him during his entire lifetime. In fact, the fulfillment is explicitly stated in God's words to Solomon: " 'Since this is your attitude and you have not kept my covenant and my decrees, which I commanded you, I will most certainly tear the kingdom away from you and give it to one of your subordinates. Nevertheless, for the sake of David your father, *I will not do it during your lifetime.* I will tear it out of the hand of your son' " (1 Kings 11:11–12). So God did keep His promise to David about Solomon.

The other text (1 Kings 2:1–4) is not speaking about God's promise to David regarding his son Solomon. Rather, it refers to God taking the kingdom from any of Solomon's sons. There was no unconditional promise made here. From his deathbed, David exhorted Solomon to " 'Walk in his [God's] ways, and keep his decrees and commands . . . so that you may prosper in all you do and wherever you go, and that the LORD may keep his promise to me: "*If your descendants* watch how they live, and *if* they walk faithfully before me with all their heart and soul, you will never fail to have a man on the throne of Israel" ' " (2:3–4). This promise was both conditional ("if") and limited to Solomon's sons. It said nothing about Solomon, from whom God had already made an unconditional promise not to take the throne away during his lifetime.

---

[15]See R. Garrigou-LaGrange, *God: His Existence and Nature* (St. Louis: B. Herder Book Co., 1946), appendix IV, 465–528.

142

Destroying assurance of salvation

One of the great motivating factors in the Christian life is the assurance of salvation. But no Arminian can be sure he will make it to heaven. The possibility of backsliding always hangs over his head. And if he does backslide, then he loses his salvation.

Thank God, the Bible assures us that we can know that we have eternal life (John 5:24; 1 John 5:13). And nothing can separate us from the love of Christ (Rom. 8:36–39). Even if we are faithless, God remains faithful (2 Tim. 2:13). These and numerous other passages of Scripture inform us that true believers are eternally secure (see chapters 6 and 7).

Hindering confidence in answered prayer

In spite of the fact that extreme Arminians make much of God's dynamic ability to answer prayer, it would appear that their concept of God actually undermines God's use of special providence in answering prayer. They admit, as indeed they should, that most answers to prayer do not involve a direct supernatural intervention in the world. Rather, God works through special providence in unusual ways to accomplish unusual things. But a God who does not know for sure what any future free act will be is severely limited in His logistic ability to do things that a God who knows every decision that will be made can do. So, ironically, the extreme Arminian God is a liability to unanswered prayer, which they consider so important to a personal God. Surely one can have much more confidence knowing that God has not only infallible foreknowledge of the future but complete control of it (see chapter 1). To pray to the extreme Arminian God who is Himself only guessing about the future encourages little confidence in the devotee that he is in firm hands.

A FINAL WORD

The Bible is a balanced Book. It affirms both God's sovereignty (see chapter 1) and man's free choice (see chapter 2). It teaches both that God is in complete control and that humans can choose to receive or reject salvation (see chapter 3).[16] Unfortunately, however,

---

[16]John F. Walvoord wrote, "The immediate problem that faces the interpreter, however, is that of human freedom. It seems evident from experience as well as from Scripture that man has choices. How can one avoid a fatalistic system where everything is predetermined and no moral choices are left? Is human responsibility just a mockery or is it real? These are the problems which face the interpreter of Scripture on this difficult doctrine." (See Lewis Sperry Chafer and John F. Walvoord, *Major Bible Themes* [Grand Rapids, Mich.: Zondervan, 1980], 233.)

there seems to be an incurable human propensity to go to one extreme or the other. Extreme Calvinism (see chapters 4 and 5) and extreme Arminianism (see chapter 6) are cases in point. And, as we have shown in this chapter, extreme views lead logically, and often practically, to extreme actions, whether they are in an extreme emphasis on God's sovereignty or on man's free will.

Again, it has been shown that there is no contradiction in the co-working of sovereignty and free will. We can be assured that (1) God is in control and that (2) we have been given the ability to choose. We are indeed chosen but free.

APPENDIX ONE

GREAT CHRISTIAN CHURCH FATHERS ON FREE WILL

With the exception of the later writings of St. Augustine, who after his experience in the Donatist controversy (see appendix 3) concluded that persons could be forced to believe, virtually all of the great thinkers up to the Reformation affirmed that human beings possess the power of contrary free choice, even in a fallen state.[1] None believed that a coerced act is a free act. In short, all would have rejected the extreme Calvinists' view that God acts irresistibly on the unwilling (see chapter 5).

JUSTIN MARTYR (A.D. 100–165)

God, wishing men and angels to follow His will, resolved to create them free to do righteousness. But if the word of God foretells that some angels and men shall certainly be punished, it did so because it foreknew that they would be unchangeably (wicked), but not because God created them so. So if they repent, all who wish for it can obtain mercy from God (*Dialogue*, CXLI).

---

[1]The citations up to St. Augustine follow Roger T. Forster and V. Paul Marston, *God's Strategy in Human History*, 245f., emphasis mine in all citations.

IRENAEUS (A.D. 130–200)

This expression, "How often would I have gathered thy children together, and thou wouldst not," set forth the ancient law of human liberty, because *God made man a free [agent] from the beginning, possessing his own soul to obey the behests of God voluntarily, and not by compulsion of God.* For there is no coercion with God, but a good will [toward us] is present with Him continually. And therefore does He give good counsel to all. And *in man as well as in angels, He has placed the power of choice (for angels are rational beings), so that those who had yielded obedience might justly possess what is good,* given indeed by God, but preserved by themselves....

If then it were not in our power to do or not to do these things, what reason had the apostle, and much more the Lord Himself, to give us counsel to do some things and to abstain from others? But because man is possessed of free will from the beginning, and God is possessed of free will in whose likeness man was created, advice is always given to him to keep fast the good, which thing is done by means of obedience to God (*Against Heresies*, XXXVII).

ATHENAGORAS OF ATHENS (SECOND CENTURY)

Just as with *men who have freedom of choice as to both virtue and vice (for you would not either honor the good or punish the bad; unless vice and virtue were in their own power,* and some are diligent in the matters entrusted to them, and others faithless), so is it among the angels (*Embassy for Christians*, XXIV).

THEOPHILUS OF ANTIOCH (SECOND CENTURY)

For *God made man free, and with power over Himself*... now God vouchsafes to him as a gift through His own philanthropy and pity, when men obey Him. For as man, disobeying, drew death on Himself; so, *obeying the will of God, he who desires is able to procure for Himself life everlasting* (*To Autolycus*, xxvii).

TATIAN OF SYRIA (LATE SECOND CENTURY)

Live to God, and by apprehending Him lay aside your old nature. We were not created to die, but we die by our own fault. *Our free will has destroyed us;* we who were free have become slaves; we have been sold through sin. Nothing evil has been created by God; *we ourselves have manifested wickedness; but we, who have manifested it, are able again to reject it (Address,* xi).

BARDAISAN OF SYRIA (c. 154–222)

How is it that God did not so make us that we should not sin and incur condemnation?—If man had been made so, he would not have belonged to himself but would have been the instrument of him that moved him. . . . And how, in that case, would a man differ from a harp, on which another plays; or from a ship, which another guides: where the praise and the blame reside in the hand of the performer or the steersman . . . they being only instruments made for the use of him in whom is the skill? But *God, in His benignity, chose not so to make man; but by freedom He exalted him to above many of His creatures (Fragments).*

CLEMENT OF ALEXANDRIA (c. 150–215)

But we, who have heard by the Scriptures that *self-determining choice and refusal have been given by the Lord to men,* rest in the infallible criterion of faith, manifesting a willing Spirit, since we have chosen life and believe God through His voice (*Stromata,* 2.4).

But nothing is without the will of the Lord of the universe. It remains to say that such things happen without the prevention of God; for this alone saves both the providence and the goodness of God. *We must not therefore think that He actively produces afflictions (far be it that we should think this!); but we must be persuaded that He does not prevent those that cause them, but overrules for good the crimes of His enemies (Stromata,* 4.12).

TERTULLIAN (155–225)

I find, then, that *man was by God constituted free, master of his own will and power;* indicating the presence of God's image and likeness in him by nothing so well as by this constitution of his nature. . . .

You will find that when He sets before man good and evil, life and death, that the entire course of discipline is arranged in precepts by God's calling men from sin, and threatening and exhorting them; and this on no other ground than that *man is free, with a will either for obedience or resistance. . . .*

Since, therefore, *both the goodness and purpose of God are discovered in the gift to man of freedom in his will* . . . (*Against Marcion*, 2.5).

NOVATIAN OF ROME (c. 200–258)

He also placed man at the head of the world, and man, too, made in the image of God, to whom He imparted mind, and reason, and foresight, that he might imitate God; and although the first elements of his body were earthly, yet the substance was inspired by a heavenly and divine breathing. And when He had given him all things for his service, *He willed that he alone should be free.* And lest, again, an unbounded freedom should fall into peril, He laid down a command, in which man was taught that there was no evil in the fruit of the tree; but he was forewarned that *evil would arise if perchance he should exercise his free will* in the contempt of the law that was given (*On the Trinity*, chap. 1).

ORIGEN (c. 185–254)

Now it ought to be known that the holy apostles, in preaching the faith of Christ, delivered themselves with the utmost clearness on certain points which they believed to be necessary to everyone. . . . *This also is clearly defined in the teaching of the church that every rational soul is possessed of free will and volition* (*De Principiis*, preface).

There are, indeed, *innumerable passages in the Scriptures which establish with exceeding clearness the existence of freedom of will* (*De Principiis*, 3.1).

METHODIUS (c. 260–311)

Now *those who decide that man is not possessed of free will, and affirm that he is governed by the unavoidable necessities of fate* . . . *are guilty of impiety toward God Himself, making Him out to be the cause and author of human evils* (*The Banquet of the Ten Virgins*, xvi).

I say that *man was made with free will,* not as if there were already existing some evil, which *he had the power of choosing* if he wished . . . but that *the power of obeying and disobeying God* is the only cause (*Concerning Free Will*).

ARCHELLAUS (c. 277)

For *all creatures that God made, He made very good, and He gave to every individual the sense of free will* in accordance with which standard He also instituted the law of judgment. To sin is ours, and that we sin not is God's gift, as *our will is constituted to choose either to sin or not to sin (The Disputation with Manes).*

ARNOBIUS OF SICCA (c. 253–327)

Does not He free all alike who invites all alike? Or does He thrust back or repel any one from the kindness of *the Supreme who gives to all alike the power of coming to Him?*—To all, He says, the fountain of life is open, and no one is hindered or kept back from drinking . . . (*Against the Heathen*, 64. 1 reply).

Nay, *my opponent says, if God is powerful, merciful, willing to save us, let Him change our dispositions, and compel us to trust in His promises. This then, is violence, not kindness nor the bounty of the Supreme God,* but a childish and vain strife in seeking to get the mastery. For *what is so unjust as to force men who are reluctant and unworthy, to reverse their inclinations; to impress forcibly on their minds what they are unwilling to receive, and shrink from* . . . (ibid., 65).

CYRIL OF JERUSALEM (c. 312–386)

Know also that *thou hast a soul self-governed,* the noblest work of God, made after the image of its Creator, immortal because of God that gives it immortality, a living being rational, imperishable, because of Him that bestowed these gifts: *having free power to do what it willeth (Lecture,* IV 18).

There is not a class of souls sinning by nature and a class of souls practicing righteousness by nature; but both act from choice, the substance of their souls being of one kind only and alike in all (ibid., 20).

The soul is self-governed: and though the Devil can suggest, he has not the power to compel against the will. He pictures to thee the thought of fornication: if thou wilt, thou rejectest. For *if thou wert a fornicator of necessity, then for what cause did God prepare hell? If thou wert a doer of righteousness by nature and not by will, wherefore did God prepare crowns of ineffable glory?* The sheep is gentle, but never was it crowned for its gentleness; since its gentle quality belongs to it not from choice but by nature (ibid., 21).

GREGORY OF NYSSA (c. 335–395)

Being the image and the likeness . . . of the Power which rules all things, *man kept also in the matter of a free will this likeness to Him whose will is over all (On Virginity,* 368, chap. X11).

JEROME (c. 347–420)

It is in vain that you misrepresent me and try to convince the ignorant that I condemn free will. Let him who condemns it be himself condemned. *We have been created, endowed with free will; still it is not this which distinguishes us from the brutes.* For human free will, as I said, depends upon the help of God and needs His aid moment by moment, a thing which you and yours do not choose to admit. Your position is that once a man has free will he no longer needs the help of God. *It is true that freedom of the will brings with it freedom of decision. Still man does not act immediately on his free will but requires God's aid who Himself needs no aid* (*Letters*, 133).

But when we are concerned with grace and mercy, free will is in part void; in part, I say, for *so much depends upon it, that we wish and desire, and give assent to the course we choose. But it depends on God whether we have the power in His strength and with His help to perform what we desire, and to bring to effect our toil and effort* (*Against the Pelagians*, Book 111, 10).

It is ours to begin, God's to finish (ibid., 3.1, see also appendix 11).

JOHN CHRYSOSTOM (347–407)

God having placed good and evil in our power, has given us full freedom of choice; he does not keep back the unwilling, but embraces the willing (*Homilies on Genesis*, 19.1).

All is in God's power, but *so that our free will is not lost. . . . It depends therefore on us and on Him. We must first choose the good, and then He adds what belongs to Him. He does not precede our willing, that our free will may not suffer. But when we have chosen, then He affords us much help. . . .* It is ours to choose beforehand and to will, but God's to perfect and bring to the end (*On Hebrews Homily*, 12).[2]

EARLY ST. AUGUSTINE (354–430)[3]

Free will, naturally assigned by the creator to our rational soul, is such a neutral power, as can either incline toward faith, or turn toward unbe-

---

[2]John Calvin consciously pitted himself against Chrysostom and virtually all the Fathers when he said, "*We must, therefore, repudiate the oft-repeated sentiment of Chrysostom, 'Whom he draws, he draws willingly'; insinuating that the Lord only stretches out his hand, and waits to see whether we will be pleased to take his aid. We grant that, as man was originally constituted, he could incline to either side,* but since he has taught us by his example how miserable a thing free will is if God works not in us to will and to do, of what use to us were grace imparted in such scanty measure?" (John Calvin, *Institutes of the Christian Religion*, 1.2.3.10, 260–61).

[3]These texts are taken from St. Augustine's earlier writings before his position changed following the controversy with schismatics known as Donatists (see appendix 3), whom Augustine believed could be coerced against their will into accepting the truth of the Catholic Church.

lief (*On the Spirit and the Letter*, 58).

In fact, *sin is so much a voluntary evil that it is not sin at all unless it is voluntary* (*Of True Religion*, 14).

Either then, *will is itself the first cause of sin, or the first cause is without sin* (*On Free Will*, 3.49).

Sin is indeed nowhere but in the will, since this consideration also would have helped me, that *justice holds guilty those sinning by evil will alone*, although they may have been unable to accomplish what they willed (*Two Souls, Against the Manichaeans*, 10.12).

Our conclusion is that *our wills have power to do all that God wanted them to do and foresaw they could do. Their power, such as it is, is a real power. What they are to do they themselves will most certainly do, because God foresaw both that they could do it and that they would do it and His knowledge cannot be mistaken* (*City of God*, 5.9).

Because *whoever has done anything evil by means of one unconscious or unable to resist, the latter can by no means be justly condemned* (*Two Souls, Against the Manichaeans*, 10.12).

For *every one also who does a thing unwillingly is compelled, and every one who is compelled, if he does a thing, does it only unwillingly. It follows that he that is willing is free from compulsion, even if any one thinks himself compelled* (*Two Souls, Against the Manichaeans*, 10.14).

The conclusion is that *we are by no means under compulsion to abandon free choice in favor of divine knowledge*, nor need we deny— God forbid!—that God knows the future, as a condition for holding free choice (*City of God*, 5.10).

ST. ANSELM (1033–1109)

No one deserts uprightness except by willing to desert it. If "against one's will" means "unwillingly," then no one deserts uprightness against his will. . . . But a man cannot will against his will because he cannot will unwillingly to will. For everyone who wills, wills willingly (*Truth, Freedom, and Evil*, 130).

Although *they [Adam and Eve] yielded themselves to sin, they could not abolish in themselves their natural freedom of choice.* However, they could so affect their state that they were not able to use that freedom except by a different grace from that which they had before their fall (ibid., 125).

And we ought not to say that they [Adam and Eve] had freedom for the purpose of receiving, from a giver, the uprightness which they didn't have, because *we have to believe that they were created with upright wills—although we must not deny that they had free-*

dom for receiving this same uprightness again, should they once desert it and were it returned to them by the one who originally gave it. We often see an evidence of this in men who are led back to justice from injustice by heavenly grace (ibid., 126).

Don't you see *it follows from these considerations that no temptation can conquer an upright will? For if temptation can conquer the will, it has the power to conquer it, and conquers the will by its own power. But temptation cannot do this because the will can be overcome only by its* own power (ibid., 132).

Now, *I wonder whether even God could remove uprightness from a man's will. Could he? I'll show you that He cannot.* For although He can reduce everything which He has made from nothing back to nothing, He does not have the power to separate uprightness from a will that has it (ibid., 136).

THOMAS AQUINAS (1224-1274)

The cause of a sin is the will's not holding to the rule of reason and divine law. Evil does not arise before the will applies itself to doing something (Aquinas, *Theological Texts,* trans. Thomas Gilby [London: Oxford University Press, 1955; reprint, Durham, N.C.: The Labyrinth Press, 1982], 132).

Necessity comes from the agent when the latter so coerces someone that he cannot do the contrary. We refer to this as "necessity by coercion." *Such necessity by coercion is contrary to the will.* For we consider violent whatever is contrary to a thing's inclination. But the will's own motion is an inclination toward something, so that something is voluntary when it follows the inclination of nature. Just as something cannot possibly be violent and natural simultaneously, so *something cannot be absolutely coerced or violent and simultaneously voluntary* (Aquinas, *An Aquinas Reader,* ed. Mary T. Clark [Garden City, N.Y.: Doubleday & Company, Inc., 1972], 291–92).

Thus of necessity man wills happiness, and it is impossible for him to will not to be happy or to be unhappy. But since choice does not deal with the end but with the means to the end, as previously discussed (*Summa Theologica,* I-II, 13, 3), it does not deal with the perfect good or happiness but with other particular goods. *Consequently man does not choose necessarily but freely* (ibid., 293).

Some have proposed that man's will is moved necessarily to making some choice, although they do not hold that the will is coerced. For not every necessity from an external principle (violent motion) is coercive, but only that which originates from without where both certain natural movements are discovered to be necessary but not coercive. *For the coercive is opposed to the natural just as it is also opposed to voluntary motion,* because the latter comes from an internal principle, while violent motion comes from an external one. *This opinion [of the Latin Averroists] is therefore heretical because it destroys merit and demerit in human actions.* For why should there be any merit or demerit for actions one cannot avoid doing? It is, moreover, to be included among the excluded opinions of philosophers: for *if there is no freedom in us but we are moved of necessity to will, then deliberate choice, encouragement, precept, punishment, praise, and blame are removed,* and these are the very problems that moral philosophy considers. Not only is this contrary to the faith, but it undermines all the principles of moral philosophy (ibid., 294–95).

Now sin cannot destroy man's rationality altogether, for then he would no longer be capable of sin (Aquinas, *Philosophical Texts,* trans. Thomas Gilby [New York: Oxford University Press, 1960], 179).

To be free is not to be obliged to one determinate object (ibid., 259).

Man has free choice, otherwise counsels, exhortations, precepts, prohibitions, rewards, and punishments would all be pointless ... (ibid., 261–62).

Man, however, can act from judgment and adaptation in the reason; *a free judgment that leaves intact the power of being able to decide otherwise* (ibid.).

Similarly, then, *sin is caused by the free will according as it turns away from God.* Hence *it does not follow that God is the cause of sin, although He is the cause of free will* (St. Thomas Aquinas, *On Evil,* trans. Jean Oesterle [Notre Dame, Ind.: University of Notre Dame Press, 1995], 106).

But nevertheless it must be noted that the movement of the first mover is not uniformly received in all movable things, but in each according to its own mode.... For *when a thing is properly disposed to receive the movement of the first mover, a perfect action in accord with the intention of the first mover follows;* but if a thing is not properly disposed and suited to receive the motion of the first mover, an imperfect action follows. And then whatever action is present is referred to the first mover as the cause, but whatever defect is present is not referred to the first mover as the cause, since such a defect in the action results from the fact that the agent departs from the order of the first mover.... And for this reason we maintain that *the action pertaining to the sin is from God, but the sin is not from God* (ibid., 110).

However *the deformity of sin in no way falls under the divine will but results from this that the free will departs or deviates from the order of the divine will* (ibid., 111).

Aquinas added,

Similarly *when something moves itself, it is not precluded that it is moved by another from whom it has this very ability by which it moves itself. And therefore it is not contrary to liberty that God is the cause of the act of free will* (ibid.).[4]

Sin wounded man in his natural powers so far as concerns his capacity for gratuitous goods but not in such a way that it takes away anything of the essence of his nature; and so it does not follow that the demon's intellect erred except about gratuitous matters (ibid., 496).

---

[4]By this he apparently means God is the primary Cause who produced the *fact* of free will, while humans are the secondary cause who perform (by the power God gives them) the *acts* of free choice.

APPENDIX TWO

WAS CALVIN A CALVINIST?

At first blush, it may seem absurd to ask whether John Calvin was a Calvinist. But he was not the first in the history of thought to have his views be distorted by his disciples. In fact, many of the great thinkers were misunderstood by their followers.

DEFINING "CALVINISM"

If Five-Point Calvinism (T-U-L-I-P), as described in chapters 4 and 5 of this book, is taken as the definition of "Calvinism" in this question, then it seems clear that Calvin was not a Calvinist, at least at one crucial point: limited atonement.[1] This is why we have preferred to call this view extreme Calvinism throughout this book; it goes beyond what Calvin himself taught on the matter. The following texts support this conclusion.

THE EXTENT OF THE ATONEMENT IS UNLIMITED

While Calvin believed that the benefits of the Atonement are *applied* only to a limited group (those who believed), he held that

---

[1] The position that Calvin rejected limited atonement is supported by the classic work of R. T. Kendall, *Calvin and English Calvinism to 1649* (Oxford, 1979).

the *extent* of the Atonement is unlimited. That is, Christ died for the sins of the whole human race.

Christ's blood expiated (satisfied) God for all the sins of the world

Calvin wrote, "This is our liberty, this our glorying against death, that our sins are not imputed to us. He says that this redemption was procured by the blood of Christ, for *by the sacrifice of His death all the sins of the world have been expiated.*[2]

Christ suffered and provided salvation for the whole human race

"We must now see in what ways we become possessed of the blessings which God has bestowed on his only begotten Son, not for private use, but to enrich the poor and needy. And the first thing to be attended to is, that so long as we are without Christ and separated from him, nothing which *he suffered and did for the salvation of the human race* is of the least benefit to us" (*Institutes*, 3.1.1).

The "many" for whom Christ died (in Romans 5) is all of mankind

"We should note, however, that Paul does not here contrast the larger number with the many, for *he is not speaking of the great number of mankind*, but he argues that since the sin of Adam has destroyed many [all], *the righteousness of Christ will be no less effective for the salvation of many [all]*" (Comments on Rom. 5:15).

The guilt of the whole world was laid on Christ

"I approve of the ordinary reading, that he alone bore the punishment of many, because *on him was laid the guilt of the whole world*. It is evident from other passages, and especially from the fifth chapter of the Epistle to the Romans, that *'many' sometimes denotes 'all'* " (Comments on Isa. 53:12).

The "many" for whom Christ died means the whole human race

"Mark 14:24. This is my blood. *I have already warned, when the blood is said to be poured out (as in Matthew) for the remission of sins*, how in these words we are directed to the sacrifice of Christ's death, and to neglect this thought makes any due celebration of the Supper impossible. In no other way can faithful souls be satisfied, if they cannot believe that God is pleased in their regard. *The word many does not mean a part of the world only, but the whole human race:* he contrasts many with one, as if to say that he would not be the

---

[2]Comments on Col. 1:15. Emphasis mine in all citations.

Redeemer of one man, but would meet death to deliver many of their cursed guilt. *It is incontestable that Christ came for the expiation of the sins of the whole world"* (*Eternal Predestination of God,* IX.5).

Salvation is limited in its effect, not in its offer

"But if it is so (you will say), little faith can be put in the Gospel promises, which, in testifying concerning the will of God, declare that he wills what is contrary to his inviolable decree. Not at all; for *however universal the promises of salvation may be,* there is no discrepancy between them and the predestination of the reprobate, provided we attend to their effect. We know that the promises are *effectual only when we receive them in faith,* but, on the contrary, when faith is made void, the promise is of no effect" (*Institutes,* 3.24.17).

Christ's death is only applied to the righteous (by faith)

"To communicate to us the blessings which he received from the Father, he must become ours and dwell in us. Accordingly, he is called our Head, and the firstborn among many brethren, while, on the other hand, we are said to be ingrafted into him and clothed with him, all which he possesses being, as I have said, *nothing to us until we become one with him.* And although it is true that we obtain this by faith, yet since we see that all do not indiscriminately embrace the offer of Christ which is made by the gospel, the very nature of the case teaches us to ascend higher, and inquire into the secret efficacy of the Spirit, to which it is owing that we enjoy Christ and all his blessings" (*Institutes,* 3.1.1).

Salvation is only applied to those who believe

"The apostle indicates that *the fruits of it do not come to any but to those who are obedient.* In saying this he commends faith to us, for neither He nor His benefits become ours unless, and in so far as, we accept them and Him by faith. At the same time he has inserted the universal term 'to all' to show that *no one is excluded from this salvation who proves to be attentive and obedient to the Gospel of Christ"* (Comments on Heb. 5:9).

Even the lost were purchased by Christ's blood

"It is no small matter to have the souls perish who were bought by the blood of Christ" (Calvin, *The Mystery of Godliness,* 83).

No men are barred from salvation

"He had commanded Timothy that prayers should be regularly offered up in the church for kings and princes; but as it seemed somewhat absurd that prayer should be offered up for a class of men who were almost hopeless (all of them being not only aliens from the body of Christ, but doing their utmost to overthrow his kingdom), he adds, that it was acceptable to God, who will have all men to be saved. By this he assuredly means nothing more than that the way of salvation was not shut against any order of men; that, on the contrary, *he had manifested his mercy in such a way, that he would have none debarred from it*" (*Institutes*, 3.24.16).

Christ suffered for the sins of the world

"I would they were even cut off. His indignation increases and he prays for destruction on the imposters by whom the Galatians had been deceived. The word 'cut off' seems to allude to the circumcision which they were pressing for. Chrysostom inclines to this view: 'They tear the Church for the sake of circumcision; I wish they were cut off entirely.' *But such a curse does not seem to fit the mildness of an apostle, who ought to wish that all should be saved and therefore that not one should perish. I reply that this is true when we have men in mind; for God commends to us the salvation of all men without exception, even as Christ suffered for the sins of the whole world*" (Comments on Gal. 5:12).

"And when he says the sin of the world *he extends this kindness indiscriminately to the whole human race*, that the Jews might not think the Redeemer has been sent to them alone. From this we infer that the whole world is bound in the same condemnation; and that since all men without exception are guilty of unrighteousness before God, they have need of reconciliation. John, therefore, by speaking of the sin of the world in general, wanted to make us feel our own misery and exhort us to seek the remedy" (Comments on John 1:29).

"We must now see in what way we become possessed of the blessings which God has bestowed on his only begotten Son, not for private use, but to enrich the poor and needy. And the first thing to be attended to is, that so long as we are without Christ and separated from him, nothing which *he suffered and did for the salvation of the human race* is of the least benefit to us. To communicate to us the blessings which he received from the Father, he must become ours and dwell in us" (*Institutes*, 1.3.2).

While Calvin affirmed that the *extent* of the Atonement is unlimited, he also held that its *application* was limited only to those who believe. This is made evident in several texts.

UNBELIEF IS THE REASON THAT SOME DO NOT RECEIVE THE BENEFITS OF CHRIST'S DEATH

"Paul makes grace common to all men, not because it in fact extends to all, but because it is offered to all. *Although Christ suffered for the sins of the world,* and is offered by the goodness of God without distinction to all men, *yet not all receive Him*" (Comments on Rom. 5:18).

"To bear the sins means to free those who have sinned from their guilt by his satisfaction. *He says many meaning all, as in Rom. 5:15.* It is of course certain that *not all enjoy the fruits of Christ's death, but this happens because their unbelief hinders them*" (Comments on Heb. 9:28).

Only believers enjoy the benefit of salvation

" 'I am come a light into the world.' The universal particle seems to have been put in deliberately, partly that *all believers without exception might enjoy this benefit* in common and partly to show that unbelievers perish in darkness because they flee from the light of their own accord" (Comments on John 12:46).

UNIVERSALISM IS DENIED: SALVATION IS NOT APPLIED TO ALL MANKIND

"He put this in for amplification, that believers might be convinced that *the expiation made by Christ extends to all who by faith embrace the Gospel.* But here the question may be asked as to *how the sins of the whole world have been expiated.* I pass over the dreams of the fanatics, who make this a reason to extend salvation to all the reprobate and even to Satan himself. Such a monstrous idea is not worth refuting. Those who want to avoid this absurdity have said that *Christ suffered sufficiently for the whole world but effectively only for the elect.* This solution has commonly prevailed in the schools. Although *I allow the truth of this,* I deny that it fits this passage. For John's purpose was only to make this blessing common to the whole Church. Therefore, under the word 'all' [in 1 John 2:2] he does not include the reprobate, but refers to all who would believe and those who were scattered through various regions of the earth. For, as is meet, the grace of Christ is really made clear when it is declared to be the only salvation of the world" (Comments on 1 John 2:2).

Note: Calvin clearly denies universalism and affirms the sufficiency of Christ's death for the whole world, even though he denies that this particular passage can be used to teach this.

Christ's "blood" received in communion is not for unbelievers

"How can the wicked drink Christ's blood 'which was not shed to expiate their sins' and Christ's flesh 'which was not crucified for them'?" (*Theological Treatises*, 285).[3]

CONCLUSION

Whatever else Calvin may have said to encourage extreme Calvinism's T-U-L-I-P (see chapters 4 and 5), he certainly denied limited atonement as they understand it. For Calvin, the Atonement is universal in *extent* and limited only in its *application*, namely, to those who believe.

---

[3]Calvin seems to have verbally overstated his point here in the heat of the battle against Heshusius's heretical claim that even the wicked can receive benefit from Communion "by the mouth bodily without faith." In context his point is clear, namely, only those who believe actually enter into the benefits of Christ's death.

APPENDIX THREE

THE ORIGINS OF EXTREME CALVINISM

A VIRTUALLY UNBROKEN TRADITION

There is an almost unbroken tradition among the great Fathers of the church affirming the power of contrary free choice. This includes the writings of Irenaeus, the early St. Augustine, St. Anselm, and Thomas Aquinas (see appendix 1). This means that virtually the whole of the Christian tradition up to the Reformation stands against the characteristic views of what we have called extreme Calvinism in this book. This includes not only the ability of fallen human beings to exercise free choice in their own salvation, but the rejection of the doctrine of irresistible grace on the unwilling (see chapter 5) and, at least logically and implicitly, the other concomitant doctrines of limited atonement, unconditional election, and total depravity as conceived by extreme Calvinism.

THE ORIGINS OF EXTREME CALVINISM

Were it not for one significant blip in pre-Reformation history, there would have been no notable extreme "Calvinists" for the first 1,500 years of the church. This exception is found in the late writings of St. Augustine (A.D. 354–430). As a result of his controversy with the Pelagians (who emphasized free will at the expense of grace), Augustine overreacted with an emphasis on grace at the expense of free will. Likewise, in response to the Donatists, a schismatic group that had broken away from the Catholic Church, St. Augustine overreacted by affirming that heretics could be coerced to believe *against* their free choice to confess the Catholic faith. The logic seemed irresistible to him: If the Church can coerce heretics to believe against their will, then why can't God force sinners to believe against their will? This, of course, fit with his long-held belief that infants could be regenerated apart from any free choice on their part. Why, then, he reasoned, could not God force adults to be saved against their will?

However, even in his early anti-Pelagian writings, Augustine never adopted the radical view on free will and limited atonement that he manifested in his later works, particularly those written after A.D. 417. The hardening of Augustine's theological arteries is manifested in several areas. In his early view, the same one held by all the Fathers throughout church history up to Luther, he embraced *unlimited* atonement; later he affirmed *limited* atonement. In the early period, he held that God never coerces a free act; this was discarded in favor of irresistible grace on the unwilling in his later years. This, of course, resulted in a hardened view of predestination where God was active in both the destiny of the elect and the non-elect, and in a denial that there are any conditions for receiving God's gift of unconditional salvation. In fact, for the later Augustine, in contrast to the earlier, mankind is so totally depraved that he has no free choice with regard to spiritual matters. In short, Augustine moved from moderate "Calvinism" to extreme "Calvinism" (see chapter 7).

Even John Calvin noted the difference between Augustine's earlier and later views, observing that the earlier Augustine explained God "hardening" unbelievers' hearts as His foreseeing their act of will, while later on he held that God was actively hardening their hearts. Calvin wrote, "Even Augustine was not always free from this superstition, as when he says that *blinding and hardening have respect not to the operation of God* but to prescience (*Lib. De Predestina. Et Gratia*). But this subtlety is repudiated by *many passages of Scripture, which clearly show that the divine interference amounts to something more than prescience.*" Calvin continues, "And Augustine himself, in his book against Julian, contends at length that sins are manifestations not merely of divine permission or patience, but also of divine power, that thus former sins may be punished. In like manner, what is said of permission is too weak to stand. God is very often said to blind and harden the reprobate, to turn their hearts, to incline and impel them, as I have elsewhere fully explained" (Book I. c. xviii.).[1]

THE MODERATE "CALVINISM" OF THE EARLIER AUGUSTINE

From the very beginning, Augustine followed the teachings of the church fathers before him. Human beings, even fallen ones, possess the power of free choice. This is true of his anti-Manichaean writings as well as his early anti-Pelagian works. More precisely, as late as A.D. 412 (*On the Spirit and the Letter*), and perhaps later, Augustine still held a moderate view. But by A.D. 417 (*On the Correction of the Donatists*) his view had radicalized.[2]

All sin is voluntary

> In fact, *sin is so much a voluntary evil that it is not sin at all unless it is voluntary (Of True Religion, 14).*

Sin is nowhere but in the will

> Sin is indeed nowhere but in the will, since this consideration also would have helped me, that justice holds guilty those

---

[1]John Calvin, *Institutes of the Christian Religion*, 1.2.4.3, 267.
[2]Select Early Works of Augustine
  On True Religion (390)
  On Two Souls (A.D. 391)
  On Free Will (388–95)
  On the Spirit and the Letter (412)
  City of God, Books 1–10 (413f.)
  On Nature and Grace (415)
  On Man's Perfection in Righteousness (415)
  On the Proceedings of Pelagius (417)
Select Later Works of Augustine
  *On the Correction of the Donatists** (417)
  On the Grace of Christ (418)
  On Original Sin (418)
  Against Two Letters of the Pelagians (420)
  Enchiridion (421)
  City of God, Books 11–22 (up to 426)
  On Grace and Free Will (426)
  On Rebuke and Grace (426)
  On Predestination of the Saints (428–29)
  On the Gift of Perseverance (428–29)
*This was the turning point, manifesting the later extreme "Calvinistic" view of Augustine. The works of Augustine listed above are found in *A Select Library of the Nicene and Post-Nicene Fathers of the Christian Church*, ed. Philip Schaff (Grand Rapids, Mich.: Wm. B. Eerdmans Publishing Co., 1956).

sinning by evil will alone, although they may have been unable to accomplish what they willed (*Two Souls, Against the Manichaeans,* 10.12).

Free will is the first cause of sin

Either then, *will is itself the first cause of sin,* or the first cause is without sin (*On Free Will,* 3.49).

Free will is neutral

Free will, naturally assigned by the Creator to our rational soul, *is such a neutral power,* as can either incline toward faith, or turn toward unbelief (*On the Spirit and the Letter,* 58).

All evil is resistible

Because *whoever has done anything evil by means of one unconscious or unable to resist, the latter can by no means be justly condemned* (*On Two Souls, Against the Manichaeans,* 10.12).

God wills all to be saved

(*On the Spirit and the Letter;* cf. *Reply to Faustus* 12.36).

God's will can be resisted

This being the case, *unbelievers indeed do contrary to the will of God when they do not believe the gospel;* nevertheless they do not therefore overcome His will, but rob their own selves of the great, nay the very greatest, good, and implicate themselves in the penalties of punishment (*On the Spirit and the Letter,* 58).

God gives the power of choice but not the acts of choice

As He is the Creator of all natures, so is *He the giver of all powers—though He is not the maker of all choices.* Evil choices are not from Him, for they are contrary to the nature which is from Him (*City of God,* 5.9).

Even the gift of faith must be freely received

A man cannot be said to have even that will with which he believes in God, without having received it . . . but *yet not so as to take away from the free will,* for the good or the evil use of which they may be most righteously judged (*On the Spirit and the Letter,* 58).

If evil cannot be resisted, we are not responsible

*Because whoever has done anything evil by means of one uncon-
scious or unable to resist, the latter can by no means be justly condemned* (*Two Souls, Against the Manichaeans*, 10.12).

Responsibility implies ability to respond

Our conclusion is that *our wills have power to do all that God
wanted them to do and foresaw they could do.* Their power, such
as it is, is a real power. What they are to do they themselves
will most certainly do, because God foresaw both that they
could do it and that they would do it and His knowledge
cannot be mistaken (*City of God,* 5.9).

An unwilling act is compelled and a compelled act is not free

For *every one also who does a thing unwillingly is compelled,
and every one who is compelled, if he does a thing, does it only unwillingly.* It follows that *he that is willing is free from compulsion,*
even if any one thinks himself compelled (*Two Souls, Against
the Manichaeans,* 10.14).

We sin free, not because God foresaw it

For, no one sins because God foreknew that he would sin. In fact,
the very reason why *a man is undoubtedly responsible for his own
sin,* when he sins, is because He whose foreknowledge cannot
be deceived foresaw, not the man's fate or fortune or what not,
but that the man himself would be responsible for his own sin.
*No man sins unless it is his choice to sin; and his choice not to sin,
that, too, God foresaw* (*City of God,* 5.10).

God's predetermination is in accordance with our free choice

The conclusion is that *we are by no means under compulsion
to abandon free choice in favor of divine knowledge, nor need we
deny—God forbid!—that God knows the future, as a condition for
holding free choice* (*City of God,* 5.10).

The will to believe comes from ourselves

*If we believe that we may attain this grace (and of course believe
voluntarily),* then the question arises, whence we have this
will?—If from nature, why is it not at everybody's command,
since the same God made all men? If from God's gift, then
again, why is not the gift open to all; since "He will have all

men to be saved, and to come unto the knowledge of the truth? ..." *God no doubt wishes all men to be saved and to come into the knowledge of the truth; but yet not so as to take away from them free will, for the good or the evil use of which they may be most righteously judged* (*On the Spirit and the Letter*, 57.58).

Soul must consent in receiving gifts from God

For the soul cannot receive and possess these gifts, which are here referred to, except by yielding its consent. And thus whatever it possesses, and whatever it receives is from God; and yet the act of receiving and having belongs, of course, to the receiver and possessor (*On the Spirit and the Letter*, 60).

We must consent to God's summons

To yield our consent, indeed, to God's summons, or to withhold it, is (as I have said) the function of our will (ibid.).

THE EXTREME "CALVINISM" OF THE LATER AUGUSTINE

Working from his belief that infants could be saved apart from their free choice and that schismatic Donatists could be forced to believe against their free choice, Augustine drew out the logic of these positions in his later extreme "Calvinistic" views.

We killed ourselves in the Fall but can't bring ourselves back to life

For it was by the evil use of his free will that man destroyed both it and himself. For, as a man who kills himself must, of course, be alive when he kills himself, but after he has killed himself ceases to live, and cannot restore himself to life; so, when man by his own free will sinned, then sin being victorious over him, the freedom of his will was lost (*Enchiridion*, 30).

True freedom lost in the Fall

Take the case of the will. Its choice is truly free only when it is not a slave to sin and vice. *God created man such a free will, but once that kind of freedom was lost by man's fall from freedom, it could be given back only by Him who had the power to give it* (*City of God*, 14.11).

God creates a new heart in us

We should remember that *He says, "Make you a new heart and a new spirit," who also promises, "I will give you a new heart,*

166

and a new spirit will I put within you." How is it, then, that He who says, "Make you," also says, "I will give you"? Why does He command, if He is to give? Why does He give if man is to make, except it be that *He gives what He commands* when He helps him to obey whom he commands? ... (*On Grace and Free Will*, 31).

God makes us act by efficaciously exerting power on our will

Of the same Lord again it is said, "It is God who worketh in you, even to will!" It is certain that it is we that act when we act; *but it is He who makes us act, by applying efficacious powers to our will*, who has said, "I will make you to walk in my statutes, and to observe my judgments, and to do them" (*On Grace and Free Will*, 32).

Faith is the gift of God

And *lest men should arrogate to themselves the merit of their own faith* at least, not understanding that *this too is the gift of God*, this same apostle, who says in another place that he had "obtained mercy of the Lord to be faithful," here also adds: "and that not of yourselves; it is the gift of God: not of works, lest any man should boast" (*Enchiridion*, 31).

Even our free choice is a gift of God

And further, *should any one be inclined to boast, not indeed of his works, but of the freedom of his will, as if the first merit belonged to him, this very liberty of good action being given to him as a reward he had earned*, let him listen to this same preacher of grace, when he says: "For it is God which worketh in you, both to will and to do of His own good pleasure" (*Enchiridion*, 32).

Double-predestination

As the Supreme Good, he made good use of evil deeds, for the damnation of *those whom he had justly predestined to punishment* and for the salvation of those whom he had mercifully predestined to grace (*Enchiridion*, 100).

God turns evil wills of men as He wills

Furthermore, *who would be so impiously foolish as to say that God cannot turn the evil wills of men—as he willeth, when he willeth, and where he willeth—toward the good?* But when he acteth, he acteth through mercy; when he doth not act, it is through justice (*Enchiridion*, 98).

God does not have to show love to anyone

For then he perceives that the whole human race was condemned in its rebellious head by a divine judgment so just, that if not a single member of the race had been redeemed, no one could justly have questioned the justice of God; and that it was right that those who are redeemed should be redeemed in such a way as to show, by the greater number who are unredeemed and left in their just condemnation, what the whole race deserved, and whither the deserved judgment of God would lead even the redeemed, *did not His undeserved mercy interpose, so that every mouth might be stopped of those who wish to glory in their own merits,* and that he that glorieth might glory in the Lord (*Enchiridion*, 99).

Compelling Donatists is acceptable

Wherefore, if the power which the Church has received by divine appointment in its due season ... be the instrument by which *those who are found in the highways and hedges—that is, in heresies and schisms—are compelled to come in, then let them not find fault with being compelled, but consider whether they be so compelled* (*Corrections of the Donatists*, 6.24).

Christ used violence on Paul

Where is what the Donatists were wont to cry: Man is at liberty to believe or not believe? Towards whom did Christ use violence? Whom did He compel? Here they have the Apostle Paul. Let them recognize in his case Christ first compelling and afterwards teaching; first striking, and afterwards consoling. For it is wonderful how he who entered the service of the gospel in the first instance under the *compulsion* of bodily punishment, afterwards labored more in the gospel than all they who were called by word only; and he who was *compelled* by the greater influence of fear to love, displayed that perfect love which casts out fear.

Why, therefore, should not the Church use force in compelling her lost sons to return, if the lost sons compelled others to their destruction? (*Correction of the Donatists*, 6.22–23).

Jesus says to compel people into the kingdom

Whence also *the Lord Himself bids the guests in the first instance to be invited to His great supper; and afterwards compelled;*

for on His servants making answer to Him, "Lord, it is done as Thou hast commanded, and yet there is room," He said to them, "Go out into the highways and hedges, and compel them to come in." In those, therefore, who were first brought in with gentleness, the former obedience is fulfilled; but *in those who were compelled, the disobedience is avenged* (*Correction of the Donatists*, 6.24).

Let compulsion be found outside, the will will arise within. Whom thou shalt find wait not till they choose to come, compel them to come in (*Sermons on the New Testament: LXII*, 8).

God's grace is irresistible

Great indeed is the help of the grace of God, so that He turns our heart in whatever direction He pleases. But according to this writer's foolish opinion, however great the help may be, we deserve it all at the moment when, without any assistance beyond the liberty of our will, we hasten to the Lord, desire His guidance and direction, suspend our own will entirely on His, and by close adherence to Him become one spirit with Him. Now all these vast courses of goodness we (according to him) accomplish, forsooth, simply by the freedom of our own free will; and by reason of such antecedent merits we so secure His grace, that *He turns our heart which way soever He pleases* (*On the Grace of Christ*, 24).

God makes the unwilling willing

We read in Holy Scripture, both that God's mercy 'shall meet me,' and that His mercy 'shall follow me.' *It goes before the unwilling to make him willing;* it follows the willing to make his will effectual. *Why are we taught to pray for our enemies, who are plainly unwilling to lead a holy life, unless that God may work willingness in them?* And why are we ourselves taught to ask that we may receive, unless that He who has created in us the wish, may Himself satisfy the wish? (*Enchiridion*, 32).

God's initial grace operative without our free will

He operates, therefore, without us, in order that we may will; but when we will, and so will that we may act, He cooperates with us. We can, however, ourselves do nothing to effect good works of piety without Him either working that we may will, or co-working when we will. *Now, concerning His working that we may will, it is said: "It is God which worketh in you, even to will."* While of His co-working with us, when we will and act by willing, the apostle says, "We know that in all things there is co-working for good to them that love God" (*On Grace and Free Will*, 33).

God creates a new heart in unbelievers

... We should remember that He says, 'Make you a new heart and a new spirit,' who also promises, '*I will give you a new heart*, and a new spirit will I put within you.' How is it, then, that He who says, 'Make you,' also says, 'I will give you'? Why does He command, if He is to give? *Why does He give if man is to make, except it be that He gives what He commands when He helps him to obey whom he commands?* ... (*On Grace and Free Will*, 31).

Even the free action to accept salvation is given by God

And further, should any one be inclined to boast, not indeed of his works, but of the freedom of his will, as if the first merit belonged to him, *this very liberty of good action being given to him as a reward he had earned*, let him listen to this same preacher of grace, when he says: "For it is God which worketh in you, both to will and to do of His own good pleasure" (*Enchiridion*, 32).

We cannot will good without God's grace

Therefore, when the will turns from the good and does evil, it does so by the freedom of its own choice, but when *it turns from evil and does good, it does so only with the help of God* (*City of God*, 15.21).

"All men" in 1 Timothy 2:4–6 means only all whom He wills

Accordingly, when we hear and read in Scripture that He "will have all men to be saved," although we know well that all men are not saved, we are not on that account to restrict the omnipotence of God, but are rather to understand the Scripture, "*Who will have all men to be saved*," *as meaning that no man is saved unless God wills his salvation: not that there is no man whose salvation He does not will, but that no man is saved apart from His will*; and that, therefore, we should pray to Him to will our salvation, because if He wills it, it must necessarily be accomplished (*Enchiridion*, 103; cf. 97).

" 'He wills all men to be saved,' is so said that *all the predestined may be understood by it, because every kind of man is among them*" (*On Rebuke and Grace*, 44).

Matthew 23:37 doesn't mean God wants all to be saved

Our Lord says plainly, however, in the Gospel, when up-braiding the impious city: "How often would I have gathered thy children together; even as a hen gathereth her chickens under her wings, and ye would not!" *as if the will of God had been overcome by the will of men. . . . But even though she was unwilling, He gathered together as many of her children as He wished: for He does not will some things and do them, and will others and do them not;* but "He hath done all that He pleased in heaven and in earth" (*Enchiridion,* 97).

John 1:9 doesn't mean God enlightens everyone

And on the same principle we interpret the expression in the Gospel: "The true light which lighteth every man that cometh into the world;" *not that there is no man who is not enlightened, but that no man is enlightened except by Him* (*Enchiridion,* 103).

God can change evil wills whenever He wants

And, moreover, *who will be so foolish and blasphemous as to say that God cannot change the evil wills of men, whichever; whenever; and wheresoever He chooses, and direct them to what is good?* But when He does this, He does it of mercy; when He does it not, it is of justice that He does it not; for "He hath mercy on whom He will have mercy, and whom He will He hardeneth" (*Enchiridion,* 98).

Note: It is interesting to note that in spite of the hardened and coercive nature of God's acts on human beings affirmed in Augustine's later writings, he still held to the belief that unsaved persons possessed the power of free choice. For example: "It is He who when He foreknew that man would in his turn sin by abandoning God and breaking His law, *did not deprive him of the power of free will,* because He at the same time foresaw what good He Himself would bring out of the evil . . ." (*City of God,* 22.1). Of course, as extreme Calvinists argue, this power is for all practical purposes inoperative in fallen man. So the question is whether this freedom is genuine or merely circumstantial.

In heaven we are not free to sin

The souls in bliss will still possess the freedom of will, though sin will have no power to tempt them. They will be more free than ever—so free, in fact, from all delight in sinning as to find, in not sinning, an unfailing source of joy. . . . *Freedom is that more potent freedom which makes all sin impossible* (*City of God*, 22.30).

VISIBLE PROBLEMS: CONTRASTING THE EARLY AND LATE AUGUSTINE

There are many contrasts between the early and late Augustine that bear on the origin of extreme Calvinism. The essential ones can be summarized as follows:

Early Augustine	Late Augustine
God Wills All to Be Saved	God Wills Only Some to Be Saved
God Never Compels Free Will	God Compels Free Will
God Loves All	God Loves Only Some
Faith Is Not a Special Gift to Some	Faith Is a Special Gift to Some
Fallen Men Can Receive Salvation	Fallen Men Cannot Receive Salvation

There are, of course, several problems with the later position of Augustine. First, it involves, in practice, a denial of human free choice. As Augustine himself stated earlier, *"he that is willing is free from compulsion. . . ."*[3] For in the final analysis, man has no choice in his own salvation. As Jonathan Edwards held, "free choice" is doing what we desire, but it is God who gives the desire. But since God only gives the desire to some (not all), this leads to the dilemma of extreme Calvinism: either God is not omnibenevolent or universalism is tenable.

THE PAINFUL DILEMMA OF EXTREME CALVINISM

Extreme Calvinists cannot hold all the following premises:

(1) God can do anything He wills, including save all He wills to save.

(2) God wills only to save some persons (the elect), not all.

(3) God is all-loving, that is, He loves all persons.

[3]St. Augustine, *Two Souls, Against the Manichaeans* 10.14, quoted in Norman L. Geisler, *What Augustine Says* (Grand Rapids, Mich.: Baker, 1982), 158.

Yet extreme Calvinists cannot and do not deny (1) or (2). Therefore, they must deny that (3) God is all-loving. For if God were all-loving, then He would do what He could do, namely, save everyone. Since He does not do that, then He must not be all-loving.

The problem can be stated as follows:

(1) If God is all-powerful, then He could save all persons.

(2) If God is all-loving, then He would save all persons.

But according to extreme Calvinism:

(3) God is all-powerful;

(4) God will not save all persons.

(5) Therefore, God is not all-loving.

If an all-powerful God *can* save all, but He *will not* save all, then God is not all-loving. For a God who is all-loving would save all, if He could save all.

AVOIDING THE DILEMMA BY MODERATE CALVINISM

The only way to avoid this conclusion is to say that (1) even an all-powerful God cannot do what is impossible, and (2) it is impossible to force free creatures to act contrary to their freedom. This is the moderate Calvinistic view.

EXTREME CALVINISTS' MISUNDERSTANDING OF AUGUSTINE

R. C. Sproul admits that "at times Augustine seems to deny all freedom to the will of fallen man. In the *Enchiridion*, for example, he writes: '. . . when man by his own free-will sinned, then sin being victorious over him, the freedom of his will was lost' " (chapter 30).[4] Yet he acknowledges that elsewhere Augustine said, " 'there is . . . always within us a free will—but it is not always good,' " for " 'it is either free from righteousness when it serves sin—and then it is evil—or else it is free from sin when it serves righteousness—and then it is good' " (*On Grace and Free Will*, chapter 31).

Brushing aside the view that the later Augustine hardened his view against free will, Sproul attempts to reconcile these by making a distinction between liberty and free will. He argues that the former is lost in the Fall but the latter is not. "For Augustine the sin-

---

[4]Sproul, *Willing to Believe*, 63.

ner is both free and in bondage at the same time, but not in the same sense. He is free to act according to his own desires, but his desires are only evil. . . . This corruption greatly affects the will, but it does not destroy it as a faculty of choosing."[5]

However, Sproul's explanation fails for several important reasons. First, the early Augustine admitted free will of fallen humans in the sense of the uncoerced ability to do otherwise (see appendix 4), which Augustine later gave up. Second, Sproul's explanation of freedom being reduced to desire does not work. For one thing, it makes God responsible for the free choice of Lucifer and Adam to sin. Also, it is a clear case of double-speaking, for while it denies that God coerces free acts on the one hand, on the other hand it is forced to admit that God gives the desire to love him by regenerating them contrary to free choice. Finally, the idea that God regenerates only some, when He could regenerate all, destroys our belief in His omnibenevolence. Thus, Sproul violates his own charge that "any view of human will that destroys the biblical view of human responsibility is seriously defective." And "any view of the human will that destroys the biblical view of God's character is even worse."[6]

---

[5]Ibid.
[6]Ibid., 29.

APPENDIX FOUR

ANSWERING OBJECTIONS TO FREE WILL

DEFINITION OF FREE WILL

Much, if not most, of the problem in discussing "free will" is that the term is defined differently by various persons in the dispute. As explained in chapter 2, logically there are only three basic views: self-determinism (self-caused actions), determinism (acts caused by another), and indeterminism (acts with no cause whatsoever). Indeterminism is a violation of the law of causality that every event has a cause, and determinism is a violation of free will, since the moral agent is not causing his own actions.

There are, of course, several varieties of self-determinism. Some contend that all moral acts must be free only from all external influence. Others insist they must be free from both external and internal influence, that is, truly neutral. But they all have in common that, whatever influence there may be on the will,[1] the agent could have done otherwise. That is, they could have chosen the opposite course of action.

---

[1] The Bible makes it evident that there are divine influences on the human will both before and after conversion (Rom. 2:4; Phil. 2:13).

SOME PHILOSOPHICAL OBJECTIONS TO SELF-DETERMINISM

Moral and spiritual self-determination, the ability to choose the opposite, has come under several criticisms. The first has to do with the principle of causality.

Self-determinism violates the principle of causality

The principle of causality holds that every event has an adequate cause. If this is so, then it would seem that even the act of free choice has a cause and so on back to God (or infinity). In any case, if the act of free choice is caused by another, then it cannot be caused by one's self. Thus self-determination would be contrary to the principle of causality that it embraces.

Response

There is a basic confusion in this objection. This confusion results in part from an infelicitous expression of the self-determinism view. Representatives of moral self-determinism sometimes speak of free will as though it were the *efficient* cause of moral actions. This would lead one naturally to ask: What is the cause of the act of free choice, and so on? But a more precise description of the process of a free act would avoid this problem. Technically, free will is not the efficient cause of a free act; it is simply the power through which the agent performs the free act. *I* (my Self) act *by means of* my will. The *efficient* cause of a free act is really the free *agent*, not the free choice. Free choice is simply the power by which the free agent acts. We do not say that person *is* free choice but simply that he *has* free choice. Likewise, we do not say man *is* thought but only that he *has* the power of thought. So it is not the power of free choice that causes a free act, but the *person* who has this power.

Now, if the real cause of a free act is not an *act* but an *actor*, then it makes no sense to ask for the cause of the actor as though it were another act. The cause of a performance is the *performer*. Likewise, the cause of a free act is not another free act, and so on. Rather, it is a free agent. And once we have arrived at the free agent, it is meaningless to ask what caused its free acts. For if something else caused its actions, then the agent is not the cause of them and thus is not responsible for them. The free moral *agent* is the cause of free moral actions. And it is as senseless to ask what caused the free agent to act as it is to ask: Who made God? The answer is the same in both cases: Nothing can cause the first cause because it is first.

There is nothing before the first. Likewise, a person is the first cause of his own moral actions. If he were not the cause of his own free actions, then they would not be *his* actions.

If it is insisted that a person cannot be the first cause of his moral actions, then it is also impossible for God (who is also a Person) to be the first cause of His moral actions. Tracing the cause of human actions back to God does not solve the problem of finding a cause for every action. It simply pushes the problem back further. Sooner or later those proposing this argument will have to admit that a free act is a self-determined act that is not caused by another. Eventually it must be acknowledged that all acts come from an actor, but that the actor (i.e., free agent) is the first cause of his action, and who, therefore, has no prior cause of his actions.

The real question, then, is not whether there are agents who cause their own actions but whether God is the only true Agent (i.e., Person) in the universe. Christians have always denounced as a form of pantheism the belief that there is ultimately only one Person (Agent) in the universe. But a denial of human free agency is reducible to this charge.

Self-determinism leads to uncaused events

It is objected that if we say that human actions are not caused, then we have admitted that there are uncaused events in the universe! If so, this would be a violation of the principle of causality.

Response

This charge is based on a misunderstanding of the difference between uncaused and self-caused actions. The moral self-determinist does not claim there are any uncaused moral actions. He, in fact, believes all moral actions are caused by moral agents. But unlike the moral determinist who believes all human acts are caused by another (e.g., by God), the self-determinist believes that ultimately there are more selves (agents) than God who cause actions. Either way, the self-determinist believes that there is a cause for every moral action and that the cause is a moral agent, whether it is God or some other moral creature.

Self-determinism is contradictory

It is further objected that self-determined acts are a contradiction in terms. For are not self-determined actions self-caused? And is it not impossible to cause one's self?

Response

Here again there is a confusion of act and actor. It is true that no actor (agent) can cause itself to exist, for a cause is ontologically prior to its effect. And one cannot be prior to himself; therefore, a self-caused *being* (actor) is impossible. However, a self-caused *action* is not impossible, since the actor (cause) must be prior to its action (effect). So self-caused *being* is impossible, but self-caused *becoming* is not. We determine what we will become *morally*. But God determines what we are *ontologically* (i.e., in our being). So while man cannot cause his own *being*, he can cause his own moral *behavior*.

Perhaps some of the confusion could be cleared away if we did not speak of self-determinism as though one were determining his *Self*. For moral self-determinism does not refer to the determination *of* one's Self but determination *by* one's self. So it would be more proper not to speak of a *self-caused* action but of an action *caused by one's Self*. Yet even without this distinction, there is a significant difference between a self-caused *being* and a self-caused *action*. The former is clearly impossible but the latter is not. For a being cannot be prior to itself, but an actor must be prior to his action.

Self-determined actions are contrary to God's foreknowledge

Traditional theists, both Calvinists and Arminians, hold that God knows infallibly all that will come to pass. But how can this be, if there are free creatures? It is not difficult to understand how God can bring about a necessary end through *necessary* means (such as determining in advance that the last domino in a falling series will drop, too). But how can God bring about a necessary end through *contingent* means (such as free choice)?

Response

The answer lies in the fact that God knows—for sure—(infallibly) precisely how everyone will use his freedom. So, from the vantage point of His omniscience, the act is totally determined. Yet from the standpoint of our freedom it is not determined. God knows *for sure* what we will *freely* do. Both Augustine (see *City of God*, 5.9) and Aquinas (*Summa Theologica*, 1a, 14, 4) answered this way. This is not to deny that God uses *persuasive* means to convince us to choose in the way that He desires. It is only to deny that God ever uses *coercive* means to do so.

Self-determinism is contrary to God's grace

The Bible teaches that all the regenerate (justified) will ultimately be saved (see chapter 7). None shall perish (John 10:26–30) or ever be separated from Christ (Rom. 8:36–39). Indeed, all believers are in Christ (2 Cor. 5:17; Eph. 1:4) and are part of His body (1 Cor. 12:13). Hence, if any were severed from Christ, then part of Christ would have to be severed from Himself! Man can be faithless to God, but God cannot deny Himself (2 Tim. 2:13). Salvation is not dependent on man but on God, and so it cannot be lost by man. Salvation was not gained by man's will (John 1:13; Rom. 9:16); therefore, it cannot be lost by it. Salvation is totally of grace, not of works, lest anyone should boast (Eph. 2:8–9).

Response

If salvation is conditioned wholly on God's grace and not on man's will, then how can man's free choice play any part in his salvation? The answer to this question is found in an important distinction between two senses of the word "condition." There are no conditions for God's *giving* of salvation; it is wholly of grace. But there is one (and only one) condition for *receiving* this gift—true saving faith.

There is absolutely nothing *in man* that is the basis for God saving him. But there was something *in God* (love) that is the basis for man's salvation. It was not because of any merit in man but only because of grace in God that salvation was initiated toward man. Man does not *initiate* salvation (Rom. 3:11), and he cannot *attain* it (Rom. 4:5). But he can and must *receive* it (John 1:12). Salvation is an unconditional act of God's election. Man's faith is not a condition for God *giving* salvation, but it is for man *receiving* it. Nonetheless, the act of faith (free choice) by which man receives salvation is not meritorious. It is the *Giver* who gets credit for the gift, not the receiver.

Why, then, does one person go to heaven and another not? Because God willed that all who receive His grace will be saved and that all who reject it will be lost. And since God knew infallibly just who this would be, both the elect and non-elect were determined from all eternity. And this determination was not based on anything in man, including their free choice. Rather, it was determined on God's choice to save all who would accept His unconditional grace.

THE DEGREE OF INFLUENCE ALLOWED

The degree of influence self-determinists acknowledge as to free actions will vary according to their accepted degree of "Calvinism" or "Arminianism." The maximum allowable for a self-determinist is high persuasion short of coercion. The minimum is zero.

The scale of "persuasion allowed" ranges as follows:

- No influence allowed—Pelagian (no grace needed)
- Some influence allowed—Semi-Pelagianism (some grace needed)
- Much influence allowed—Arminianism (much grace needed)
- Great influence allowed—Moderate Calvinism (great grace needed; irresistible grace on the willing allowed)
- Overwhelming influence allowed—Extreme Calvinism (irresistible grace on the unwilling needed)

Some illustrations of acceptable and unacceptable influence will help make the point. If one decides to sit on his front porch where he can view the mountains, and hornets come and chase him inside, this last was not a truly free choice. He was coerced into doing it. If one proposes to a lover and is turned down, yet continues to court and woo her, this is compatible with free choice. However, if he attempts to force her to love him against her will, this is not love. If one is offered a dangerous job for $40,000 a year and turns it down, yet later accepts the same job for $80,000 a year, this is acceptable influence.

What about an "offer that is too good to refuse"? Is this compatible with a self-determinist's view of free will? Say that one is offered $100 million a year for doing a job he hates. Is this not too good to refuse, and would not the acceptance of such an offer be a violation of self-determinism? The answer is no, since there is no coercion involved. He could have turned it down. Take as an example a wife who lives such a pure life that she would not even consider being unfaithful to her husband for $100 million or more. The fact that an attractive male offers her $100 million to commit adultery with him is in no way coercive. The faithful wife may be highly tempted, but she still has the power to say NO.

No matter how tempting or how persuasive an overture may be, as long as it is not coercive of the will, the act is still free. Again, just how much influence, both of sin and grace, is appropriate will have to be settled by other doctrines, particularly, how depraved human beings are. But no matter what the influence, either for evil or good, a self-determinist's view of free will demands that the act is not coerced, whether externally or internally. This is in accord with what both good reason and a proper understanding of Scripture teach (see chapters 2, 3, and 6, and appendices 1 and 9).

APPENDIX FIVE

IS FAITH A GIFT ONLY TO THE ELECT?

Along with the other elements of the extreme Calvinists' T-U-L-I-P (see chapters 4 and 5) is the belief that faith is a gift of God given only to a select group of people (the elect). The famous Calvinistic *Canons of Dort* (1619; see appendix 8) uses Ephesians 2:8–9 to prove this point. Louis Berkof declared that "the seed of faith is implanted in man in regeneration."[1]

The belief that faith is a special gift of God fits with the extreme Calvinist understanding of total depravity and the need for regeneration prior to faith (see appendix 10). A dead person cannot believe, they insist; he must first be made alive by God and given the faith to believe.[2] Objections against this view have already been set forth (see

---

[1] Louis Berkof, *Systematic Theology*, 2nd ed. (Grand Rapids, Mich.: Wm. B. Eerdmans Publishing Co., 1977), 503.

[2] Commenting on John 6:44, Calvin himself said, "Faith does not depend on the will of men, but that it is God who gives it." He adds, "He [Paul] does not say that the power of choosing aright is bestowed upon us, and that we have afterwards to make our own choice. . . ." But "he says that we are God's work, and that everything good in us is His creation. . . . Whoever, then, makes the very smallest claim for man, apart from the grace of God, allows him to that extent ability to procure salvation" (Calvin, "Comments on Eph. 2:10" in *Calvin's Commentaries: The Epistles of Paul the Apostle to the Galatians, Ephesians, Philippians, and Colossians*, trans. T. H. L. Parker, and eds. David W. Torrance and Thomas F. Torrance [Grand Rapids, Mich.: Wm. B. Eerdmans Publishing Co., 1979]). Calvin seems to confuse the *source* of salvation, which is absolutely God, and the *receiver* of salvation, who is man. Of course, we cannot do anything to "procure" our own salvation, but we can receive it as a gift from God, namely, we can believe (cf. John 1:12; 3:16). And believing is not a work in any meritorious sense of the word.

chapter 4). It remains here to show that verses used by extreme Calvinists to support their contentions are misinterpreted.[3]

SAVING FAITH IS NOT A SPECIAL GIFT OF GOD TO THE ELECT

Ephesians 2:8–9

"For it is by grace you have been saved, through faith—and this not from yourselves, *it* is the gift of God—not by works, so that no one can boast." Extreme Calvinists often take the "it" here to refer to "faith," mentioned just before this. Indeed, this reference was used by the Calvinistic Synod of Dort (see appendix 8) to prove this very point. Zealous defender of extreme Calvinism R. C. Sproul is so confident that this is what the text means that he triumphantly concludes: "This passage should seal the matter forever. The faith by which we are saved is a gift of God."[4]

Response

But even John Calvin said of this text that "he does not mean that *faith* is the gift of God, but that *salvation* is given to us by God, or, that we obtain it by the gift of God."[5] In addition, however plausible this interpretation may seem in English, it is very clear from the Greek that Ephesians 2:8–9 is not referring to faith as a gift from God. For the "it" (*touto*) is neuter in form and cannot refer to "faith" (*pistis*), which is feminine. The antecedent of "it is the gift of God" is the salvation by grace through faith (v. 9). Commenting on this passage, the great New Testament Greek scholar A. T. Robertson noted: " 'Grace' is God's part, 'faith' ours. *And that* [it] (*kai touto*). Neuter, not feminine *taute*, and so refers not to *pistis* [faith] or to *charis* [grace] (feminine also), but to the act of being saved by grace conditioned on faith on our part."[6]

While some have argued that a pronoun may agree in sense, but not in form, with its antecedent, this view is refuted by Gregory Sapaugh, who notes that "if Paul wanted to refer to *pistis* ('faith'), he could have written the feminine *haute*, instead of the neuter, *touto*, and his meaning would have been clear." But he did not. Rather, by the

---

[3]For a brief but solid discussion of this topic, see Roy Aldrich, "The Gift of God," *Bibliotheca Sacra* (July–September 1965): 248–53.
[4]See Sproul, *Chosen by God*, 119.
[5]See Calvin, *Calvin's Commentaries*, vol. 11, 145, emphasis mine.
[6]See A. T. Robertson, *Word Pictures in the New Testament*, (Nashville: Broadman Press, 1930; reprint, New York: R. R. Smith, Inc., 1931), 4:525.

"it" (*touto*) Paul refers to the whole process of "salvation by grace through faith." Sapaugh notes that "this position is further supported by the parallelism between *ouk hymon* ('and this not of yourselves') in 2:8 and *ouk ex ergon* ('not of works') in 2:9. The latter phrase would not be meaningful if it referred to *pisteos* ('faith'). Instead, it clearly means salvation is 'not of works.' "[7]

Philippians 1:29

"For it has been granted to you on behalf of Christ not only to believe on him, but also to suffer for him. . . ." This is taken to mean that faith is a gift of God to certain persons, namely, the ones who are elect.

Response

There are several indications here that Paul had no such thing in mind. First, the point is simply that God has not only provided us with the opportunity to trust Him but also to suffer for Him. The word "granted" (Greek: *echaristhe*) means "grace" or "favor." That is, both the opportunity to suffer for Him and to believe on Him are favors with which God has graced us. Further, Paul is not speaking here of initial faith that brings salvation but of the daily faith and daily suffering of someone who is already Christian. Finally, it is noteworthy that both the suffering and the believing are presented as things that we are to do. He says it is granted for "you" to do this. It was not something God did for them. Both were simply an opportunity God gave them to use "on the behalf of Christ" by their free choice.

Philippians 3:8–9

Paul prayed: "That I may gain Christ and be found in him, not having a righteousness of my own that comes from the law, but that which is through faith in Christ—the righteousness *that comes from God and is by faith.*"

Response

Here it is not faith that comes from God but "righteousness." And the righteousness from God comes to us "by faith," namely, by the exercise of our faith.

---

[7] See Gregory Sapaugh, "Is Faith a Gift? A Study of Ephesians 2:8," *Journal of the Grace Evangelical Society* 7, no. 12 (Spring 1994): 39–40.

1 Corinthians 4:7

"What do you have that you did not receive? And if you did receive it, why do you boast as though you did not?" The strong Calvinist insists that if everything we receive is from God, then so is faith.

Response

It should be noted first that the apostle makes no application of this verse to the faith that receives God's gift of salvation. Rather, he is referring to gifts given to believers (cf. 1 Cor. 12:4–11), which should be exercised in humility. There is no thought here of giving faith to unbelievers so that they can be saved. In addition, even if faith for unbelievers had been envisioned here, there is no affirmation that God gives it only to some. What is more, even if faith were a gift, it is something we must "receive" or reject. It is not something forced on us. Finally, the uniform presentation of Scripture is that faith is something unbelievers are to exercise to receive salvation (e.g., John 3:16, 18, 36; Acts 16:31), and not something they must wait upon God to give them.

1 Corinthians 7:25

"I give my judgment, as one that hath obtained mercy of the Lord to be faithful" (KJV). St. Augustine used this verse (*Enchiridion*, 31) to support his belief that faith is a gift of God prior to regeneration.

Response

In actual fact this verse is not speaking about unsaved persons (the elect) receiving faith unto salvation but of believers receiving mercy from God that enables them to be faithful. Yet it is only by a prior act of our faith that we become believers in the first place (John 1:12; Eph. 2:8–9). In fact, this verse is speaking about believing virgins having the grace to remain faithful sexually. The quote begins: "Now concerning virgins I have no commandment of the Lord." The NIV captures the meaning: "Now about virgins: I have no command from the Lord, but I give a judgment as one who by the Lord's mercy is trustworthy."

1 Corinthians 12:8–9

"To one *there is given* through the Spirit the message of wisdom, to another the message of knowledge by means of the same Spirit, to another *faith* by the same Spirit. . . ." It is evident that faith is spoken of here as a gift of God.

Response

To be sure, faith *is* referred to here as a gift from God. However, Paul is not talking about faith given to *unbelievers* by which they can be *saved*. Rather, it is speaking of a special gift of faith given to some *believers* by which they can *serve* (cf. vv. 5, 12). One can plainly see the difference by looking at the context.

Acts 5:31

" 'God exalted him to his own right hand as Prince and Savior that *he might give repentance* and forgiveness of sins to Israel.' " This is supposed to support the extreme Calvinists' contention that repentance is a gift only to the elect. Second Timothy 2:25 adds that we "must gently instruct, in the hope that *God will grant them repentance* leading them to a knowledge of the truth" (cf. Acts 11:18).

Response

First of all, the contention is that according to these verses repentance is a gift in the same sense that forgiveness is a gift, since they are tied together. If this is so, then all Israel must have been saved, since both were given "to Israel." But only a remnant of Israel will be saved (Rom. 9:27), not all. The same clarification is true of Acts 11:18, which says, " 'God has granted even the Gentiles repentance unto life.' " This clearly does not mean that all Gentiles will be saved but that all have the opportunity to be saved. Likewise, it means that all have the God-given opportunity to repent (cf. 2 Peter 3:9).

Second, the *opportunity* to repent is a gift of God. He graciously allows us the opportunity to turn from our sins, *but we must do the repenting*. God is not going to repent for us. Repentance is an act of our will supported and encouraged by His grace.

Further, if repentance is a gift, then it is a gift in the same sense that forgiveness is a gift. But forgiveness was obtained by Jesus on the Cross for "everyone who believes" (Acts 13:38–39), not just for the elect (see chapters 4 and 5). Hence, by the same logic, all men must have been given saving faith—a conclusion emphatically rejected by extreme Calvinists.

John 6:44–45

" 'No one can come to me unless the Father who sent me draws him, and I will raise him up at the last day. It is written in the Prophets: "They will all be taught by God." Everyone who listens to the Father and learns from him comes to me.' "

Response

It should be observed that it does not say here that faith is a gift of God. It merely says that they were "taught" by God. The method of obtaining faith is not mentioned. The Bible says elsewhere that "faith comes by hearing, and hearing by the word of God" (Rom. 10:17 NKJV). Faith grows in the heart of the one who "receives it [the Word] with joy" (Matt. 13:20).

Acts 16:14

"One of those listening was a woman named Lydia, a dealer in purple cloth from the city of Thyatira, who was a worshiper of God. *The Lord opened her heart to respond* to Paul's message." Acts 18:27 adds that salvation is "to those *who by grace had believed.*" Without this gracious work of God, no one would believe and be saved.

Response

Moderate Calvinists do not deny that God moves upon the hearts of unbelievers to persuade and prompt them to exercise faith in Christ. They only deny that God does this coercively by irresistible grace (see chapters 4 and 5) and that He only does it on some persons (the elect). The Holy Spirit is convicting "the world [*all men*, not just some; cf. John 3:16–18; 1 John 2:15–17] of sin, righteousness, and judgment" (John 16:8). And God does not force anyone to believe in Him (Matt. 23:37).

Romans 10:17

"Consequently, faith comes from hearing the message, and the message is heard through the word of Christ." Here it would appear that faith is produced in a person by the Word of God; the Word of God is prior to faith, not the reverse.

Response

First of all, there is no reference here to faith as a gift. That is an assumption that has to be read into the text. Second, the order of events is sending, preaching, hearing the Word of God, believing, calling on (Rom. 10:14–15). But it does not affirm that in every case the prior is the cause of the latter. For not everyone who is sent goes. And not everyone who hears the Word of God believes to salvation (cf. Matt. 13:19). Again, consider Acts 16:14: It is true that God opened Lydia's heart to believe, but (1) she did the believing, and (2) God didn't open her heart against her will. Finally, whatever role the

Word of God has in prompting saving faith, the faith must come from us, for the context says faith is something we are called upon to do. Paul says, "If *you* ... believe in your heart that God raised him [Christ] from the dead, you will be saved" (Rom. 10:9). For "it is with *your heart* that *you believe* ... and are saved" (10:10).

Romans 12:3

"For by the grace given me I say to every one of you: Do not think of yourself more highly than you ought, but rather think of yourself with sober judgment, *in accordance with the measure of faith God has given you.*"

Response

Paul is speaking to believers (1:7; 12:1–2), not to or about un-believers. This is not the faith that unbelievers exercise for salvation (Acts 16:31); it is a special gift of faith given to some believers. Paul lists it among the gifts of the Spirit in 1 Corinthians 12.

1 Peter 1:21

"*Through him you believe* in God, who raised him [Christ] from the dead and glorified him, and so your faith and hope are in God."

Response

The phrase "through Him you believe" does not necessarily mean that faith is a gift of God. It simply means that apart from Christ we would never have come to believe. As A. T. Robertson renders it, "Who through him are believers in God."[8] Ellicott comments, "It is in that same God that *you have been led thereby to believe.*"[9] There is no affirmation here, or anywhere else in the Bible, that God gives faith unto salvation only to a select few.

2 Peter 1:1

"Simon Peter, a servant and apostle of Jesus Christ, *To those who* through the righteousness of our God and Savior Jesus Christ *have received a faith* as precious as ours."

Response

Peter claims only that they have "received" or "obtained" (NKJV) their faith, but does not inform us as to exactly how they got it.

---

[8]Robertson, *Word Pictures in the New Testament*, vol. VI, 91.
[9]See Charles John Ellicott, *Ellicott's Commentary on the Whole Bible*, vol. VIII (Grand Rapids, Mich.: Zondervan, 1954), 397, emphasis mine.

Using such a vague, undefined statement as this to support their belief only demonstrates how desperate the extreme Calvinists are to find support of this unscriptural dogma.

1 Thessalonians 1:4–6

"For we know, brothers loved by God, that he has chosen you, because *our gospel came to you* not simply with words, but also *with power*, with the Holy Spirit and *with deep conviction. . . .* You became imitators of us and of the Lord; in spite of severe suffering, you welcomed the message with the joy given by the Holy Spirit."

Response

It should be plain to anyone who examines this text that it says nothing about faith being a gift of God only to the elect. For starters, neither "faith" nor "gift" is present in the text. Further, the gospel is "the power of God *to those who believe*" (Rom. 1:16). Or, as the text here points out, it is God's power to those who "*welcomed*" it. Finally, here again it is faith that precedes salvation, not salvation preceding faith.

TWO IMPORTANT POINTS

Even if it could be demonstrated from Scripture—and none of these texts do this—that faith for salvation is a gift of God, there are still some crucial problems with the extreme Calvinists' view on the matter.

First, salvation involves "gifts" that *must be received* or rejected.[10] John wrote, "He came to that which was his own, but his own *did not receive* him. Yet to all who *received* him, to those who believed in his name, *he gave* the right to become children of God" (John 1:11–12).[11]

---

[10]Contrary to popular belief, Arminius was so "Calvinistic" that he held that grace is absolutely necessary for bestowing salvation; nonetheless, an act of free will is necessary for receiving it. He wrote, " 'What then,' you ask, 'does Free Will do?' I reply with brevity, 'It saves.' Take away Free Will, and nothing will be left to be saved: Take away Grace, and nothing will be left as the source of salvation. . . . No one, except God, is able to bestow salvation; and nothing, except Free Will, is capable of receiving it" (*The Works of James Arminius: The London Edition,* 2.196, 11; reprint, *The Writings of James Arminius,* trans. James Nichols and W. R. Bagnall [Grand Rapids, Mich.: Baker Book House, 1956]).

[11]Sproul succinctly describes extreme Calvinism by contrast: "To receive the gift of faith, according to Calvinism, the sinner also must stretch out his hand. But he does so only because God has so changed the disposition of his heart that he will most certainly stretch out his hand. By the irresistible work of grace, he will do nothing else except stretch out his hand" (Sproul, *Willing to Believe,* 133–34). But "irresistible" means this condition is forced upon, and few have seen that *forced freedom is a contradiction in terms.*

Second, if faith is a gift from God, then it is offered to all men, not only some. "For God so loved *the world* that He gave His only begotten Son . . ." (John 3:16). Christ "is the atoning sacrifice for our sins, and not only for ours but also *for the sins of the whole world*" (1 John 2:2). God is not willing that any should perish but that all should repent (2 Peter 3:9). Numerous other passages affirm that Christ's atonement is unlimited in its extent (see appendix 6).

SAVING FAITH IS SOMETHING ALL CAN EXERCISE

Nowhere does the Bible teach that saving faith is a special gift of God only to a select few. Further, everywhere the Bible assumes that anyone who wills to be saved can exercise saving faith.[12] Every passage where the Scriptures call upon unbelievers to believe or repent to be saved implies this truth. A few familiar passages will suffice to make the point:

Luke 13:3—" 'But unless you repent, you too will all perish.' "

John 3:16—" 'For God so loved the world that he gave his one and only Son, that *whoever believes* in him shall not perish but have eternal life.' "

John 3:18—" '*Whoever believes* in him is not condemned, but whoever does not believe stands condemned already because he has not believed in the name of God's one and only Son.' "

John 6:29—"Jesus answered and said unto them, 'This is the work of God, that *ye believe* on him whom he hath sent' " (KJV).[13]

John 11:40—" 'Did I not tell you that if *you believed*, you would see the glory of God?' "

John 12:36—" 'Put *your trust* in the light while you have it, so that you may become sons of light.' "

Acts 16:31—" '*Believe* in the Lord Jesus, and you will be saved— you and your household.' "

Acts 17:30—" 'In the past God overlooked such ignorance, but now he *commands all people everywhere to repent.*' "

Acts 20:21—" 'I have declared to both Jews and Greeks that *they must turn to God in repentance and have faith* in our Lord Jesus.' "

---

[12]Contrary to insistence of the extreme Calvinists (see Sproul, *Willing to Believe*, 99), this is not merely a "possible" inference but a natural and reasonable one. For it would be unreasonable to condemn someone for not doing something it was impossible for him to do either by himself or with God's help.

[13]"Believing" is not actually a work. Jesus uses the word "work" of faith in an ironic sense to respond to the Jews' preceding question, "What shall we do, that we might work the works of God?"

Hebrews 11:6—"And without faith it is impossible to please God, because *anyone who comes* to him *must believe* that he exists and that he rewards those who earnestly seek him." There are numerous other Scriptures that affirm the same truth (cf. Rom. 3:22; 4:11, 24; 10:9, 14; 1 Cor. 1:21; Gal. 3:22; Eph. 1:16; 1 Thess. 1:7; 4:14; 1 Tim. 1:16).

Finally, the Bible describes faith as *ours* and not God's. It speaks of *"your* faith" (Luke 7:50), *"his* faith" (Rom. 4:5), and *"their* faith" (Matt. 9:2), but never of *"God's* faith."

EXERCISING FAITH IS NOT A MERITORIOUS WORK

The dispute here is not over whether or not salvation is based on works. All orthodox Protestants believe that salvation is *not* based on works. The question is whether an act of "faith" on man's part constitutes a meritorious work. A negative answer to this is supported by both Scripture and good reason.

First of all, faith is clearly contrasted and opposed to works in the Bible. The Bible constantly places faith in opposition to works, as is evident in the passages just cited and many more (cf., e.g., Rom. 3:26–27; Gal. 3:11). Romans 4:4 affirms that "when a man works, his wages are not credited to him as a gift, but as an obligation." It is either faith or works, but not both. Thus, the faith exercised to receive the gift of salvation is not a work. It is the admission that we cannot work for it but must accept it by pure grace.

Furthermore, the act of receiving a gift by faith is not any more meritorious than is that of a beggar receiving a handout. It is a strange logic that asserts that the receiver gets credit for receiving a gift rather than the giver who gives it! The act of faith in receiving God's unconditional gift accrues no merit to the receiver. Rather, all praise and glory goes to the Giver of "every good and perfect gift" (James 1:17).

CAN FAITH NONETHELESS BE CONSIDERED A WORK?

J. I. Packer and O. R. Johnson charge that Reformed Theology condemned Arminianism as being in principle a return to Rome "because in effect it turned faith into a meritorious work...."[14] R. C.

---

[14]J. I. Packer and O. R. Johnson, "Historical and Theological Introduction," in Martin Luther, *The Bondage of the Will*, trans. Henry Cole (Grand Rapids, Mich.: Baker Book House, 1976), 59.

Sproul seems to agree, adding, "The Arminian acknowledges that faith is something a person does. It is a work, though not a meritorious one. Is it a good work? Certainly it is not a bad work. It is good for a person to trust in Christ and in Christ alone for his or her salvation." Thus, "the Arminian finds it difficult to escape the conclusion that ultimately his salvation rests on some righteous act of the will he has performed. He has 'in effect' merited the merit of Christ, which differs only slightly from the view of Rome."[15] This, however, involves an equivocation on the word "do." Faith is something we "do" in the sense that it involves an act of our will prompted by God's grace. However, faith is not something we "do" in the sense of a meritorious work necessary for God to give us salvation.

J. Gresham Machen, himself a strong Calvinist, emphatically denied that faith is a kind of good work: "The faith of man, rightly conceived, can never stand in opposition to the completeness with which salvation depends upon God: it can never mean that man does part while God merely does the rest; for the simple reason that faith consists not in doing something but in receiving something."[16]

RECEIVING A GIFT IS NOT MERITORIOUS

Arminius asked these poignant questions: "A rich man bestows, on a poor and famished beggar, alms by which he may be able to maintain himself and his family. Does it cease to be a pure gift, because the beggar extends his hand to receive it? Can it be said with propriety, that 'the alms depend partly on the liberality of the Donor, and partly on the liberty of the Receiver, though the latter would not have possessed the alms unless he had received it by stretching out his hand?' " He continued: "If these assertions cannot be truly made about a beggar who receives alms, how much less can they be made about the gift of faith, for the receiving of which far more acts of Divine Grace are required!"[17]

---

[15]Sproul, *Chosen by God*, 25–26.
[16]J. Gresham Machen, cited in J. I. Packer, *Fundamentalism and the Word of God* (Grand Rapids, Mich.: Wm. B. Eerdmans Publishing Co., 1958), 172.
[17]Arminius, *Works*, 2.52, article 27.

APPENDIX SIX

BIBLICAL SUPPORT FOR UNLIMITED ATONEMENT

VERSES THAT TEACH *UNLIMITED* ATONEMENT

Not only are there no verses that, properly understood, support limited atonement (see chapter 5), but there are numerous verses that teach unlimited atonement, that is, that Christ died for the sins of all mankind. Extreme Calvinists have not offered any satisfactory interpretations of these texts that support unlimited atonement.

CHRIST IS THE ATONING SACRIFICE FOR THE WHOLE WORLD

The plain meaning of John 1:29

"The next day John saw Jesus coming towards him and said, 'Look, the Lamb of God, *who takes away the sin of the world!*'" In light of the context and other uses of the word "world" in John's gospel, it is evident that the word "world" here does not mean "the church" or "the elect" but all fallen human beings. The apostle records later that "'God so loved the world that He gave His one and only son'" (John 3:16). What is meant by the word "world" is clarified only three verses later: " 'This is the verdict: Light has come into *the world*, but men loved darkness instead of light because *their deeds were evil.*' " This is clearly the whole fallen world, as is John 16:8: "When he [the Holy Spirit] comes, he will convict *the world* of *guilt in regard to sin* and righteousness and judgment."

Implausible interpretation by extreme Calvinists

In light of John's explicit use of the word "world" in salvation passages to mean all fallen human beings, it is painful to watch the contorted logic of extreme Calvinists in response, claiming "that often the Bible uses the words *world* and *all* in a restricted, limited sense," adding "it is clear that *all* is not *all*."[1] Then, in support they cite passages (like Luke 2:1–2) from another book, in another context, used in a geographical (not a redemptive) sense in a futile attempt to prove their point.[2] If "all" does not mean "all" fallen human beings, then what does it mean in Romans 3:23: "*All* have sinned, and come short of the glory of God"? (KJV). Does it mean that only the elect have sinned?

The plain meaning of John 3:16–17

" 'For *God so loved the world that he gave his one and only Son*, that whoever believes in him shall not perish but have eternal life. For God did not send his Son into the *world* to condemn the world, but to save the *world* through him.' "

The clear statement is that God loves the "world," and the clear implication is that Christ was given to die for the world (cf. v. 14). What is more, verse 17 makes it unmistakably clear that "world" here means the whole fallen world, for it is the same world that is under His condemnation (vv. 17–18).

Implausible interpretation by extreme Calvinists

Arguably, the best defense of extreme Calvinism on limited atonement comes from John Owen. His response to this passage is a shocking retranslation to: "God so loved his elect throughout the world, that he gave his Son with this intention, that by him believers might be saved"![3] This needs no response, simply a sober reminder that God repeatedly exhorts us not to add to or subtract from His words (Deut. 4:2; Prov. 30:6; Rev. 22:18–19).

---

[1]Palmer, *The Five Points of Calvinism*, 52.
[2]The attempt to show texts used in a redemptive context where "all" means "only the elect" have failed. See comments on page 203 on 2 Cor. 5:14–19 and elsewhere (chapter 4) on 1 Cor. 15:22.
[3]John Owen, *The Death of Death in the Death of Christ* (Carlisle, Pa.: The Banner of Truth Trust, 1995), 214.

The plain meaning of John 12:47

" 'For *I did not come to judge the world, but to save the world'* " (NASB). It is evident that the word "world" stated in the first part of the verse and in the last part is the same universal fallen, sinful world that will be judged in "the last day" (v. 48).

Implausible interpretation by extreme Calvinists

As elsewhere, extreme Calvinists claim the world is used here in a limited sense, meaning part of the world, namely, the elect. They point to John 12:19 as an illustration of the limited use of the word "world": "The Pharisees said to one another, 'See, this is getting us nowhere. Look how the whole world has gone after him!' "

But this is a false comparison for several reasons. First, the word is used *geographically* in John 12:19, not generically. Second, this is not giving the words of Jesus but those of the Pharisees.[4] Finally, the statement of the Pharisees is obviously an exaggeration or hyperbole. Yet even the extreme Calvinists admit that this is not true of John 12:47, where it is Jesus' statement, and it refers to the whole fallen world generically.[5]

The plain meaning of 1 John 2:2

John writes clearly, "He [Christ] is the atoning sacrifice for our sins, *and not only for ours but also for the sins of the whole world."* This seems so evident that were it not for the skewed claim of extreme Calvinists, no comment would be needed.

Implausible interpretation by extreme Calvinists

The groundless claim of extreme Calvinists is that "world" here refers to "Christian world," namely, to the elect. The later St. Augustine (see appendix 3) said John here "means 'of the world,' all the faithful scattered throughout the whole earth."[6] This is such an obvious case of *eisegesis* (reading into the text) that it does not deserve

---

[4]Likewise, it was not Jesus but His unbelieving brothers who used the word "world" in an exaggerated sense when they said, " 'No one who wants to become a public figure acts in secret. Since you are doing these things, show yourself to the world' " (John 7:4). Here, the phrase "show yourself to the world" is used as a figure of speech meaning to do in "public" and not in "secret," to use the very words of the text.

[5]Paul used the word "world" geographically in Romans 1:8 and in a limited sense in Colossians 1:5–6 (cf. v. 23), but no extreme Calvinist would admit that Paul does not use it generically of the condemnation of the whole human race in Romans 3:19. Why then should they deny it is used in an unlimited sense when referring to providing salvation for the world?

[6]St. Augustine, *Epistle of John:* Homily V, 9, in *A Select Library of the Nicene and Post-Nicene Fathers of the Christian Church,* vol. VII, ed. Philip Schaff (Grand Rapids, Mich.: Wm. B. Eerdmans Publishing Co., 1956), 491.

an extensive treatment. One needs only to make a study of the generic[7] use of the word "world" (*cosmos*) in John's writings to confirm that he speaks here of the fallen, sinful world (cf. John 1:10–11; 3:19). In fact, John defines his use of the term "world" only a few verses later. In the same chapter, he claims Christ's death is a satisfaction for the sins of the "whole world." He says, "Do not love the world or anything in the world. If anyone loves the world, the love of the Father is not in him. For *everything in the world*—the *cravings of sinful man*, the *lust of his eyes* and the *boasting of what he has and does*—comes *not from the Father* but from the world" (2:15–16). This is clearly a description of the fallen, sinful world that includes the non-elect—for whom Christ died (v. 2). Later he adds, "We know that we are children of God, and that *the whole world* is under the control of the evil one" (1 John 5:19). By no stretch of the imagination does this refer only to the elect (if indeed to them at all)!

CHRIST "BOUGHT" EVEN APOSTATES BY HIS BLOOD

The plain meaning of 2 Peter 2:1

Peter speaks of Christ purchasing the redemption of even those who are apostate. Since Calvinists believe those who are saved will never lose their salvation, and since this passage speaks clearly of lost persons, then when it affirms Christ "bought" these lost souls, it means the atonement is not limited to the elect. In Peter's own words, "But there were also false prophets among the people, just as there will be false teachers among you. They will secretly introduce destructive heresies, even *denying the sovereign Lord who bought them*—bringing swift destruction on themselves" (2 Peter 2:1). The terms used to describe these people leave little doubt that they are lost souls. They are called "false prophets," "false teachers," those "denying the Lord" (v. 1), who are themselves "destructive" (v. 2 NKJV), and bringing "judgment" (v. 3). What is more, they are compared to fallen and unredeemable angels who were cast "into hell" (v. 4), the "wicked" (v. 7 NKJV), the "unjust" (v. 9 KJV), "natural brute beasts" (v. 12 KJV), a "dog" (v. 22), and "slaves of corruption" (v. 19 NKJV)—none of which are descriptions of the elect in Scripture.

[7]Extreme Calvinists attempt in vain to avoid this conclusion by pointing to the limited *geographical* uses of words like "world" ("all" [Rom. 1:8] or "every nation" [Acts 2:5]). But this misses the point that the *generic* use of these terms is truly universal (cf. Rom. 3:19, 23; 5:12).

What is more, for them "is reserved the blackness of darkness forever" (v. 17). It is these apostate, reprobate, non-elects that Christ "bought" with His own precious blood (cf. 1 Peter 1:19).

Implausible interpretation by extreme Calvinists

Commenting on this text, John Owen skillfully but futilely attempts to shift the burden of proof onto those who claim that "sovereign Lord" really refers to Christ, or that "bought" refers to His redemption for us.[8] As to the first point, (1) he admits that the word "Lord" (Greek: *despoten*) is used elsewhere of Christ, as indeed it is. As a matter of fact, other than the few times it is used of earthly masters (cf. 1 Tim. 6:1–2; Titus 2:9; 1 Peter 2:18), as is the Greek word *kurios* (Lord), all other references to *despoten* are of Christ or God the Father (cf. Luke 2:29; Acts 4:24; 2 Tim. 2:21; Jude 4; Rev. 6:10). In point of fact, in the parallel book (of Jude) on the same topic the reference is made clear: "For certain men whose condemnation was written about long ago have secretly slipped in among you. They are godless men, who change the grace of our God into a license for immorality and *deny Jesus Christ* our only Sovereign and *Lord (despoten)*" (Jude 1:4). At least two things are evident: (a) Jude is speaking of Christ, and (b) it is in a redemptive context, not simply of an early deliverance from the corruption of idolatry, as Owen suggests. For Jude refers to "salvation" and God's "grace" (vv. 3–4). (2) Owen acknowledges that the term is used of God, which amounts to the same thing, since even the Bible speaks of God's blood (Acts 20:28).[9] And even if it did not, since Christ *is* God, His blood is the blood of God in the same sense that Mary is the Mother of God (cf. Luke 1:43), namely, it is the blood of the Person (Christ), who is God. And Mary was the human mother of the Person (Christ), who is God.

As to the second point, there are good indications that the word "bought" (*agorazo*) refers to Christ's redemptive work: (1) Otherwise, why should they be lost unless they denied Christ's redemptive work for them? (2) Other than buying tangible things (cf. Matt. 13:44; 21:12), this word "bought" (*agorazo*) is almost always used redemptively in the New Testament, and never of redeeming someone socially from the corruption and pollution of idolatry. For example, Paul said to the "saints" at Corinth (1:1), "You were *bought* at a price. Therefore honor God with your body" (1 Cor. 6:20). He

---

[8] Owen, *The Death of Death in the Death of Christ*, 250–56.
[9] The NIV renders Acts 20:28: "Keep watch over yourselves and all the flock of which the Holy Spirit has made you overseers. Be shepherds of *the church of God, which he bought with his own blood.*"

added, "You were *bought* at a price; do not become slaves of men" (1 Cor. 7:23). Likewise John recorded the saints saying, "You are worthy to take the scroll and to open its seals, because you were slain, and with your blood you *purchased* men for God from every tribe and language and people and nation" (Rev. 5:9). He adds twice more, "No one could learn the song [of redemption] except the 144,000 who had been *redeemed* from the earth. These are those who did not defile themselves with women, for they kept themselves pure. They follow the Lamb wherever he goes. They were *purchased* from among men and offered as firstfruits to God and the Lamb" (Rev. 14:3–4). In view of this New Testament usage, the burden of proof rests on the extreme Calvinists to prove that Peter is using this term in any other than a redemptive sense here.

CHRIST DIED FOR THE UNGODLY

The plain meaning of Romans 5:6

Romans 5:6 informs us that "Christ died for the ungodly." Verse 10 adds, "For if, when we were God's *enemies*, we *were reconciled* to him through the death of his Son, how much more, having been reconciled, shall we be saved through his life!'"

But it is not only the elect that were ungodly and enemies of God, but also the non-elect. Therefore, Christ must have died for the non-elect as well as for the elect. Otherwise, He would not have died for all the ungodly and enemies of God. Further, if Paul meant Christ died only for the "elect" he could easily have said it and avoided any misunderstanding. The word "elect" was a regular part of New Testament vocabulary (cf. Matt. 24:24, 31; Mark 13:22, 27; Luke 18:7; 1 Peter 1:2), including Paul's (cf. Rom. 8:33; Col. 3:12; 1 Tim. 5:21; Titus 1:1). The same is true of the words "some" and "few."

Implausible interpretation by extreme Calvinists

John Owen repeatedly insists that in such passages the indefinite is not to be confused with the universal. In short, he says we cannot argue that "because Christ died for sinners, therefore he died for all sinners,"[10] for in other places the Bible affirms that God "justifies the ungodly" (Rom. 4:5 NASB), yet no one in this dispute believes that all the ungodly are justified.

---

[10]See Owen, *The Death of Death in the Death of Christ,* 260.

While this is true logically and formally, it is not true actually and contextually in Romans 5:6, for the context indicates that Paul is plainly speaking of "all" and "all men" as lost (Rom. 5:12, 18) and in need of salvation: "Just as the result of one trespass was condemnation for all men, so also the result of one act of righteousness was justification that brings life for *all men*" (5:18).

CHRIST RECONCILED THE WORLD TO GOD

The plain meaning of 2 Corinthians 5:14–19

According to the apostle Paul, "For Christ's love compels us, because we are convinced that *one died for all*, and therefore all died. . . . God was *reconciling the world* to Himself in Christ, not counting men's sins against them" (2 Cor. 5:14, 19). He adds, "And *he died for all*, that those who live should no longer live for themselves but for him who died for them and was raised again" (v. 15).

Now it is evident that this reconciliation of all did not guarantee the salvation of all, but only their savability. For it goes on to say that on the basis of what Christ did on the Cross, we must still plead with the world: "We are therefore Christ's ambassadors, as though God were making his appeal through us. We implore you on Christ's behalf: *Be reconciled to God*" (v. 20). Thus, their reconciliation by Christ makes their salvation *possible*. They themselves, by faith, must make it *actual*. Nonetheless, "One [Christ] died for all" (v. 14) to make this possible.

Implausible interpretation by extreme Calvinists

Palmer claims: "Obviously, the *all* in both cases means all the believers—*not the whole world*, reprobate as well as elect."[11] Here again, this is the reading of one's own theological system into the text rather than reading the proper meaning out of the text. Palmer argues, "The 'all died' refers to the spiritual death of the believer." Hence, "the 'all died' cannot refer to the natural death of all men, for Christ's death is not the cause of man's physical death."

But this is implausible for many reasons. First, whatever the "all died" means in verse 14, it is clear that Paul identifies the object of Christ's reconciliation in verse 19 as *"the world,"* not only believers. Second, verse 15 contrasts the "those who live"—Christians with eternal life—with the "all" for whom Christ died, saying, "And he

---

[11]Palmer, *The Five Points of Calvinism*, 49.

died for *all*, that *those who live* should no longer live for themselves. ...." Third, the connection in verse 14 between the "[Christ] died for all" and the "all [who] died" is to show why Christ's love should impel us to reach them with a "word of reconciliation," pleading with the "world" to be reconciled to God (vv. 19–20). It has nothing to do with our spiritual death but rather with our compassion toward the "world," which is spiritually dead and needs to be reconciled to God.

GOD DESIRES ALL TO BE SAVED

The plain meaning of 2 Peter 3:9

God is love, and as such "[He is] not willing that *any* should perish but that all should come to repentance" (2 Peter 3:9 NKJV). He "wants *all men* to be saved and to come to a knowledge of the truth" (1 Tim. 2:4). And contrary to the unreasonable view of the extreme Calvinists, this does not mean "all classes of men," namely, the elect from all nations. Words have limits to their meaning by context. And when "any," "all men," and the "whole world" (1 John 2:2) are taken to mean only "some" (unless used as figures of speech), then language has lost its meaning.

Implausible interpretation by extreme Calvinists

Extreme Calvinists are not unaware that many texts refer to Christ dying for "the world," "all men," etc. Some attempt to avoid the obvious impact of these verses by creating an artificial distinction. They speak of Christ as dying for all men without *distinction* but not all men without *exception*.[12] While this is a clever turn of a phrase, it is both without content and without ground. It amounts to saying that "all" really means "some"—something they would not tolerate in other verses such as "All have sinned and fall short of the glory of God" (Rom. 3:23). Further, as we shall see, there is no basis in these texts to support such an interpretation.

Others offer an even less plausible suggestion: that "God does not will that any of us (the elect) perish."[13] As a firm believer in inerrancy, R. C. Sproul is aware of how dangerous it is to change the Word of God. God the Holy Spirit was surely capable of using the word "some" instead of "all." But He did not. Furthermore, the

---

[12]Steele and Thomas, *The Five Points of Calvinism*, 46.
[13]Sproul, *Chosen by God*, 197. R. K. McGregor offers the same reasoning. See his *No Place of Sovereignty* (Downer's Grove, Ill.: InterVarsity Press, 1996), 169.

"any" and "all" are called upon to repent. Also, the "all" who need to repent cannot mean the "beloved," (vv. 1, 8), since they were already saved and in no need of repenting. In addition, this would mean that God is not calling on the non-elect to repent, which is clearly opposed to other Scriptures where "he commands *all people everywhere* to repent" (Acts 17:30). "All people everywhere" does not mean "some people everywhere" or "some people somewhere." The text speaks for itself.

The plain meaning of Matthew 23:37

Weeping over Jerusalem, Jesus said, " 'O Jerusalem, Jerusalem, you who kill the prophets and stone those sent to you, *how often I have longed to gather your children together*, as a hen gathers her chicks under her wings, but you were not willing.' " What could be more clear: God wanted all of them, even the unrepentant, to be saved.

Implausible interpretation by extreme Calvinists

John Gill proposed this is to be understood not of gathering to salvation but only of a gathering to hear him preach and thus to be brought to historical faith "sufficient to preserve them from temporal ruin." Likewise, the will of Christ to gather them "is not to be understood of his divine will ... but of his human will, or of his will as a man; which ... [is] yet not always the same with it, nor always fulfilled."[14] A clear exposition of the extreme Calvinists' view here is perhaps the best refutation of it, for it forces us to believe that God's concern for the temporal conditions of all men is greater than that of His concern for their eternal souls!

GOD OFFERED SALVATION TO MORE THAN THE ELECT

The plain teaching of Matthew 20:16

Jesus said, "Many are called, but few chosen" (Matt. 20:16 NKJV). While God knew that only the elect would believe (Acts 13:48), He desires all to be saved (2 Peter 3:9; 1 Tim. 2:4). Thus, "God so loved the world that he gave his only begotten Son" (John 3:16 NKJV) to provide an atoning sacrifice for the sins of "the whole world" (1 John 2:2). Since God called all, He provided salvation for all and com-

---

[14]John Gill, *The Cause of God and Truth*, (London, 1814, new ed.), 1.87–88; cf. 2.77.

manded all to repent (Acts 17:30) and believe (Acts 16:31). Now, it would be both deceptive and absurd for God to command all to repent when He had not provided salvation for all.

Implausible interpretation by extreme Calvinists

John Owen offers the unlikely suggestion that "God's commands and promises had revealed our duty, not his purpose; what God would have us to do, and not what he will do."[15] This clever turn of a phrase conceals hidden errors. First, it implies that God commands the impossible, which would make the Omniscient irrational: it is irrational to expect someone to do what cannot be done. Second, it overlooks the obvious, namely, that there is another alternative: God commands not only what He would have us do but also what He actually desires to be done. It is not, as Owen misleadingly suggests, what God "will do," but what He wills to be done that He commands.[16]

GOD DESIRES ALL TO BE SAVED

The plain meaning of 1 Timothy 2:3–4

Paul expressly says, "This is good, and pleases *God our Savior, who wants all men to be saved* and to come to a knowledge of the truth." Even Charles Spurgeon, who believed in limited atonement, could not deny the obvious meaning of this text.

Implausible interpretation by extreme Calvinists

From the time of the later Augustine[17] this text has been manhandled by extreme Calvinists. Spurgeon summarizes their attempts to avoid the obvious. He said here is how "our older Calvinistic friends deal with this text. 'All men,' say they,—'that is, some men': as if the Holy Ghost could not have said 'some men' if he had meant some men. 'All men,' say they; that is, 'some of all sorts of men'; as if the Lord could not have said 'All sorts of men' if he had meant that. The Holy Ghost by the apostle has written 'all men,' and unquestionably he means all men."[18] Spurgeon continues, "I

---

[15]Owen, *The Death of Death in the Death of Christ*, 200.
[16]Extreme Calvinists often offer God's command to keep the laws as a parallel illustration of commanding the impossible. But now it is not actually impossible to keep the Law, otherwise Jesus would not have been able to do it (cf. Matt. 5:17–18; Rom. 8:1–4). Anything God commands is possible to do, either in our own God-given strength or else by His special grace.
[17]See appendix 3.
[18]Cited by Murray, *Spurgeon v. Hyper-Calvinism*, 150.

was reading just now the exposition of a very able doctor who explains the text so as to explain it away: he applies grammatical gunpowder to it, and explodes it by way of expounding it." He aptly adds, "I thought when I read his exposition that it would have been a very capital comment upon the text if it had read: 'Who *will not* have all men to be saved, nor come to a knowledge of the truth.' "[19]

Of course, the problem is that this is what the text should say if limited atonement were true, but it does not. Even Spurgeon was aware of his apparent inconsistency here, saying, "I do not know how that squares with this" but added, *"I would sooner a hundred times over appear to be inconsistent with myself than be inconsistent with the word of God."*[20]

The plain meaning of 1 Timothy 2:6

Paul affirms that Christ "gave Himself as *a ransom for all men*—the testimony given in its proper time" (1 Tim. 2:6). It is plain here that Christ paid the price with His own precious blood (1 Peter 1:19) for the sins of *all men.*

Implausible interpretation by extreme Calvinists

Of this and like passages John Owen offers the dubious view that "all" does not mean "all" here. His tactic is to divert the issue to other passages where "all" does not mean the whole human race.[21] This only proves that "all" means "all" in its category or context, and that sphere is designated by the passage. But here the category and context is the whole human race, for the use of "all" as an object of God's love and redemption is used generically, not geographically. And what the extreme Calvinist must do, and does not, is demonstrate that this and like passages where "all" is used generically are not being used of the entire human race.

Even if "all" can and does mean less than literally all men in some passages, it still leaves open the question of what "all" means in this particular passage. And there is ample evidence that Paul has reference to the entire human race in 1 Timothy 2:4–6.

First, he could have used the word "some," if he had chosen to do so, but he did not. Second, his reference to "men" in verse 5 is

---

[19]Ibid., 151.
[20]From Spurgeon's sermon "A Critical Text—C. H. Spurgeon on 1 Timothy 2:3, 4" cited in Iain Murray, *Spurgeon v. Hyper-Calvinism: The Battle for Gospel Preaching* (Carlisle, Pa.: The Banner of Truth Trust, 1995), 150, 154, emphasis mine.
[21]See Owen, *The Death of Death in the Death of Christ,* 222f.

clearly generic—meaning all men, since it is used as the other pole from God that the Mediator, Christ, brings together. But generic usages of "all" in a redemptive context are usually, if not always, of the entire human race. Third, the desire for "all men" to be saved is parallel with that same desire expressed in other passages (cf. 2 Peter 3:9). Finally, the Bible tells us elsewhere that what hinders His desire from being fulfilled is not the universal scope of His love (John 3:16) but the willing rejection of some creatures—"*you were not willing*" (Matt. 23:37).

The plain meaning of Hebrews 2:9

"But we see Jesus, who was made a little lower than the angels, now crowned with glory and honor because he suffered death, so that by the grace of God *he might taste death for everyone.*" Christ died for everyone, not just the elect. This is the plain meaning of the text.

Implausible interpretation by extreme Calvinists

Responses to this follow the same line as those just discussed. Since we have already replied to them, it will suffice to add here only a couple of words about the context. First of all, "everyone" is used generically of humans, as is indicated not only by the contrast of humans with angels (v. 7) but also by the reference to human "flesh and blood" (i.e., enfleshed human nature). This generic use is almost always universal. Furthermore, since the result of the death (and resurrection) of Christ destroys death and defeats the devil (v. 14), it must have reference to all of Adam's race. Otherwise, Christ was not victorious in reversing what the devil did. In short, His victory would not have been complete.

NOT ALL CHRIST DIED FOR WILL BE SAVED

The plain teaching of other Scriptures

The doctrine of limited atonement claims that all Christ died for will be saved. But the above passages and many others reveal that: (1) Christ died for all, and (2) All will not be saved (cf. Matt. 25:41; Rev. 20:10). Thus, not all Christ died for will be saved. The doctrine of limited atonement is contrary to the clear teaching of Scripture.

ANSWERING QUESTIONS POSED BY EXTREME CALVINISTS

Spurgeon's question

Charles Spurgeon is often cited as defending limited atonement by insisting that it is the opponents, not the Calvinists, who limit the atonement, since they do not believe that: (1) Christ died so as to secure the salvation of all men, nor that (2) He died to secure the salvation of any man in particular. Then Spurgeon goes on to boast that those who believe in limited atonement believe that Christ died for "multitudes that no man can number," namely, the elect.[22]

However, this inverted logic is a good example of Spurgeon's eloquence gone to seed. It is an upside down logic indeed that can get anyone to think twice about the assertion that limited atonement is more unlimited than unlimited atonement! For one thing, the first assertion diverts the issue, for it is not a question of *securing* the salvation of all (this is universalism) but of *providing* salvation for all (as in moderate Calvinism and Arminianism), as opposed to extreme Calvinism, which holds that Christ died to *provide* and to *secure* the salvation of only the elect. So first, Spurgeon in the case of (1) gives the right answer to the wrong question! Further, in the case of (2) he gives the wrong answer to the right question, for both the moderate Calvinist and traditional Arminian opponents of extreme Calvinism surely do believe that Christ died to secure the salvation of the elect and that God foreknew from all eternity exactly who they would be.

Sproul's question

Many extreme Calvinists believe they have trapped their opposition by asking: "For whom was the atonement *designed?*"[23] If it was intended for all, then why are not all saved? How can a sovereign God's intention be thwarted? If it was intended for only some (the elect), then limited atonement follows. Thus the dilemma is this:

(1) Either Christ's atonement was intended for all, or only for some (the elect).

(2) If it was intended for all, then all will be saved (since God's sovereign intentions *will* come to pass).

(3) If it was not intended for all, then it was intended only for some (the elect).

---

[22]Cited by Steele and Thomas, *The Five Points of Calvinism*, 40.
[23]See Sproul, *Chosen by God*, 205.

(4) Therefore, either universalism is true or else limited atonement is true.

Of course, both moderate Calvinists and traditional Arminians deny universalism. Therefore, they would seem to be driven by this logic to accept limited atonement.

In response to the question and the dilemma it is only necessary to point out that premise (1) is a false dilemma. There is a third alternative: (1a) Christ's atonement was intended to *provide* salvation for all as well as to *procure* salvation for all who believe. The false dilemma wrongly assumes that there was only one intention for the atonement. Or, if understood in terms of a primary or single intention, then *the* purpose of the atonement was to *procure* salvation for all who believe. But since God also wanted everyone to believe, He also intended that Christ would die to *provide* salvation for all people. It is the denial that God really wants all persons to be saved that is such a hideous error of extreme Calvinism.

CONCLUSION

The plain meaning of numerous texts of Scripture is that Christ died for the sins of the whole world. Atonement is unlimited in its extent. Only by straining and stretching the texts can any other meaning be attributed to these passages. The clear contextual meaning of numerous texts is that Christ died for the sins of the whole human race.

APPENDIX SEVEN

DOUBLE-
PREDESTINATION

All Calvinists, like it or not, must hold some form of double-predestination—the logic of their position demands it. St. Augustine said, "As the Supreme Good, he [God] made good use of evil deeds, for the damnation of those whom he had justly predestined to punishment and for the salvation of those whom he had mercifully predestined to grace."[1] R. C. Sproul admits, "If there is such a thing as predestination at all, and if that predestination does not include all people, then we must not shrink from the necessary inference that there are two sides to predestination."[2]

Nonetheless, there is an intramural debate among extreme Calvinists whether God actively predestines both the elect and non-elect or whether the non-elect are predestined only passively. At the same time, less radical Calvinists call the active predestination of both the elect and the reprobate double-predestination. Those who hold it are called hyper-Calvinists.[3] It can be differentiated

---

[1]St. Augustine, *Enchiridion*, 100.
[2]Sproul, *Chosen by God*, 141.
[3]Hyper-Calvinism is a term that entails more than simply this stance on predestination. In its English manifestation in the late eighteenth century and early nineteenth century, it involved people like James Wells (1803–1872) and Charles Waters Banks (1806–1886). Earlier it was manifest in the works of Joseph Hussey, who wrote *God's Operations of Grace* (1707), and John Gill (1697–1771), author of *The Cause of God and Truth*. Charles Spurgeon identified and op-

from other forms of Calvinism on how predestination is willed as follows:[*]

Hyper-Calvinists	Other Calvinists
Active of both elect and non-elect	Active only of elect
Active in choosing both	Passive in not choosing non-elect
Positive election of both	Positive of elect and negative of non-elect
Faith given to the elect	Unbelief given to the non-elect
Symmetrical relation	Asymmetrical relation
Equal ultimacy	Unequal ultimacy

WHAT BOTH HOLD IN COMMON

Both hyper- and non-hyper Calvinists hold to all articles of the acronym T-U-L-I-P (see chapters 4 and 5). They both believe in T (total depravity), that all men are so totally sinful that they cannot initiate or attain salvation of their own free choice. As to the U (unconditional election), they both believe that God chooses on the basis of unconditional grace alone—that some will be saved and that some will not be saved. Likewise, they both hold that Christ died only for the elect (L is for limited atonement), and that God will work with irresistible grace (I) so as to ensure that all the elect will believe, and with efficacious grace to ensure that all the elect will persevere (P) in their faith and enter heaven.

HOW HYPER-CALVINISTS DIFFER ON PREDESTINATION

There is, however, a significant difference between the hyper-Calvinists and other Calvinists regarding election. It can be summarized as follows:

posed four characteristics of the movement (see Iain H. Murray, *Spurgeon v. Hyper-Calvinism: A Battle for Gospel Preaching*): (1) A denial that the offer of salvation is universal; (2) A denial that the warrant to believe lies in the command and promise of Scripture; (3) A denial that sinners are responsible to trust Christ; and (4) A denial that God desires the salvation of the non-elect. See Peter Toon, *The Emergence of Hyper-Calvinism in English Non-Conformity 1689–1765* (London: The Olive Tree, 1967).

[*]This chart is similar to one employed by R. C. Sproul in *Chosen by God*, 143.

Hyper-Calvinists	Other Calvinists
God also elects unbelievers	God elects only believers
God also elects to hell	God elects only to heaven
God's election of unbelievers is active	God's election of unbelievers is passive

Three great Calvinistic confessions appear to oppose the hyper-Calvinist view.

The Belgic Confession of Faith (1561)

"God then did manifest Himself such as He is: that is to say, merciful and just: *merciful*, since He delivers and preserves from this perdition all whom He in His eternal and unchangeable counsel of mere goodness has elected in Christ Jesus our Lord, without any respect to their works; *just*, in *leaving* others in the fall and perdition wherein they have involved themselves" (emphasis mine).

The Synod of Dort (1619)

"Of Divine Predestination," Article VI states: "He [God] graciously softens the hearts of the elect, however obstinate, and inclines them to believe; while he *leaves* the non-elect in his just judgment to their own wickedness and obduracy" (emphasis mine).

The Westminster Confession of Faith (1648)

"As God has *appointed the elect to Glory*, so has He, by the eternal and most free purpose of His will, foreordained all the means thereto.... *The rest of mankind* God was pleased, according to the unsearchable counsel of His own will, whereby He extends or withholds mercy, for the glory of His sovereign power over His creatures, *to pass by*; and to ordain them to dishonor and wrath for their sin, to the praise of His glorious justice" (III., 6–7, emphasis mine).

GOD'S GENERAL REDEMPTIVE LOVE FOR ALL MEN

Hyper-Calvinists also deny that God has any redemptive love for the non-elect. Even strong Calvinist Charles Spurgeon took a moderate view of this, saying, "Beloved, the benevolent love of Jesus is more extended than the lines of his electing love.... That [i.e., the love of Christ revealed in Matthew 23:37] is not the love which beams resplendently upon his chosen, but it is true love for all that."

In addition, God has a special love for the elect that "is not love for all men. . . . There is an electing love, discriminating, distinguishing love, which is settled upon a chosen people . . . and it is this love which is the true resting place for the saint."[5] The hyper-Calvinist believes only in electing love and no general redemptive love for the non-elect. Arminians (Wesleyans), on the other hand, believe in no special elective love but only in a general redemptive love for all sinners.

As mentioned before, Spurgeon seemed to be aware of the inconsistency of his moderating view but said in comments on 1 Timothy 2:3–4: "I would sooner a hundred times over appear to be inconsistent with myself than be inconsistent with the word of God."[6] (After all, the text does say, "This is good, and pleases God our Savior, who wants all men to be saved and to come to a knowledge of the truth.")

THE BIBLICAL ARGUMENT AGAINST HYPER-CALVINISM

All the arguments provided elsewhere against extreme Calvinism also apply to hyper-Calvinism (see chapters 4–5 and appendices 5–6). In addition, a few can be put forward in particular against hyper-Calvinism.

First, hyper-Calvinism makes God the direct author of evil. For God does not merely permit evil, He causes it. But we know that God is absolutely Good (Matt. 5:48), and He cannot do, promote, or produce evil (Hab. 1:13; James 1:13).

Second, hyper-Calvinists explicitly confess not only that God is not all-loving but that He also hates the non-elect. John Owen bluntly confessed, "God having 'made some for the day of evil,' . . . 'hated them before they were born' . . . 'before ordained them to condemnation'. . . ."[7] William Ames affirmed, "There are two kinds of predestination: election and rejection or reprobation."[8] He added that *God "hates" them*. "This hatred is negative or privative, because it denies election. But *it has a positive content*, for God has willed

---

[5]Cited by Murray, *Spurgeon v. Hyper-Calvinism*, 98.
[6]Ibid., 150.
[7]Owen, *The Death of Death in the Death of Christ*, 115.
[8]Ames, *The Marrow of Theology*, 154.

that some should not have eternal life"![9] May it never be! Perish the thought! God forbid!

A PASSIONATE PLEA

Charles Spurgeon, himself an ardent Calvinist, saw the dangers of the deadly doctrine of hyper-Calvinism. He said, "I cannot image a more ready instrument in the hands of Satan for the ruin of souls than a minister who tells sinners it is not their duty to repent of their sins," and "Who has the arrogance to call himself a gospel minister, while he teaches that God hates some men infinitely and unchangeably for no reason whatever but simply because he chooses to do so. O my brethren! May the Lord save you from the charmer, and keep you ever deaf to the voice of error."[10]

---

[9]Ibid., 156.
[10]Cited by Murray, *Spurgeon v. Hyper-Calvinism*, 155–56.

AN EVALUATION OF THE CANONS OF DORT (1619)

Our purpose in providing a selective analysis of this famous statement of Calvinism is to expound on what is widely considered to be a modern origin of extreme Calvinism and to express a moderate Calvinistic view by way of interaction with it. In fact, in some respects *Dort* appears not to support extreme Calvinism. In other cases, it is often not what is said that is radical Calvinism, but rather what it leaves unsaid and what may be implied that could be a more extreme form of Calvinism.

OF DIVINE PREDESTINATION

Article I

"As all men have sinned in Adam ... God would have done no injustice by leaving them all to perish...."

Response

This does not give exclusive support to extreme Calvinism. It is true as far as it goes, and moderate Calvinists could agree as well. However, it is wrong to imply that God's justice could have condemned all to hell without His love doing anything about it.

God is more than just; He is also all-loving. It is true that all men are justly condemned because of their sin. But it is wrong to assume that one attribute of God (justice) operates in isolation from another (love). There was nothing in sinful man that necessitated any attempt to save him, but there was something *in a sinless God* that did (namely, His infinite love).

Article V

"The cause or guilt of this unbelief, as well as of all other sins, is nowise in God, but in man himself: whereas faith in Jesus Christ, and salvation through him is the free gift of God . . . (Eph. ii. 8)."

Response

It is correct to say man's unbelief is the "cause" of all his evil actions. Likewise, salvation is totally a gift from God. But there is no biblical support, including Ephesians 2:8–9 (see appendix 5), for the idea that faith is a gift of God to only the elect. "*It* [neuter] is a gift of God" does not refer to "faith" (which is feminine) but to salvation by grace. It is doubtful whether any Bible text teaches that faith is a gift given only to the elect. Faith is a gift from God, it is offered to everyone, and it is not forced on anyone against his or her will (see chapters 4 and 5). It must be received by an act of free choice prompted by God's persuasive and efficacious grace.

Article VI

"He [God] graciously softens the hearts of the elect, however obstinate, and inclines them to believe; while he leaves the non-elect in his just judgment to their own wickedness and obduracy."

Response

This rightly avoids "double predestination" (see appendix 7), which would attribute eternal condemnation directly to God. God does graciously soften the hearts of the elect, and the non-elect are left to condemnation in their own unbelief.

However, it would be wrong—and contrary to Scripture (1 Tim. 2:3–4; 2 Peter 3:9)—to imply that God does not truly desire to save all men (see chapters 4–6). To imply this suggests that God is not *all*-loving. Also, it would be fallacious to assume that the "obstinate" will always respond to "gracious softening" that is less than coercive. The only *guarantee* that all the unwilling will respond is to ungraciously *force* some against their wills. For most extreme Calvinists, regeneration apart from (or prior to) faith is such an act.

Article VII

This article speaks of "election" of only a "certain number of persons" who are "effectually" called. This is true to a degree. God foreknew, chose, and secured the salvation of only a limited number of persons. Thus, the atonement is limited in its *application*. Moderate Calvinists agree (see appendix 6).

Response

However, it would be wrong to imply that God is partial and arbitrary in His choice, and not *all*-loving. God's grace is effective on the *willing*. But it cannot be "effectual" without being coercive when some unsaved persons are set in stubborn unwillingness to believe (Matt. 23:37; Acts 7:51).

Article IX

"This election was not *founded upon* foreseen faith ... or any other good quality or disposition in man, as the prerequisite, cause, or condition on which it depended."

Response

This article correctly points out that God's election is not *based on* His foreknowledge of any good works man will do. Even so, it would be wrong to assume, contrary to Scripture (e.g., Rom. 8:29), that election is not "in *accordance with* the foreknowledge of God" (1 Peter 1:2). Further, man's faith is not the *ground* of God's choice to provide salvation, but it is the *means* through which we receive His grace (Rom. 5:1; Eph. 2:8–9). The ground for election is in God's good will, not in man's good works. But while the gift of salvation is unconditional from the standpoint of the Giver (God), it is conditional from the standpoint of the receiver. That is, the gift of salvation must be received by faith in order to be obtained.

Article X

"The good pleasure of God is the sole cause of this gracious election ... (Rom. ix. 1113)." This is true. For God alone is the total efficient primary cause of salvation.

Response

Nonetheless, we should not wrongly posit that God does not use secondary causes (such as free choice) when He accomplishes this salvation. Even the Calvinistic *Westminster Confession of Faith* speaks of human free will as a "secondary cause" of our receiving salvation. It declares, "Although in relation to the foreknowledge and decree of God, the first cause, all things come to pass immutably and infallibly, yet by the same providence he ordereth them to fall out, according to the nature of second causes, either necessarily, freely, or contingently" (V, ii).

Nor should we assume that God's will operates independently of His "unchangeable" nature. If God is simple, as classical theists acknowledge, then His nature and will are absolutely one. Hence, He cannot will to love only some. An all-loving God by nature must love all.

Article XVIII

"To those who murmur at the free grace of election, and just severity of reprobation, we answer with the Apostle: 'Nay but, O man, who art thou that repliest against God?' (Rom. ix. 20)." Of course, it is wrong to murmur against God (cf. Num. 11:1). He has a sovereign right to choose what He chooses.

Response

However, it is wrong to imply that God is not consistent with His own unchangeably just and loving nature (see chapter 1). Further, doing *systematic* theology properly is not murmuring against God. It *must* show how God's own attributes of love and justice are not *inconsistent.* God Himself has told us to be "avoiding . . . contradictions" (1 Tim. 6:20 NKJV). Questioning a false concept of God (e.g., an arbitrary, partially loving God) is not the same as questioning the true God (who is the all-just *and* all-loving One).

OF THE DEATH OF CHRIST

Article III

"The death of the Son of God is the only and most perfect sacrifice and satisfaction for sin; is of infinite worth and value, abundantly sufficient to expiate the sins of the whole world." This is true, as such. It gives rise to the Calvinist's dictum that Christ's death is sufficient for all and efficient for the elect.

Response

But this is not what the debate is about between extreme Calvinists and those who oppose them. The question is whether Christ actually died for the sins of the whole world. John Calvin seemed to think He did (see appendix 2). And, the New Testament clearly affirms that He did (see appendix 6).

Article VI

"Whereas many who are called by the gospel do not repent nor believe in Christ, but perish in unbelief; this is ... wholly to be imputed to themselves." This is true. All who hear the Gospel are responsible to repent and believe it. And "the Lord is ... patient" (2 Peter 3:9).

Response

Regardless, since God is not irrational or unjust, He would never hold persons responsible for actions they could not have avoided. Further, their unbelief could not be *"wholly"* their fault if, as extreme Calvinists claim, it was because God *could have* but *did not* give them the irresistible desire to believe and the faith to believe. How could they justly be expected to repent or believe if neither is within their power to do so and God chose not to give them the power to do so?

OF MAN'S CORRUPTION AND CONVERSION

Article I

"Man was originally formed after the image of God ... and abusing the freedom of his own will, he ... became wicked...." This makes it clear that Adam before the Fall had the power of free will to obey or disobey God's command.

Response

If this is so, then extreme Calvinists, like Jonathan Edwards and his modern-day proponents in John Gerstner and R. C. Sproul, are wrong in claiming that God had to give the desire to Adam to will something before it could be willed (since Adam had no evil nature before his fall).

Article II

"All the posterity of Adam ... have derived corruption from their original parents, not by imitation, as the Pelagians of old asserted, but by propagation of a vicious nature."

Response

The article is correct as far as it goes. It correctly rejects Pelagianism and affirms that man is born with a fallen nature. The problem only arises when extreme Calvinists carry depravity to the point of claiming that fallen human beings do not even have the capability of receiving God's gracious and efficacious gift of salvation (see appendix 6).

Article III

"Therefore all men are conceived in sin, and are by nature . . . incapable of any saving good . . . and without the regenerating grace of the Holy Spirit, they are neither able nor willing to return to God. . . ."

Response

It is true that man is incapable of *doing* any saving good, but this does not mean he is incapable of *receiving* any saving good. And even here moderate Calvinists can agree provided this grace is not irresistible on the unwilling (see chapter 5). For there is a difference in claiming that grace *aids* the will and that grace *forces* it. The latter is contrary both to the nature of God and the nature of free will (see chapters 1 and 2).

If this attitude is taken to imply that irresistible regeneration comes before our willingness to accept it, then it is contrary to Scripture (see appendix 10), which affirms that faith is logically prior to being regenerated or justified (Rom. 5:1; 1:17; Eph. 2:8–9).[1]

Article IV

"These remain, however, in man since the fall, the glimmerings of natural light, whereby he retains some knowledge of God, of natural things, and of the difference between good and evil. . . . But so far is this light of nature from being sufficient to bring him to a saving knowledge of God, and to true conversion, that he is incapable of using it aright even in things natural and civil."

Response

Following Calvin (*Institutes*, Book I), moderate Calvinists agree with this statement. It correctly notes that there is a natural reve-

---

[1] Faith is *logically prior* to justification in the sense that it is the condition for receiving justification. But faith and justification are *actually simultaneous*, since one is justified the very instant he believes.

lation (cf. Rom. 1:19–20; 2:12–14), although it is begrudging in the amount of natural light (e.g., "glimmerings"). And it correctly (I believe) notes that natural revelation is insufficient for salvation. It fits with Romans 1 by noting that although depraved persons "know it," for "God made it evident to them," nonetheless, by an act of free will they "suppress the truth" (Rom. 1:18) they clearly know.

Article VIII

"He [God], moreover, seriously promises eternal life and rest to as many as come to Him, and believe on Him."

Response

Here the universal offer of salvation to all men is affirmed. While moderate Calvinists certainly agree, nonetheless, they deny that this is consistent with the extreme Calvinists' interpretation of limited atonement and irresistible grace (see chapters 4 and 5). A sincere promise to save all who believe implies that Christ died for all and that all are capable of believing this promise to be saved (see appendix 6).

Article X

"But that others who are called by the gospel obey the call and are converted, is not to be ascribed to the proper exercise of free will . . . but it must be wholly ascribed to God. . . ."

Response

If "wholly" is taken to mean that God is the sole source of both the gift of salvation and the persuasive and effective grace to receive it, then moderate Calvinists would agree. If, on the other hand, "wholly" of God means it is irresistible apart from man's free choice, moderate Calvinists would respond that God would not be wholly God (namely, wholly good) and man would not be wholly man (namely, really free). Salvation is "wholly" of God in the sense that He *initiates* and *accomplishes* it, but not in the sense that man is forced to accept it against his will by some alleged God-given desires that are "irresistible."

Article XI

"But when God accomplishes his good pleasure in the *elect* or *works* in them true conversion . . . he opens the closed and softens the hardened heart . . . infuses new qualities into the will, which, though heretofore dead, he quickens . . . renders it good, actuates and strengthens it . . ." (emphasis mine).

Response

If this means that God as primary cause does the work of actualizing salvation in the elect, then this is not unique to extreme Calvinism. However, if words like "infuses" and "actuates" are taken to imply that man is being treated as a passive *object* instead of a subject (an "it," not an "I"), then it is contrary to God's Word as well as the *Westminster Confession,* which speaks of God working through "secondary causes" of free will (V, ii).

Article XIV

"Faith is therefore to be considered as a gift of God, not on account of its being offered by God to man, to be accepted or rejected at his pleasure, but because it is in reality conferred, breathed, and infused into him; nor even because God bestows the power or ability to believe and expects that man should, by the exercise of his own free will, consent to the terms of salvation; but because he . . . produces both the will to believe and the act of believing also."

Response

It is difficult to interpret this in any other than an extreme Calvinist sense. Supposedly, both the gift and act of believing are caused by God. If so, then man has no choice in even receiving the gift. Grace must be irresistible on the unwilling, and this view of God is open to the charge that He is not all-loving, for though He has the power, He does not have the will to save all. As discussed elsewhere (chapter 5 and appendix 6), there is no biblical support for this conclusion.

Article XV

"God is under no obligation to confer this grace upon any; for how can he be indebted to man who has no previous gifts to bestow as a foundation for such recompense?"

Response

There are several ways this can be understood as true, even by moderate Calvinists. For it is true that God is in no way indebted to man. Further, there is nothing in depraved humans that merits anything except God's justice, namely eternal separation from God.

However, this does not mean God is under *no* obligation of His own unchangeably loving nature to show love to His creatures. God is obligated by His own essentially loving nature to love all His creatures (1 John 4:16; 2 Peter 3:9; 1 Tim. 2:3–4).

Article XVI

"But as man by the fall did not cease to be a creature endowed with understanding and will, nor did sin ... deprive him of the human nature ... so also this grace of regeneration does not treat men as senseless stocks and blocks, nor take away their will and its properties, neither does violence, thereto; but ... sweetly and powerfully bends it ... [toward that wherein] true spiritual restoration and freedom of our will consist."

Response

This clearly and correctly affirms that even fallen man retains the image of God, along with the power of free choice. However, it is inconsistent with other statements (cf. Article XIV) affirming that God forces the elect to believe against their will by irresistible power. The extreme Calvinist cannot have his cake (of unforced freedom) and yet deny it, too (by forced freedom). This is not a mystery; it is a contradiction.

OF THE PERSEVERANCE OF THE SAINTS

Article III

"But God is faithful, who having conferred grace, mercifully confirms and powerfully preserves them therein, even to the end."

Response

There is no disagreement here. Both sides concur with "once saved, always saved." This is not because we have in ourselves the power to endure but because God will give us the power to do so.

Article VIII

"Thus, it is not in consequence of their own merit or strength, but of God's free mercy, that they do not totally fall from faith and grace. ..."

Response

True again. The drowning man can claim no credit for his rescue; all praise goes to the one who rescued him. Otherwise, he would have drowned.

Even so, this does not mean that the act of believing is meritorious. Faith is not a meritorious "work." Faith and works are placed in opposition in Scripture (Rom. 4:4–5), as are grace and works (Rom. 11:6).

APPENDIX NINE

JONATHAN EDWARDS ON FREE WILL

The extreme Calvinistic perspective on free will is rooted in the radicalized view of the later Augustine (see appendix 3). This was born out of his controversy with the Donatists, whom he maintained could be forced to believe against their wills. Jonathan Edwards' *Freedom of the Will* is an example of this theistic determinism. The late John Gerstner and R. C. Sproul hold the same view. It is at the heart of extreme Calvinism.

Ironically, as stated previously, R. C. Sproul declares that "Any view of human will that destroys the biblical view of human responsibility is seriously defective. Any view of human will that destroys the biblical view of God's character is even worse."[1] Yet, as we will see, this is exactly what the extreme Calvinists' view does, for it robs humans of their responsibility and defrocks God of His essential omnibenevolence (all-lovingness).

JONATHAN EDWARDS' VIEW OF FREE WILL

Edwards argued that all actions are caused, since it is irrational to claim that things arise without a cause. But for him a self-caused

---

[1]Sproul, *Willing to Believe*, 29.

action is impossible, since a cause is prior to an effect, and one cannot be prior to himself. Therefore, all actions are ultimately caused by a First Cause (God). "Free choice" for Edwards is doing what one desires—but God gives the desire to do good. Hence, all good human actions are determined by God. Evil actions are determined by the strongest desires of an evil nature left to itself.

Edwards wrote: ". . . that which appears most inviting, and has . . . the greatest degree of previous tendency to excite and induce the choice, is what I call the 'strongest motive.' And in this sense, I suppose the will is always *determined* by the strongest motive."[2] Not only are our choices determined by our natures but they are actually necessary. And in this sense, adds Edwards, "necessity is not inconsistent with liberty."[3] As Sproul summarizes it, "The will cannot choose against its strongest inclination."[4]

Jonathan Edwards saw a dilemma for all who reject his view: Either there is an infinite regress of causes or else there is no motive to act. On the one hand, "if the will determines all its own free acts, then every free act of choice is determined by a preceding act of choice, choosing that act" and so on to infinity.[5] On the other hand, if there is no cause of the choice, then one would never act. But we do act. Therefore, our actions must be determined by our motives or desires.

As we shall see, Edwards has posed a false dilemma, since the actions *can* be caused by the Self and not by another. True, every action is caused. But from this it does not follow that every actor is caused to act by another actor. This is not true of God's free actions; they are self-caused (i.e., caused by His Self). Likewise, creatures made in God's image have the God-given power to cause their own moral actions. This alternative is not only logically possible, but it is the only one that can explain how Lucifer and Adam were able to sin (see chapter 2 and appendix 4). On Edwards' view that God could not have given them the desire to sin, nor did they have a sinful nature to determine their actions, then they must have been the first cause of their own evil actions. But this is the very view of freedom that Edwards rejects.

---

[2] Edwards, *Freedom of the Will*, 142, emphasis mine.
[3] Ibid., 152.
[4] Sproul, *Willing to Believe*, 163.
[5] Edwards, *Freedom of the Will*, 172–73.

THE PROBLEMS WITH EDWARDS' FORM OF DIVINE DETERMINISM

Opponents to Edwards' determinism respond as follows. First, defining free choice as "doing what one desires" is contrary to experience. For people do not always do what they desire, nor do they always desire to do what they do (cf. Rom. 7:15–16).

Second, Edwards also misunderstands self-determinism as causing itself. Rather, it means simply that a self can cause something else to happen. That is, a free agent can cause a free action, and causing an action is not the same thing as causing one's Self (i.e., being self-caused).

Third, Edwards has a faulty, mechanistic view of human personhood. He likens human free choice to balancing scales in need of more pressure in order to tip the scales one way or the other. But humans are not machines; they are persons made in the image of God (Gen. 1:27).

Fourth, Edwards wrongly assumes that self-determinism is contrary to God's sovereignty. But God pre-determined things *in accordance with* free choice, rather than in contradiction to it (see chapter 3). Even the Calvinistic *Westminster Confession of Faith* declares that "although in relation to the foreknowledge and decree of God, the first cause, all things come to pass immutably and infallibly, yet by the same providence he ordereth them to fall out, according to the nature of second causes, either necessarily, freely, or contingently" (V, ii).

A BETTER ALTERNATIVE

There are three basic alternatives with regard to free actions. Either (1) they are determined (caused) by another (as Edwards held); or (2) they could be undetermined (that is, uncaused), but this is contrary to the principle of causality, which holds that every event has a cause; or, finally, (3) they could be self-determined, that is, caused by our Selves. According to this third view, a person's moral acts are self-caused (see chapter 4).

The arguments for self-determinism

The arguments for this view are as follows (see also chapter 2): First, either moral actions are uncaused, caused by another, or caused by one's self. However, no action can be uncaused, since this violates the fundamental rational principle that every event has a cause. Neither can a person's actions be caused by another, for in that case they would not be *his* actions. Further, if one's acts are caused by another, then how can *he* be held responsible for them? Both the early Augustine (in *On Free Will* and *On Grace and Free Will*) and Thomas Aquinas were self-determinists, as were virtually all church fathers up to the Reformation (see appendix 1).

Second, human beings have moral responsibility. But moral responsibility demands the ability to respond (free choice).

Third, the Bible insists that there are actions that people *ought* to perform (cf. Ex. 20). But *ought* implies *can* (free choice).[6]

Fourth, *both* the Bible *and* common understanding state that some acts are praiseworthy (e.g., heroism), and some are blameworthy (e.g., cruelty). But if one is not free to perform the act, then it makes no sense to praise or blame him for doing it.

Fifth, if God determines all acts, then *He*, not Satan, is responsible for the origin of sin. For if a free choice is doing what one desires, and if God gives the desire, then God must have given Lucifer the desire to rebel against Him (Rev. 12). But this is morally absurd, since it would be God working against Himself.

Answering some objections (see also appendix 4)

One objection to self-determinism is that if everything needs a cause, then so do acts of the will, in which case they are not caused by one's Self. In response, self-determinists claim that this confuses the *actor* (agent) who causes the act and the *act* being caused. The principle of causality does not demand that every *thing* (or person) has a cause but only that every *event* has a cause. God, the First Cause, is a person, and He needs no cause. Now, all finite beings *do* need a cause. But once they are caused (by the First Cause) and given free choice, then they are the cause of their own moral actions. And if a free agent (e.g., a human person) is the first cause of his own free actions, then it is meaningless to ask, "What caused him to do it?" Again, God caused the *fact* of free choice (by making free agents), but free agents are the cause of the *acts* of free choice.

Others object that self-determinism is contrary to God's predestination. But self-determinists respond that God can predetermine in accordance with His foreknowledge (1 Peter 1:2), insisting that "those he foreknew he also predestined" (Rom. 8:29). God, they insist, can determine the future by means of free choice,

---

[6]This does not mean that everything God commands we can do in our own strength, but we *can* do it by God's grace (Phil. 4:13; 2 Cor. 12:9; 1 Cor. 10:13).

since He omnisciently knows how moral free agents will freely act.

Still others hold that, regardless of what free choice Adam may have had (Rom. 5:12), fallen human beings are in bondage to sin and not free to respond to God. But this view is contrary to both God's consistent call on all people to believe (e.g., John 3:16; Acts 16:31; 17:30) and to direct statements that even unbelievers have the ability to respond to God's grace (Matt. 23:37; John 7:17; Rom. 7:18; 1 Cor. 9:17; Philem. 14; 1 Peter 5:2).

Finally, some argue that if humans have the ability to respond, then salvation is not of grace (Eph. 2:8–9) but by human effort. However, this is a confusion about the nature of faith. The ability of a person to receive God's gracious *gift* of salvation is not the same as *working* for it. To think so is quite obviously to give the credit for the gift to the receiver rather than to the Giver who graciously gave it.

CONCLUSION

Jonathan Edwards' view of free choice, which is at the heart of extreme Calvinism, is a form of determinism. It destroys true freedom, lays the credit (and blame) for our actions on another (God), and eliminates the grounds for rewards and moral responsibility. What is more, it makes God ultimately responsible for evil.

Further, Edwards overlooks the only viable concept of free will, namely that it is the power of *self*-determination. That is, a free act, whatever persuasion is placed upon it, is the uncoerced ability to cause one's own actions.

IS REGENERATION PRIOR TO FAITH?

A fundamental pillar in the extreme Calvinists' view is the belief that regeneration is logically prior to faith. That is, we are saved in order to believe; we do not believe in order to be saved. As R. C. Sproul succinctly states: "In regeneration, God changes our hearts. He gives us a new disposition, a new inclination. He plants a desire for Christ in our hearts. We can never trust Christ for our salvation unless we first desire him. This is why we said earlier that *regeneration precedes faith.*"[1]

As we will see, nothing could be more contrary to the clear statements of Scripture. But before we look at the text, a clarification must be made in the question. The word "prior" is not used in a chronological sense, but in a logical sense. For salvation and faith are simultaneous, since one cannot be saved without faith, and faith cannot be present without our being saved. The question is: Which one is *logically* prior to the other?

VERSES OFFERED BY EXTREME CALVINISTS IN SUPPORT OF THEIR VIEW

As anyone familiar with Scripture can attest, verses allegedly supporting the contention that regeneration precedes faith are in

---

[1]Sproul, *Chosen by God*, 118 (italics his).

short supply. In fact, some extreme Calvinists acknowledge that this belief is more of a logical consequence of their system than it is the result of the analysis of any given verses. Nonetheless, many extreme Calvinists do make inferences from some texts to support their conclusion.

Acts 13:48

"When the Gentiles heard this, they were glad and honored the word of the Lord; and *all who were appointed for eternal life believed.*" From the fact that all who were preordained to salvation eventually believed, some extreme Calvinists conclude that salvation is prior to belief.

Response

The text says no such thing. What it affirms is that *all who are preordained* to be saved will eventually believe. It does not say that *all who are saved* will believe, but that those whom God fore-ordained will eventually get eternal life. It doesn't speak to the matter of whether faith is a condition for getting this salvation, which the Bible everywhere says is faith *first* and then regeneration.

Ephesians 2:1–2

"And you He made alive, who were dead in trespasses and sins" (NKJV). Extreme Calvinists deduce from this that since dead persons cannot believe, they must be made alive (regenerated) first in order that they can believe.

Response

This does not follow from the text for two basic reasons. First, spiritually "dead" persons *can* believe (see chapter 4 and appendix 5), since "dead" means separation from God, not annihilation. The image of God is not erased by the Fall (Gen. 9:6; James 3:9) but only effaced. Otherwise, God would not call on unsaved people to believe (John 3:16–18; Acts 16:31; 20:21), and the second death (Rev. 20:14) would be annihilation—which extreme Calvinists reject. Second, in this very passage the apostle lists faith as logically prior to salvation.[2] He declares: "For it is by grace *you have been saved, through faith*—and this not from yourselves, it is the gift of God" (v. 8). Clearly, faith is the means here and salvation is the end.

---

[2] Again, in a chronological sense, faith is simultaneous with salvation, for one receives salvation the very moment he believes.

But the means come before the end. Hence, faith is logically prior to being saved.

Ephesians 2:8–9

"For it is by grace you have been saved, through faith—and this not from yourselves, *it is the gift of God.*" Strong Calvinists from the later Augustine (see appendix 3) through the Synod of Dort (see appendix 8) to R. C. Sproul[3] have used this verse and others to prove that salvation is prior to faith.

Response

These texts have been thoroughly examined and these interpretations refuted elsewhere (see appendix 5). Here we will only mention that the "it" (*touto*) is neuter in form and cannot refer to "faith" (*pistis*), which is feminine. The antecedent of "it is the gift of God" must be the salvation by grace (v. 9). Commenting on this passage, A. T. Robertson noted, " 'Grace' is God's part, 'faith' ours. *And that* [it] (*kai touto*). Neuter, not feminine *taute*, and so refers not to *pistis* [faith] (feminine) or to *charis* [grace] (feminine also), but to the act of being saved by grace conditioned on faith on our part."[4]

VERSES THAT DEMONSTRATE THAT FAITH IS PRIOR TO SALVATION

Contrary to the claims of extreme Calvinists, there are no verses properly understood that teach regeneration is prior to faith. Instead, it is the uniform pattern of Scripture to place faith logically prior to salvation as a condition for receiving it. Consider the following selection of numerous texts on the topic.

Romans 5:1

"Therefore, since we have been justified *through faith*, we have peace with God through our Lord Jesus Christ." According to this text, faith is the means by which we get justification; justification is not the means by which we get faith. Since the means is logically prior to the end, it follows that faith is prior to justification.

---

[3]In his zeal to defend this view, R. C. Sproul triumphantly concludes: "This passage should seal the matter forever. The faith by which we are saved is a gift of God." See R. C. Sproul, *Chosen by God*, 119.
[4]See Robertson, *Word Pictures in the New Testament*, 4:525.

Luke 13:3

" 'I tell you, no! But *unless you repent*, you too will all perish.' "
Here repentance is the condition for avoiding judgment. It is the
means prior to the end of salvation. This is the uniform pattern
throughout Scripture.

2 Peter 3:9

"The Lord is not slow in keeping his promise, as some understand slowness. He is patient with you, not wanting anyone to perish, but *[he wants]* *everyone to come to repentance.*" The order here is
the same: repentance comes before salvation. Those who do not repent will perish. Those who repent will not perish.

John 3:16

" 'For God so loved the world that he gave his one and only
Son, that *whoever believes in him shall not perish* but have eternal
life.' " Again, belief is the precondition for salvation. If the extreme
Calvinists were correct it should affirm the opposite, namely, that
having eternal life is the condition of believing.

Acts 16:31

" 'Believe in the Lord Jesus, and you will be saved—you and
your household.' " Again, the order is the same: belief comes before
salvation. Faith is a condition of being saved.

Romans 3:24–25

"And *[we]* *are justified* freely by his grace through the redemption that came by Christ Jesus. God presented him as a sacrifice of
atonement, *through faith* in his blood. He did this to demonstrate his
justice." In this great didactic passage on justification Paul does not
fail to mention that justification comes to us *through faith*. While
God *planned* it before the world was—and, hence, before we could
believe—when we *receive* it, faith comes before justification. Nowhere is this pattern broken in the New Testament: it is uniform in
affirming that faith is first.

John 3:6–7

" 'Flesh gives birth to flesh, but *the Spirit gives birth to spirit*. You
should not be surprised at my saying, *"You must be born again."* ' "
The new birth is when regeneration occurs. It is when we get
spiritual life from God. But Jesus makes it absolutely clear in this

passage that faith is the condition for receiving the new birth. It is received by "whoever *believes* in Him" (v. 15 NKJV). It is "whoever *believes* in him [that] shall not perish but have eternal life" (v. 16). Faith is the means to the end—regeneration.

Titus 3:5–7

"He saved us, not because of righteous things we had done, but because of his mercy. *He saved us through the washing of rebirth and renewal by the Holy Spirit,* whom he poured out on us generously through Jesus Christ our Savior, so that, having been justified *by his grace,* we might become heirs having the hope of eternal life."

It has been observed that this great passage on regeneration says nothing about faith but simply that God regenerated us *"by his grace."* However, this does not prove that regeneration precedes grace, for two reasons. First, the very next verse affirms, "And I want you to stress these things, so that *those who have trusted in God* may be careful to devote themselves to doing what is good" (v. 8). Faith is logically prior to regeneration,[5] just as it is prior to good works. Second, the parallel passage in Ephesians 2:8–9 by the same author (Paul) explicitly declares that we are saved *"by faith,"* as does virtually every other passage in the New Testament that deals with the question.

Emery Bancroft put it this way:

> Man is never to wait for God's working. If he is ever re-generated, it must be in and through a movement of his own will, in which he turns to God as unconstrainedly and with as little consciousness of God's operation upon him as if no such operation of God were involved in the change. And in preaching we are to impress upon men the claims of God and their duty of immediate submission to Christ, with the certainty that they who do so submit will subsequently recognize this new and holy activity of their own will as due to a working within them of divine power.[6]

CONCLUSION

The extreme Calvinists' view that regeneration precedes faith is based on their extreme view of total depravity, which also lacks

---

[5]See C. C. Ryrie, *The Holy Spirit* (Chicago: Moody Press, 1965), 64–65.
[6]Emery H. Bancroft, *Christian Theology: Systematic and Biblical,* ed. Ronald B. Mayers, 2nd rev. ed. (Grand Rapids, Mich.: Zondervan, 1976).

biblical support (see chapter 4). Further, it is contrary to what the Bible (chapter 2) and the church fathers (appendix 1) teach about the nature of free choice. What is more, it is opposed to the character of God as all-loving (omnibenevolent) and to the nature of free will as the ability to choose otherwise (see appendix 4).

APPENDIX ELEVEN

MONERGISM VS. SYNERGISM

Extreme Calvinists maintain that the very first moment of conversion (regeneration) is totally a result of God's operation, without any cooperation on man's part. This is sometimes called operative grace, as opposed to cooperative grace. It is also said to be a monergistic act (literally, "[God's] work alone"), since at every point after that, man's will cooperates with God's action. This cooperation is called synergistic (literally, "work together").[1]

For the extreme Calvinist, man is purely passive with regard to the beginning of his salvation, but is active with God's grace after that point. This view was held by the later Augustine (see appendix 3), Luther, Calvin, Edwards (see appendix 9), and Turretin. The Synod of Dort (see appendix 8), following Augustine, even uses the illustration of the "resurrection from the dead" of God's work on the unregenerate (*Canons of Dort*, articles 11–12).[2]

SORTING OUT THE ISSUES

The issues involved as to which view is correct are discussed elsewhere in this book. The extreme Calvinists' view of an initial

---

[1]See Sproul, *Willing to Believe*, 119.
[2]See Sproul, *Willing to Believe*, 139.

monergism is based on their belief that irresistible grace is exercised by God on the unwilling. We have shown that this is wrong for several reasons.

It is not supported by the Bible

There is no biblical support for the extreme Calvinists' view of irresistible grace on the unwilling (see chapter 5). The Bible affirms that all can, and some do, resist the grace of God (Matt. 23:37; cf. 2 Peter 3:9).

It is not supported by the church fathers

With the explainable exception of the later Augustine (see appendix 3), no major church fathers up to the Reformation held to irresistible grace on the unwilling (see appendix 1). Even Luther's view, the first major one after the later Augustine, was reversed by his disciple and systematizer, Melanchthon. And Calvin's view was opposed by Arminius and is rejected by all moderate Calvinists (see chapters 6 and 7).

It is not supported by the attribute of God's omnibenevolence

One of the primary problems with extreme Calvinism (see chapters 4 and 5) is the denial of God's essential omnibenevolence. By the admission of this view, God is not all-loving in a redemptive sense. He loves, sent Christ to die for, and attempts to save only the elect. However, this is contrary to Scripture (see appendix 6). An all-loving God (1 John 4:16) loves all (John 3:16) and wants all to come to salvation (1 Tim. 2:3–5; cf. 2 Peter 3:9).

It is not supported by man's God-given free will

Since love is always persuasive but never coercive, God cannot force any one to love Him—which is what irresistible love on the unwilling would be. God's persuasive, but resistible love, goes hand in glove with human free choice. Free will is self-determination (see chapter 2 and appendix 4). It involves the ability to choose otherwise. One can either accept or reject God's grace.

CONCLUSION

God's grace works synergistically on free will. That is, it must be received to be effective. There are no conditions for giving grace, but there is one condition for receiving it—faith. Put in other terms, God's justifying grace works cooperatively, not operatively. Faith is a precondition for receiving God's gift of salvation (see appendix 10). Faith is logically prior to regeneration, since we are saved "through faith" (Eph. 2:8–9) and "justified by faith" (Rom. 5:1 NASB).

A fitting conclusion to this brief study on man's needed response by faith is to read the dynamic words of Revelation 22:17. Here, John the apostle clearly holds out God's gracious invitation to *all*: "The Spirit and the bride say, 'Come!' and let him who hears say, 'Come!' Whoever is thirsty, let him come; and whoever wishes, let him take the free gift of the water of life."

APPENDIX TWELVE

EXTREME CALVINISM AND VOLUNTARISM

At the root of extreme Calvinism is a radical form of voluntarism, which affirms that something is right simply because God willed it, rather than God willing it because it is right in accordance with His own unchangeable nature (a view called essentialism). If voluntarism is accurate, then there is no moral problem with irresistible grace on the unwilling, limited atonement, or even double-predestination. If, on the other hand, God's will is not ultimately arbitrary, then extreme Calvinism collapses.

AN EVALUATION OF VOLUNTARISM IN EXTREME CALVINISM

All extreme Calvinists are voluntarists, either explicitly or implicitly, and no extensive passage in the Bible is used by them more than Romans 9. Since few expositions of this passage are more comprehensive than John Piper's *The Justification of God*, we will cite it extensively on this matter. A selection of his quotes will set forth the view.

Or to put it more precisely, *it is the glory of God and his essential nature mainly to dispense mercy (but also wrath, Ex. 34:7) on whomever he pleases apart from any constraint originating outside his own will. This is the essence of what it means to be God. This is his name....*

If we paraphrase and bring out the implicit understanding of righteousness, the argument runs like this: since God's *righteousness* consists basically in his acting unswervingly for his own glory, and since his glory consists basically in his *sovereign freedom* in the bestowal and withholding of mercy, there is no unrighteousness with God (Rom. 9:11ff.). On the contrary, he must pursue his "electing purpose" apart from man's "willing and running," for *only in his sovereign, free bestowal of mercy on whomever he wills is God acting out of a full allegiance to his name and esteem for his glory....*

In a nutshell it goes like this: Paul's conception of God's righteousness is that it consists basically in his commitment to act always for his own name's sake, that is, to preserve and display his own glory (cf. chapters 7 and 8). Therefore, since according to Exodus 33:19 *God's glory or name consists basically in his sovereign freedom in the bestowal of mercy (cf. chapter 4), there is no unrighteousness with God when his decision to bless one person and not another is based solely on his own will* rather than on any human distinctive. On the contrary, he *must* pursue his 'purpose of election' in this way in order to remain righteous, for only in his sovereign, free bestowal (and withholding) of mercy on whomever he wills is God acting out of a full allegiance to his name and esteem for his glory....

The thesis that I formulate in chapter 5 in answer to this question is that for Paul *the righteousness of God must be his unswerving commitment always to preserve the honor of his name and display his glory.* If this is what it means for God to be righteous, and if his glory (or name) consists mainly in his sovereign freedom to have mercy on whom he wills, then the quotation of Exodus 33:19 as an argument for the righteousness of God in unconditional election does in fact make good sense.[1]

In brief, according to voluntarists like Piper, something is right simply because God wills it. And He wills whatever He pleases.

A CRITIQUE OF VOLUNTARISM IN EXTREME CALVINISM

There are many serious, even fatal, flaws with voluntarism, both biblical and theological. Consider the following:

---

[1]Piper, *The Justification of God,* 89, 122, 157, 219 (italics his).

First, neither Piper nor other extreme Calvinists offer any real biblical proof of their position. All the verses they offer are capable of interpretations contrary to voluntarism (see chapters 4 and 5).

Second, they are inconsistent with their own position on the nature of God. On the one hand, they claim God's mercy is based in His supreme and sovereign will—He can will anything He wants to will and show mercy on anyone to whom He wants to show mercy. On the other hand, they claim that God's holiness and justice are unchanging. He cannot be unholy or unjust, even if He wanted to be. By His very nature God must punish sin.

But they cannot have it both ways. For as a simple unchangeable being, all of His attributes are unchangeable. If He is just (and He is), then He must be unchangeably just at all times to all persons in all circumstances. And if He is loving (and He is), then He must be unchangeably loving to all persons at all times in all circumstances. To be other than this would be to act contrary to His unchangeable nature, which is impossible.

Third, virtually all strong Calvinists hold to the classical view of God's attributes. Some of them, like John Gerstner and R. C. Sproul, give specific allegiance to Thomas Aquinas, and the rest follow Augustine, who held the same position, namely, that God is simple, necessary, and unchangeable in His essence. All God's attributes are part of this unchangeable nature. Further, God can will nothing contrary to His immutable nature. But if this is the case, then voluntarism is wrong, since it makes God's will supreme over everything else, even over whatever "nature" He has.

R. C. Sproul does not appear to see the inconsistency in his own view. He says on the one hand, "Is not God necessarily good? God can do nothing but good."[2] Yet elsewhere he insists that "God may owe people justice, but never mercy."[3] If this means that God is not obligated by His own nature to love sinners—all sinners—then God's attribute of mercy is not necessary. But God is a simple and necessary Being, as even Sproul admits. Thus, while it follows that while there is *nothing* in fallen human beings that merits God's love, nonetheless, there *is* something in God's unchangeable love that necessitates that He loves them.

Fourth, there are serious theological problems with voluntarism. Essential to voluntarism is the premise that God has nothing either outside of Him or inside Him that places any limits on His

---

[2]See Sproul, *Willing to Believe*, 111.
[3]Sproul, *Chosen by God*, 33.

will. Whatever He wills is *ipso facto* right. If this were so, then God *could* will that love is wrong and hate is right, or that injustice is right and justice is wrong. But this is absurd and contradictory, for something cannot even be in-just (not just) unless there is an ultimate standard of justice (such as the nature of God) by which we know what is not just.

Finally, the voluntarism of extreme Calvinism is a classic example of the fallacy known as a theologism. It takes a single theological principle and uses it as the ultimate determiner of all truth. Often the principle is: *Whatever gives most glory to God is true.* And since *they believe* that making God's will supreme over everything else brings more glory to Him, then it would follow that voluntarism is true.

However, one can challenge both premises. Not that it is wrong to do everything for the glory of God, but that "glory" is an ambiguous term that needs definition. When properly defined it refers to the manifestation and radiation of God's eternal and unchangeable essence, not His arbitrary will. Further, the second premise is likewise flawed, for making God's will supreme, even over His nature, does not bring the most glory to God. In fact, it contradicts His unchangeable nature. And nothing that contradicts God's nature can be glorifying to Him.

A DEFENSE OF CHRISTIAN ESSENTIALISM

Either voluntarism is true, or else some form of essentialism is true. The former claims something is right because God willed it. The latter contends that God wills it because it is right. Saints Augustine, Anselm, and Aquinas defended this latter view, as did C. S. Lewis in modern times.

There are two basic forms of essentialism: either God is bound to will things in accordance to some standard outside Himself (as in Plato's Good) or else by the standard inside Himself (namely, His own nature). The latter is held by Christian essentialists. Three basic lines of argument in favor of this view are:[4] philosophical, biblical, and practical. First, the philosophical view will be discussed.

---

[4]See Norman L. Geisler, "Essentialism," in *Baker's Encyclopedia of Christian Apologetics* (Grand Rapids, Mich.: Baker Book House, 1999), 216–18.

PHILOSOPHICAL ARGUMENTS FOR DIVINE ESSENTIALISM

Christian theist Thomas Aquinas offered three basic arguments for God's unchangeable nature in his famous *Summa Theologica* (ST 1.2.3.).

The argument from God's pure actuality

The first argument is based on the fact that a God of pure Actuality ("I AM-ness") has no potentiality. For everything that changes has potentiality, and there can be no potentiality in God (He is pure Actuality, Ex. 3:14). Whatever changes has to have the potential to change. But as pure Actuality God has no potential; therefore, He cannot change.

The argument from God's perfection

The second argument for God's unchangeability stands on His absolute perfection. Briefly put, whatever changes acquires something new. But God cannot acquire anything new, since He is absolutely perfect; He could not be better. Therefore, God cannot change. God is by His very nature an absolutely perfect Being. If there were any perfection that He lacked, then He would not be God. To change one must gain something new, but to gain a new perfection is to have lacked it to begin with. If God could change, He would not be God; rather, He would be a being lacking in some perfection, not the absolutely perfect God He is. Hence, He cannot change.

The argument from God's simplicity

The third argument for God's immutability follows from His simplicity. Everything that changes is composed of what changes and what does not change. But there can be no composition in God (He is an absolutely simple being). Again, then—God cannot change.

An absolutely simple being has no composition. But whatever changes must be composed of what does change and what does not change. For if everything about a being changed, then it would not be the same being but an entirely new being. In fact, it would not be change but annihilation of the one and recreation of another entirely new. Now, if when change occurs in a being something remains the same and something does not, then the being must be composed of these two elements. But an absolutely simple being, such as God is, has no composition. Therefore, it follows that God cannot change.

THE BIBLICAL ARGUMENTS FOR DIVINE ESSENTIALISM

There are numerous Scriptures that declare that God is unchangeable in His nature. First, the Old Testament passages will be discussed.

Old Testament evidence for God's immutability

The psalmist declared: "In the beginning you [Lord] laid the foundations of the earth, and the heavens are the work of your hands. They will perish, but you remain; they will all wear out like a garment. Like clothing you will change them and they will be discarded. But you remain the same, and your years will never end" (Ps. 102:25–27). 1 Samuel 15:29 affirms that " 'He who is the Glory of Israel does not lie or change his mind; for he is not a man, that he should change his mind.' " The prophet added, "For I am the LORD, I change not; therefore ye sons of Jacob are not consumed" (Mal. 3:6 KJV).

New Testament evidence for God's immutability

The New Testament is equally strong about God's unchangeable nature. Hebrews 1:10–12 cites the psalmist with approval, repeating, " 'You [Lord] will roll them up like a robe; like a garment they will be changed. But you remain the same, and your years will never end' " (v. 12). A few chapters later the author of Hebrews asserts, "God did this so that, by two unchangeable things in which it is impossible for God to lie..." (Heb. 6:18). The apostle Paul adds in Titus 1:2, "God, who does not lie, promised before the beginning of time...." James 1:17 points out that "Every good gift and every perfect gift is from above, and cometh down from the Father of lights, with whom is no variableness, neither shadow of turning" (KJV).

Now, if God is unchangeable in His nature, then His will is subject to His unchangeable nature. Thus, whatever God wills must be good in accordance with this nature. In fact, since God is simple His will is identical to His unchangeable nature. God cannot will contrary to His nature. He cannot lie. He cannot be unloving, nor unjust. In short, divine essentialism must be correct in contrast to extreme Calvinism.

PRACTICAL ARGUMENTS FOR GOD'S MORAL IMMUTABILITY

In addition to the philosophical and biblical arguments for God's nature being unchangeable, there are many practical arguments.

The argument from moral repugnance

Divine essentialists insist that it is morally repugnant to assume, as voluntarists do, that God could change His will on whether love is essentially good and could will instead that hate be a universal moral obligation. Likewise, it is difficult to conceive how a morally perfect Being could will that rape, cruelty, and genocide be morally good. Since it is morally repugnant for creatures made in God's image to imagine such a change in God's will, how much more must it be for the God in whose image we are made?

The argument from the need for moral stability

According to this argument, if all moral principles were based on God's changing will, then there would be no moral security. For example, how could one commit himself/herself to a life of love, mercy, or justice only to find out that God could change at any moment the fact of whether these were the right things to do? Indeed, how could we serve God as supreme if He could will that our ultimate good was not to love Him but hate Him?

Argument from God's trustworthiness

The Bible presents God as eminently trustworthy. When He makes an unconditional promise He never fails to keep it (cf. Gen. 12:1–3; Heb. 6:16–18). Indeed, the gifts and callings of God are without change of mind on His part (Rom. 11:29). God is not a man that He should repent (1 Sam. 15:29 KJV). He can always be counted on to keep His word (Isa. 55:11). But this ultimate trustworthiness of God would not be possible if He could change His will at any time about anything. The only thing that makes God morally bound to keep His Word is His unchangeable nature. Otherwise, He could decide at any moment to send all believers to hell. He could reward the wicked for murder and cruelty. Such a God would not be eminently trustworthy, as is the God of the Bible, who is unchangeably good.

What is ironic here is that the very Calvinists who depend on an essentially unchanging God to support their beliefs in unconditional election and eternal security, depend on a non-essentialistic (i.e, voluntaristic) view of God to ground their view in limited atonement. Thus, extreme Calvinism has at its heart an incoherent view of God.

CONCLUSION

Extreme Calvinism stands or falls with voluntarism. It is at the root of both its biblical interpretation and theological expressions. But, as we have seen, Calvinistic voluntarism is biblically unfounded, theologically inconsistent, philosophically insufficient, and morally repugnant. Thus, extreme Calvinism is subject to the same criticisms.

BIBLIOGRAPHY

Aldrich, Roy. "The Gift of God." *Bibliotheca Sacra* (July-September 1965): 248–53.

Ames, William. *The Marrow of Theology*. Trans. and ed. John D. Eusden. Durham, N.C.: The Labyrinth Press, 1983.

Aquinas, Thomas. *Summa Theologica*. In *The Basic Writings of St. Thomas Aquinas*. Vol. 1. Edited and Annotated. Introduction by Anton C. Pegis. New York: Random House, 1944.

Arminius, James. *Remonstrance* (1610). In *The Creeds of Christendom*, Ed. Philip Schaff. Grand Rapids, Mich.: Baker Book House, 1983.

————. *Works*. In *The Writings of James Arminius*. Trans. James Nichols and W. R. Bagnall. 3 vols. Grand Rapids, Mich.: Baker Book House, 1956.

Armstrong, Brian. *Calvinism and the Amyraut Heresy*. Madison, Wis.: University of Wisconsin Press, 1969.

Arndt, William F., and F. Wilbur Gingrich. *A Greek-English Lexicon of the New Testament and Other Early Christian Literature*. Chicago, Ill.: The University of Chicago Press, 1957.

Augustine, Saint. *City of God*. In *A Select Library of the Nicene and Post-Nicene Fathers of the Christian Church*. Ed. Philip Schaff. Vol. 2. Grand Rapids, Mich.: Wm. B. Eerdmans Publishing Co., 1956.

————. *Enchiridion*. In *A Select Library of the Nicene and Post-Nicene Fathers of the Christian Church*. Ed. Philip Schaff. Vol. 3. Grand Rapids, Mich.: Wm. B. Eerdmans Publishing Co., 1956.

————. *Epistle of John*: Homily V, 9. In *A Select Library of the Nicene and Post-Nicene Fathers of the Christian Church*. Ed. Philip Schaff. Vol. 7. Grand Rapids, Mich.: Wm. B. Eerdmans Publishing Co., 1956.

————. *On the Correction of the Donatists*. In *A Select Library of the Nicene and Post-Nicene Fathers of the Christian Church*. Ed. Philip Schaff. Vol. 4. Grand Rapids, Mich.: Wm. B. Eerdmans Publishing Co., 1956.

————. *Two Souls, Against the Manichaeans* 10.14, 158. Quoted in Norman L. Geisler, *What Augustine Says*. Grand Rapids, Mich.: Baker Book House, 1982.

Bancroft, Emery H. *Christian Theology: Systematic and Biblical*. Ed. Ronald B. Mayers. 2nd rev. ed. Grand Rapids, Mich.: Zondervan Publishing House, 1976.

Basinger, David, and Randall, eds. *Predestination and Free Will*. Downers Grove, Ill.: InterVarsity Press, 1986.

Berkof, Louis. *Systematic Theology*. 2nd ed. Grand Rapids, Mich.: Wm. B. Eerdmans Publishing Co., 1977.

Boyd, Greg. *Letters From a Skeptic*. Wheaton, Ill.: Victor, 1994.

————. *Trinity and Process*. New York: Peter Lang, 1992.

Buswell, James Oliver, Jr. *A Systematic Theology of the Christian Religion, Vol. II.* Grand Rapids, Mich.: Zondervan Publishing House, 1962–63.

Calvin, John. *Calvin's Commentaries: The Acts of the Apostles.* Trans. John W. Fraser and W. J. G. McDonald. Eds. David W. Torrance and Thomas F. Torrance. Grand Rapids, Mich.: Wm. B. Eerdmans Publishing Co., 1979.

————. *Calvin's Commentaries: The Epistles of Paul the Apostle to the Galatians, Ephesians, Philippians and Colossians.* Trans. T. H. L. Parker. Eds. David W. Torrance and Thomas F. Torrance. Grand Rapids, Mich.: Wm. B. Eerdmans Publishing Co., 1979.

————. *Calvin's Commentaries: A Harmony of the Gospels Matthew, Mark and Luke and the Epistles of James and Jude.* Trans. A. W. Morrison. Eds. David W. Torrance and Thomas F. Torrance. Grand Rapids, Mich.: Wm. B. Eerdmans Publishing Co., 1972.

————. *The Institutes of the Christian Religion.* Trans. Henry Beveridge. Grand Rapids, Mich.: Wm. B. Eerdmans Publishing Co., 1957.

Chafer, Lewis Sperry, and John F. Walvoord. *Major Bible Themes.* Grand Rapids, Mich.: Zondervan Publishing, 1974.

Charnock, Stephen. *Discourses Upon the Existence and Attributes of God.* Grand Rapids, Mich.: Baker Book House, 1979, reprint.

Craig, William Lane. *The Kalam Cosmological Argument.* London: The Macmillan Press, Ltd., 1979.

————. *The Only Wise God.* Grand Rapids, Mich.: Baker Book House, 1987.

Darwin, Charles. *The Autobiography of Charles Darwin.* Ed. Nora Darwin Barlow. New York: W. W. Norton & Co., 1993.

Davis, Stephen T. *Logic and the Nature of God.* Grand Rapids, Mich.: Wm. B. Eerdmans Publishing Co., 1983.

Dillow, Jodie. *The Reign of the Servant King.* Hayesville, N.C.: Schoettle Publishing Co., 1992.

Edwards, Jonathan. *Freedom of the Will.* In *Jonathan Edwards: Representative Selections*, rev. ed. Introduction, bibliography, and notes by Clarence H. Faust and Thomas H. Johnson. New York: Hill and Wang, 1962.

————. *Jonathan Edwards: Representative Selections*, rev. ed. Introduction, bibliography, and notes by Clarence H. Faust and Thomas H. Johnson. New York: Hill and Wang, 1962.

————. *Works.* In *The Works of Jonathan Edwards.* 2 vols. Carlisle, Pa.: Banner of Truth, 1974.

Ellicott, Charles John. *Ellicott's Commentary on the Whole Bible.* Grand Rapids, Mich.: Zondervan Publishing House, 1954.

Forster, Roger T., and V. Paul Marston. *God's Strategy in Human History.* Wheaton, Ill.: Tyndale House Publishers, 1974.

Friedrich, Gerhard, gen. ed. *Theological Dictionary of the New Testament.* Trans. and ed. Geoffrey W. Bromiley. Vol. VI. Grand Rapids, Mich.: Wm. B. Eerdmans Publishing Co., 1964–76.

Garrigou-LaGrange, R. *God: His Existence and Nature.* St. Louis: B. Herder Book Co., 1946.

Geach, Peter. *Providence and Evil.* Cambridge: Cambridge University Press, 1977.

Geisler, Norman L. *Baker's Encyclopedia of Christian Apologetics.* Grand Rapids, Mich.: Baker Book House, 1999.

———. *Creating God in the Image of Man?* Minneapolis: Bethany House Publishers, 1997.

———. "Essentialism." In *Baker's Encyclopedia of Christian Apologetics.* Grand Rapids, Mich.: Baker Book House, 1999.

———. "Prophecy as Proof of the Bible." In *Baker's Encyclopedia of Christian Apologetics.* Grand Rapids, Mich.: Baker Book House, 1999.

———. *What Augustine Says.* Grand Rapids, Mich.: Baker Book House, 1982.

Geisler, Norman L., and Thomas A. Howe. *When Critics Ask.* Grand Rapids, Mich.: Baker Book House, 1992.

Gill, John. *The Cause of God and Truth.* London: 1814, new ed.

Hasker, William. *God, Time and Knowledge.* Ithaca, N.Y.: Cornell University Press, 1989.

Haykin, Mike. *One Heart and One Soul.* Phillipsburg, N.J.: Evangelical Press, n.d.

Hodge. A. A. *Outlines of Theology.* Grand Rapids, Mich.: Wm. B. Eerdmans Publishing Co., 1949.

Hume, David. *The Letters of David Hume,* ed. J. Y. T. Greig. 2 vols. Oxford: Clarendon Press, 1932.

Hussey, Joseph. *God's Operations of Grace.* London: D. Bridge, 1707.

Kendall, R. T. *Calvin and English Calvinism to 1649.* Oxford, 1979.

Lewis, C. S. *The Great Divorce.* New York: The Macmillan Company, 1946.

———. *Screwtape Letters.* New York: The Macmillan Company, 1961.

———. *Surprised by Joy.* New York: Harcourt, Brace and Company, 1955.

Lidell, Henry George, and Robert Scott, *A Greek-English Lexicon.* Oxford: Clarendon Press, 1968.

Lightner, Robert. *The Death Christ Died.* Grand Rapids, Mich.: Kregel Publications, 1998.

Locke, John. *An Essay Concerning Human Understanding.* In *The Empiricists,* Ed. Richard Taylor. Garden City, N.Y.: Doubleday & Company, Inc., 1961.

Lucas, J. R. *The Freedom of the Will.* Oxford: Clarendon Press, 1970.

———. *The Future: An Essay on God, Temporality and Truth.* London: Basil Blackwell, 1989.

Luther, Martin. *The Bondage of the Will.* Trans. Henry Cole. Grand Rapids, Mich.: Baker Book House, 1976.

Machen, J. Gresham. Quoted in J. I. Packer, *Fundamentalism and the Word of God.* Grand Rapids: Mich.: Wm. B. Eerdmans Publishing Co., 1958.

Miley, John. *Systematic Theology.* Methodist Book Concern, 1892.

Morris, Thomas V. *Our Idea of God: An Introduction to Philosophical Theology.* Downers Grove, Ill.: InterVarsity Press, 1991.

Murray, Iain H. *Spurgeon v. Hyper-Calvinism: The Battle for Gospel Preaching.* Carlisle, Pa.: Banner of Truth Trust, 1995.

Nash, Ronald, ed. *Process Theology.* Grand Rapids, Mich.: Baker Book House, 1987.

Owen, John. *The Death of Death in the Death of Christ.* Carlisle, Pa.: The Banner of Truth Trust, 1995.

Packer, J. I. *Fundamentalism and the Word of God.* Grand Rapids, Mich.: Wm. B. Eerdmans Publishing Co., 1958.

Packer, J. I., and O. R. Johnson. "Historical and Theological Introduction." In *The Bondage of the Will,* Martin Luther. Trans. Henry Cole. Grand Rapids, Mich.: Baker Book House, 1976.

Palmer, Edwin. *The Five Points of Calvinism.* Grand Rapids, Mich.: Baker Book House, 1972.

Payne, J. Barton. *Encyclopedia of Biblical Prophecy.* London: Hodder and Stoughton, 1973.

Pinnock, Clark. "Between Classical and Process Theism." In *Process Theology.* Ed. Ronald Nash. Grand Rapids, Mich.: Baker Book House, 1987.

Pinnock, Clark, et al. *The Openness of God.* Downers Grove, Ill.: InterVarsity Press, 1994.

Piper, John. *The Justification of God.* 2nd ed. Grand Rapids, Mich.: Baker Book House, 1993.

Rice, Richard. *God's Foreknowledge and Man's Free Will.* Minneapolis: Bethany House Publishers, 1985.

Robertson, A. T. *Word Pictures in the New Testament.* 5 vols. Nashville, Tenn.: Broadman Press, 1930. Reprint, New York: R. R. Smith, Inc., 1931.

Russell, Bertrand. *Why I Am Not a Christian.* New York: Simon and Schuster, 1957.

Ryrie, C. C. *The Holy Spirit.* Chicago: Moody Press, 1965.

Sapaugh, Gregory. "Is Faith a Gift? A Study of Ephesians 2:8." *Journal of the Grace Evangelical Society* (Spring 1994): 7:12, 31–43.

Schaff, Philip. *The Creeds of Christendom.* Grand Rapids, Mich.: Baker Book House, 1983.

Schaff, Philip, ed. *A Select Library of the Nicene and Post-Nicene Fathers of the Christian Church.* Grand Rapids, Mich.: Wm. B. Eerdmans Publishing Co., 1956.

Shank, Robert. *Life in the Son.* Minneapolis: Bethany House Publishers, 1989.

Shedd, W. G. T. *Dogmatic Theology.* 2nd ed. Vol. 3. Nashville, Tenn.: Thomas Nelson, Inc., 1980.

Sproul, R. C. *Chosen by God.* Wheaton, Ill.: Tyndale House Publishers, 1986.

————. *Willing to Believe.* Grand Rapids, Mich.: Baker Book House, 1997.

Spurgeon, Charles. "A Critical Text—C. H. Spurgeon on 1 Timothy 2:3, 4." Quoted in Iain Murray, *Spurgeon v. Hyper-Calvinism: The Battle for Gospel Preaching,* 150, 154. Carlisle, Pa.: The Banner of Truth Trust, 1995.

Stanley, Charles. *Eternal Security.* Nashville, Tenn.: Thomas Nelson, Inc., 1990.

Steele, David N., and Curtis C. Thomas. *The Five Points of Calvinism.* Phillipsburg, N.J.: Presbyterian & Reformed, 1963.

Stibbs, Alan M. *The Older Tyndale New Testament Commentary on First Peter.* Grand Rapids, Mich.: Wm. B. Eerdmans Publishing Co., 1959.

Strong, Augustus Hopkins. *Systematic Theology.* Old Tappan, N.J.: Fleming H. Revell Company, 1907.

Swinburne, Richard. *The Coherence of Theism.* Oxford: Clarendon Press, 1977.

Toon, Peter. *The Emergence of Hyper-Calvinism in English Non-Conformity 1689–1765.* London: The Olive Tree, 1967.

Tozer, A. W. *The Knowledge of the Holy.* New York: Harper & Row, 1978.

Walvoord, John. *The Holy Spirit.* Grand Rapids, Mich.: Zondervan Publishing House, 1958.

Watson, Richard. *Theological Institutes; or A View of the Evidences, Doctrines, Morals, and Institutions of Christianity.* 2 vols. New York: T. Mason and G. Lane, 1836.

Wright, R. K. McGregor. *No Place for Sovereignty.* Downers Grove, Ill.: InterVarsity Press, 1996.

Zagzebski, Linda. *The Dilemma of Freedom and Foreknowledge.* Oxford: Oxford University Press, 1991.

INDEX

Note: Page numbers followed by an "n" indicate citation is found in the footnote.

SCRIPTURE INDEX

SCRIPTURE INDEX